A. Beaujon

The History of Dutch sea Fisheries

Their Progress, Decline and Revival, Especially in Connection with the....

A. Beaujon

The History of Dutch sea Fisheries
Their Progress, Decline and Revival, Especially in Connection with the....

ISBN/EAN: 9783337259037

Printed in Europe, USA, Canada, Australia, Japan

Cover: Foto ©ninafisch / pixelio.de

More available books at **www.hansebooks.com**

International Fisheries Exhibition,
LONDON 1883.

THE HISTORY

OF

DUTCH SEA FISHERIES:

THEIR

PROGRESS, DECLINE AND REVIVAL,

ESPECIALLY IN CONNECTION WITH THE LEGISLATION
ON FISHERIES IN EARLIER AND LATER TIMES.

BY

A. BEAUJON.

[*PRIZE ESSAY.*]

LONDON:
WILLIAM CLOWES AND SONS, LIMITED,
13, CHARING CROSS, S.W.
1884.

LONDON:
PRINTED BY WILLIAM CLOWES AND SONS, Limited,
STAMFORD STREET AND CHARING CROSS.

CONTENTS.

PART I.

SEA FISHERY IN THE NETHERLANDS BEFORE THE
ESTABLISHMENT OF THE DUTCH REPUBLIC . 7

PART II.

SEA FISHERIES UNDER THE DUTCH REPUBLIC.

I. Grand Fishery 36
II. Whale Fishery 101
III. Cod Fishery 134
IV. Coast Fishery 144
V. "Dominium Maris" 164

PART III.

SEA FISHERIES SINCE THE END OF THE DUTCH
REPUBLIC.

I. 1795–1813 186
II. Protection at a Culminating Point 206
III. The End of Protection 230
IV. Revival 259

PREFACE.

THE following pages contain, not a complete history of the Dutch sea fisheries, but merely the outlines of their history as connected with legislation.

The subject is a vast one. Sea fishery has throughout history been either the greatest, or among the most considerable, of the industries of the Netherlands. Some of its branches have during three centuries and a half been regulated and organised by laws and bye-laws, and have been constantly in the minds of the country's rulers, legislators, and publicists; and the mass of material for their history is, of course, in proportion to the total of attention bestowed upon the subject in former times. To read this subject up and exhaust it would be the work of many years, and involve a thorough search of the archives of the present kingdom of the Netherlands, several of its provinces, and many of its cities; whereas the present author has only had the seven months before him which have elapsed since the subject for this prize essay was known in Holland, and has during that short period by no means been master of the whole of his time. Several minor parts of the subject have for this reason been left out of the range of research; such are the sea fisheries of the provinces of Zealand, Friesland, and Groningen, the whole of the oyster business, and the salmon, herring, and other fisheries in the river estuaries, which are very justly reckoned as sea fishery, and treated as such in official documents of the present day.

PREFACE.

Zuider Zee fishery has come in for a share of attention proportioned to the small area of the water so called, but perhaps rather short of the historical interest inherent to the trade and the measures taken respecting it. Even as regards deep sea fisheries, many details, a perfect insight into which might have thrown light upon the whole, have not been investigated for sheer lack of time and opportunity. I have, in short, had to be satisfied with the certainty of not having omitted, and a reasonable hope of not having misrepresented, any of the leading historical and actual features of the subject. Such as it is, however, the work contains a quantity of matter drawn from perfectly reliable authentic documents, into which no former writer on Dutch sea fisheries has ever looked, as none of them ever attempted a complete historical treatment of the subject.

There is much about laws in the book, and perhaps less about fishers and fishing. I have taken the centre of gravity of the given prize subject to lie in the former, and made it my business to show, first, what laws were made, and why they were made ; next, what they wrought. For the same reason, herring fishery, the only branch which has been constantly legislated on down to twenty-five years ago, occupies a very prominent place in the following pages. The former and present proportions of the business would perfectly warrant the pre-eminence if nothing else did.

Many details will perhaps be more interesting to the Dutch than to the British reader. The latter, I hope, will remember, that if a work like this is ever read at all, the chances are that it will be read most by the men who can trace in it some of the thoughts and actions of their own ancestors.

A. BEAUJON.

April 18*th*, 1883.

THE
HISTORY OF DUTCH SEA FISHERIES

PART I.

SEA FISHERY IN THE NETHERLANDS BEFORE THE ESTABLISHMENT OF THE DUTCH REPUBLIC.

ANYBODY may conclude from a slight survey of a map of the present Kingdom of the Netherlands, that the sea must at all times have supplied food to its inhabitants. The country is bounded by the North Sea on two sides; a gulf called Zuider Zee runs far inland and multiplies the extent of its sea-shore; and both this outer and inner sea are pregnant with fish of several kinds. The several river estuaries supply a number of ports and roadsteads for fishermen's vessels; for those river mouths, whose shallowness was until a few years ago a serious obstacle to the development of modern steam navigation in the Dutch ports, and has accordingly had to be artificially corrected in several ways, at the cost of many millions, afford, and have at all times afforded, plenty of depth for the largest of fishing craft. A glance on the map along the sandy and havenless North Sea coast north of the rivers will, moreover, at once show the existence of several villages separated from the fertile part of the country by leagues of sand-downs, and which, therefore, can never have had another source of livelihood than such sea fishing as may be carried on in vessels having no keel, and liable to be put ashore on the beach at every tide.

Sea fishing has accordingly been mentioned as a means of existence of the inhabitants of these countries by the very earliest writers. The early history of the Dutch sea fisheries is, however, fragmentary for lack of documents. Some writers mention herring to have been first caught and eaten by the Dutch in the year 1163.* But this statement can scarcely be exact, for it is likewise stated that fishermen from Kampen and Harderwijk, being two small seaports on the Zuider Zee, used to fish for herring "off Sconen," i.e. on the shores of the Baltic, before the end of the twelfth century,† and the trade must have been carried on for a considerable time before so far developing itself as to be exercised at such a distance from home. The first document on record relative to Dutch trade on the Baltic shore is a privilege granted to the men of Amsterdam by the Lords of the Germanic Order of Livonia in 1277, and confirmed by the Bishop of Livonia in 1495.‡

This privilege, indeed, does not especially mention the right of fishing; it contains simply a general promise of protection to merchants from Amsterdam in the Livonian dominions. But it has probably, judging by the unrestricted terms in which it is drawn up, been of avail to fishermen as well as to traders, inasmuch as a similar privilege granted to the men of Amsterdam, Enkhuizen and Wieringen by King Albert of Sweden, in 1368,§

* Semeyns' *Corte beschrijoinghe over de Haringvisscherije in Hollandt*, p. 1. The same date is mentioned by a writer in the periodical called *Den Koopman*, vol. i. p. 349.
† Boxhorn, *Tooneel van Hollandt*, p. 234.
‡ Luzac, *Hollands Rijkdom*, vol. i. Appendix B.
§ *Ibid.* Appendix C.

explicitly allows the said merchants to have their own boats and implements "of fishery in Schoonen aforesaid, and use them and fish at will, paying a tax of half a Schoonen merk on each boat, and no more." A certain toll on herring imported by Dutch fishermen is established by the same edict. There were regular and privileged markets for herring and other fish in the Netherlands even before this period; such market rights were granted to the town of Brouwershaven in 1344, and to that of Naarden in 1355, by the Counts of Holland then reigning; and in 1388 another fish market was established at Katwijk, a village on the North Sea coast.* The fact of Dutch sea fishery having had considerable extension in the latter part of the Middle Ages is further placed beyond doubt by an order issued by Edward I in 1295,† by which the said King "having understood that many people from Holland, Zealand, and Friesland, who are our friends, will shortly come and fish in our sea off Yarmouth," lays his commands in "*custodi orae maritimae suae Jernemuth* and *Baillivis suis de Jernemuth*," to see that these foreigners be treated civilly, and not molested, robbed, or plundered, by the king's subjects.‡

Such scanty documents as these are all the footing on which a notion of the extent of Dutch sea fisheries can be based, up to the end of the fourteenth century. But, records failing, it may be assumed as certain that their produce cannot have gone far beyond the necessities of immediate home consumption, so long as no proper method of pre-

---

* Van Mieris, *Groot. Charterboek der Graven van Holland, Zeeland*, (enz.), vols. ii. pp. 688, 826, and iii. pp. 498–9.

† Luzac, *Hollands Rijkdom*, vol. iii. p. 57. v. Mieris, *Charterbock*, vol. i. p. 566.

‡ Luzac, *Hollands Rijkdom*, vol. i. p. 136.

serving fish was in use in these parts. Fish, indeed, and herring especially, must have been salted from the very earliest times, or there could have been no possibility of catching them off Yarmouth and in the Baltic and carrying them home, in probably slow sailing vessels, with any chance of finding a market for them. Salted herrings are accordingly mentioned in a charter of Louis VII. of France, dated 1179, and, as regards the Low Countries in particular, a regulation dated 1177, and issued by Margaret of Alsatia, Countess of Flanders, on the manner of salting herring, was preserved in the town of Ostend as late as 1816.* But there is an immense distance between packing or strewing fish with salt so as to preserve them for a short time, and curing them so as to last for years and become an article of foreign trade.

The man who in any country first found out the latter method, and thereby first opened up the possibility of lucrative sea-fishing on such a scale as considerably to exceed the wants of immediate home consumption, may therefore be truly called the father of such a country's sea fishery.

The Netherlands' history records the name of such a man, which accordingly is till this day known to every school-boy in the country as that of one of the nation's benefactors. But history unfortunately does not yield much information about him beyond his name, which was William Beukelsz, and his dwelling-place, which was Biervliet, now a village in the southern part of the province of Zealand.

Volumes of subtle inquiry and learned controversy have been written about this personage, among which the above-quoted paper, read in the Brussels Academy of Science,

* Raepsaet, *Note sur la découverte de caquer le hareng*, p. 6.

in 1816, by the celebrated Belgian politician Raepsaet, is perhaps the most concise and interesting. But the prevailing feature of these many disquisitions is the extreme scantiness of the facts on which they are based. Beukelsz is universally stated to have lived at Biervliet about the middle of the fourteenth century, and been a " Stuyrman," or skipper, and concerned in the herring fishery. The year of his death has especially been the subject of much controversy, being stated by some to be 1347, by others 1397, and by a few 1401. His family are proved by deeds still extant to have been citizens of wealth and note, and his coat-of-arms is said to have consisted of two crossed " kaeckmeskens," or knives used in curing herrings (kaken) after the manner invented by him, and to which his name will be for ever attached. But how or by what circumstance he lighted upon his great invention is utterly unknown.

The operation called "kaken" is still in use with the Dutch herring fishermen, pretty much, it would appear, as first practised by Beukelsz. It is described in the same constant terms throughout Dutch history, and consists in opening and gutting the fish the moment the net is hauled aboard, salting them carefully, and packing them in barrels in a peculiar manner highly favourable for their conservation. The barrels used were anciently called " kaecken," or " kaeckjes," and the name of the curing process is probably derived from theirs.*

With further regard to the great inventor's person it is stated by all his biographers that the Emperor Charles V.

* N.B.—I am not aware of an English term for the method of curage here described. Whenever, in the course of this work, the words "*curage*" and "*cure*" are used without a further expletive, they will stand for curage in Beukelsz's fashion, or " *Kaken*."

visited his tomb at Biervliet in 1556, and there offered up prayers for the benefit of his soul. The sepulchre must have been an apocryphal one, or at best a cenotaph; for it is tolerably well established that the whole of the town of Biervliet of Beukelsz's time, including the church where he may have been buried, was destroyed by floods between the period of his death and that of the Imperial visit, the place having since then been rebuilt in a safer spot. Whether the Emperor may have been acquainted with the circumstance or not, his act of devotion is an instance of the deep veneration in which Beukelsz's name was held by his countrymen for centuries—a circumstance which may have induced Charles V., even after he had surrendered the government of the Low Countries to his son, to perform a demonstrative ceremony highly gratifying to his former subjects of Flanders and Holland, for whom he always had a strong predilection. If so, he succeeded; for whenever Beukelsz's biography has been entered into, the writer never omits to mention the Emperor's posthumous homage.

Whatever may have been Beukelsz's real character or his true merits in the case, it appears that about the time of his invention, his countrymen, the Zealanders, were the greatest herring fishermen of the Netherlands,* although, as shown above, the most ancient evidence of extensive sea fishery is relative to the more northerly provinces as well as to them. The Zealanders appear, however, to have lost their pre-eminence in the business soon afterwards, and writers of later date attribute this falling off to their having taken to the still more lucrative one of privateering. An important change in the annual migrations of the herring shoals, which about this period left the coasts of Denmark and Norway and began to concentrate about

* *Den Koopman*, vol. i. p. 237.

the shores of England and Scotland, may likewise have had something to do with the decline of the Zealand herring fishery.* At any rate, the next considerable progress in the fishing art was accomplished by men from the North; for it is stated that the first large herring-net was made at Hoorn in 1416,† and though the dimensions of this net are of course unknown, its fabrication appears to have contributed much to the rise of the trade. Leastways the latter became an object of legislation and warlike protection soon after the said period.

John Duke of Bavaria and Count of Holland issued regulations on the fabrication and marking of herring barrels and the curing of herrings in 1424.‡ Though no historical mention of cod fishery is made at the time, this branch of the fishing trade must also have been then practised to a certain extent; for the two great political parties which divided the country under the Counts of the Bavarian dynasty took their *noms de guerre* from it. The Bavarian coat-of-arms bears some resemblance to the scales of a codfish, and the followers of the first count of that dynasty, who wore his colours, were accordingly nicknamed *codfish* (*Kabeljauwen*)—an appellation from which the opposition party took occasion to style themselves *Hooks* (*Hoekschen*), and thereby transmitted to posterity a certain proof that cod was fished for in this period, in something like the manner in which it is caught to this day.

* This reason is alleged on p. 12 of the Committee's Report of 1854. But without further adstruction it is not apparent why the Zealanders could not fish off Yarmouth as well as off Sweden and Denmark.

† Velius, *Chronijk van Hoorn*, pp. 32-3. Brandt, *Historie der vermaarde Zee- en Koopstad Enkhuizen*, p. 17. Wagenaar, *Vaderlandsche Historie*, iii. p. 499.

‡ v. Mieris, *Charterboek*, vol. iv. pp. 728, 739.

The Sovereigns of the Burgundian dynasty established, or confirmed, a special tax, called *last-money*, to be paid by Dutch herring fishermen as a contribution towards the equipment of the convoying ships provided for their protection. Another edict dating from the Burgundian period prohibits herring caught by the Duke's subjects to be sold in foreign ports; and another was enacted against the salting of herring in barrels before St. Bartholomew's Day, or August 24th, and the use of salt other than of certain prescribed qualities.*

Besides this evidence of the herring fishery having had considerable importance in the course of the fifteenth century, the fact is established by a remonstrance, or memorial, delivered to the Grand Council at Malines, by the inhabitants of Brielle, in 1476. This document states herring fishery to be one of the nation's principal industries. An edict relative to trade in herring barrels, dated June 24th, 1495, has also been preserved,† in which an annual meeting of delegates of those concerned in the herring fishery is ordered to take place at the Hague, to confer on the trade's interests, as long as such conferences shall be found necessary. Beyond such general indications as these, however, no clue to the extent of the Dutch sea fisheries in the course of the fifteenth century is to be found. A placard emanated under the Emperor Charles V., on May 18th, 1519,‡ and "being very great," as its title says, inaugurated systematical legislation on sea fisheries in

* See Mr. van Limburg Brouwer's collection of *Boergoensche Charters*, pp. 51, 57, 59, 82, (1439 and 1440).

† *Eerste Memoriaelboek 's Hofs van Hollant*, fol. 451.

‡ *Placaet ende Ordonantie of 't Stuk van den Haringvaert,'t branden van de tonnen en 't zouten van den Haringh, wesende seer groot.* Derde Memoriaelboek van den Hove van Hollant, fol. 114, verso).

the Dutch provinces. The practice of *branding* barrels, in which Dutch herring laws have centred ever since, was first made obligatory by this law, and it is very remarkable that the principal warrant for the quality of the *fish* was as yet looked for in that of the *barrel.* The obligatory brand certified nothing but the latter, and stamps indicative of the quality of the fish were facultative, except in so far as early herring was to bear a peculiar mark. The principal contents of the edict are as follows :—

Every barrel of herring brought to market is to be provided with two marks or *brands;* the first to be apposed by the cooper who made the barrel, and the second by the master of the vessel on board which it was filled. Assayers (*keurmeesters*) are to be appointed in each town and village from which fishery is exercised, to control the brands ("*omme den brand te regeren*"). The attributions of these officers, however, involved a control over the barrels only, *not* over the quality of the fish. They were to test the materials and construction of each barrel, and keep a register of brands, stating the name of each brand's owner. The brand, in accordance with its meaning, was called *barrel-brand* (tonnebrand). None but new barrels were to be used; and it was prohibited to "carry to herring," i.e. to take to sea for the fishery, empty barrels already used. Besides the obligatory brands certifying the quality of barrels, towns anxious to secure a high renown for their produce were allowed to have a peculiar town brand (here called *back-brand*) apposed to the barrels exported from them as a certificate of the quality of the fish. This faculty was largely used, as will be shown hereafter.

No other salt was, by the law of 1519, allowed to be

used for salting herring than either "salt sodden from salt" (meaning *refined*) or "moor-salt."* Lisboa salt was excluded—a fact the more remarkable as no other than Spanish or Portuguese salt was allowed to be used in later years. No salt was allowed to be taken on board a herring ship unless covered by a certificate as to its quality; and skippers were to be sworn in against breach of this rule, which was considered extremely important. Four barrels of moor-salt, or five and half of "salt from salt" were to be used for one last of herring; whence it is evident that the curing qualities of the former (styled either "*moer-zout* or *zout van zelle*") were even stronger than those of refined salt.

The quality of the herring and its packing are next regulated to some extent in the law of 1519. Herring caught before St. James's Day (July 25) is prescribed to be packed in separate barrels, on which a peculiar brand representing a "St. James's shell" (*St. Jacob's schelpe*) is to be apposed. Skippers are ordered to observe peculiar "diligence" in the packing of all sorts of herring, and to have the fish carefully disposed in layers, and on no account poured out of the basket into the barrel in heaps.

* *Zout van goeden graauwen zelle.* These words refer to a peculiar industry now extinct since centuries. In the alluvial grounds of some of the Dutch river mouths, which are covered by sea-water at every tide, a kind of briny moor or turf (*darinck*) was formerly found in great quantities. This substance was burnt, and its ashes, when moistened with sea-water, yielded a peculiarly fine gray salt. This moor-salt-making industry (*zelle-neeringhe*) was of course exercised only about the mouths of the rivers, especially at Zierikzee. Boxhorn (augmented edition of *Reijgersbergen's Chronijk van Zeelandt*) describes the whole process on page 114, and adds: "No other salt than this was in times of yore used throughout the Netherlands." An engraving representing the digging and burning of "darinck" is to be found in Wagenaar, *Vad. Historie*, vol. iv.

Herrings of different quality, such as full, lean (ijdel), spawn-sick, and damaged (wrack), are to be sorted, and each description packed in separate barrels, which are to be kept asunder from the rest. But *there are as yet no separate brands* for these several qualities; and all dealers, when disposing of any herring, are enjoined to declare it to the buyer as either "full and sweet" or of inferior quality. While at sea, herring already barrelled is to be pickled, or moistened with sea-water every fortnight; whence the name of "pickle herring" (*pekelharing*) still applied to the fish salted at sea. Herring caught in the Y,* as being generally of inferior quality, is not allowed to be salted and exported, but kept for home consumption, and smoked to *bucking* when carried ashore. This is perhaps the first evidence of the existence of the smoked herring industry in these countries, and certainly the first vestige of the Grand Fishery's curing monopoly of later days. In order to enforce the rigid execution of these rules, all fishing skippers are enjoined, before dismissing their crews, to make them declare upon oath before the competent magistrate that no infraction whatever has been committed during the voyage.

This placard of Charles V. may, as already remarked, be considered as the beginning of the era of working regulations on herring fishery—an era which has lasted until twenty-five years ago, and witnessed the immense prosperity of the business, but also its most profound decline. The placard of 1519 has been often renewed, or quoted in laws of later date as the original statute on the subject. It is not, however, until a few years after its date that anything like a connecting link between the several

* An inlet of the Zuider Zee, formerly the only access to Amsterdam by sea, now drained and traversed by a canal.

facts and laws on record may be traced, by the resolutions of the States of Holland, of which a register has been kept from the year 1524 downward. As the province of Holland has always been prominent in fishery as well as in all other seafaring trades, this register is indeed the principal source from which the history both of sea fisheries and legislation relating to them may be constructed, down to the present century.

Under the government of the Emperor Charles and his son King Philip of Spain, the main feature of the fisheries' history is a succession of quarrels about money. The Sovereign wanted to raise money from the fishermen towards the equipment of convoying ships for the herring fleet, and wanted it, not in the shape of temporary subsidies, but in that of a permanent tax, as to the employment of which control would of course be inefficient. Against these pretensions the fishermen's attitude was one of constant grudging and reluctant granting. Continuous wars in the meantime occasioned constant need of efficient convoy, and kept the money question in the foreground as a subject of unceasing and painful wrangling, in the midst of which, however, the trade somehow managed to prosper. Such was, in outline, the course of affairs from the beginning of the domination of Charles V. and his successive deputies, down to his son's ultimate deposition from the sovereignty, i.e. for more than sixty years.

The wars between the Emperor and France first brought this convoying question into open dispute. The French, indeed, used much forbearance, and their admirals were in the habit of offering *sauf-conduits* for sale to the Dutch herring fishermen, subjects of a sovereign at war with theirs. These *sauf-conduits* were purchased by many for a consideration of fifteenpence per head of the crews for the cod-fishing vessels, and of twenty-five for the herring busses.* Still much damage was done to the herring fishery by the enemy, especially in the fishing season of 1537, to the effect that those who had not bought *sauf-conduits* complained of the straits of the war, and those who had were discontented about having to pay the enemy for protection which, in their estimation, was due to them from their own Government. A plan for equipping and arming six of the busses so as to be in a condition to serve as men-of-war in time of need was advised by the Emperor and much discussed in the States of Holland at the time, but suffered to drop, mainly because the shipowners who had taken out *sauf-conduits* from the enemy declined to contribute towards the costs, on the plea that such a measure had become useless. Thus, by the Government's inaction and dissensions among the parties concerned, part of the fleet remained at the enemy's mercy; and in the year 1543† the coast was infested by French privateers to such an extent that both traders and fishermen found it impossible to sail without facing imminent danger. Delegates from the fishing towns and villages met at the Hague and discussed the expediency of taking their protection into their own hands; but they did not come to a conclusion, although Government, in order to induce them to fit out their own convoy, resorted to a threat of prohibiting the fishing for the next season. In the States' sitting of May 20th, 1544,‡ the town of Schiedam's representatives again broached the convoying question;

---

* *Resol. van Holland in Aert v. d. Goes' Register*, 1537, p. 279, sqq. *Cf.* a Placard of Sept. 18, 1536 (2ᵉ *Memoriaelboek van Mr. J. de Jonge*, fol. 62, verso).

† *Resol. v. Holland, in Aert v. d. Goes' Register*, 1543, p. 357.

‡ *Resolutions of the States of Holland*, 1544, p. 30.

and as the war with Scotland added to the fishermen's distress, the point was a subject of frequent resultless deliberations in the next years. In 1547 another fruitless appeal was made to Government, who were content to advise the fishermen to equip one-tenth of their boats as ships of war,* and at last, on June 11th, issued a prohibition to fish, to last till September 1st.† This induced delegates from three of the towns most concerned, Dordrecht, Amsterdam and Rotterdam, to crave an audience from the Queen,‡ and earnestly speak up for their interests. The Emperor, they said, had been granted taxes or supplies (*beden*) by the States under promise of all available protection to the country's mercantile and industrial interests; and he therefore owed the fishermen such covering by ships of war as should enable them to fish in safety without any special contribution on their part. Having met with a flat refusal, for which the Emperor's distressed finances indeed gave the most stringent of reasons, the delegates came to terms, and after some protracted negotiations the States of Holland at length, in 1548, granted six thousand florins towards the equipment of five convoying ships. These, however, were not yet ready on the 9th of August, when a prohibition was issued against any busses sailing till the convoy should be ready to put to sea, involving the loss of the best part of the fishing season.§

The States' tardy concession by no means put an end to the disputes. What Government wanted was not a grant

* *Res. Holl.* 1547, p. 186.
† *Eerste Memoriaelboek 's Hofs van Holland, van Mr. Jan van Dam*, fol. 256. *Cf.* Wagenaar, *Vad. Hist.* v. p. 297.
‡ Mary of Austria, Queen of Hungary, appointed governess of the Dutch provinces by her imperial brother, in 1530.
§ *Eerste Memoriaelboek van Mr. Jan van Dam*, fol. 344, verso. See *Res. Holland*, 1547 and 1548, p. 197 sqq., and 245 sqq.

of money for one year, but a perpetual tax under the name of last-money, such as had formerly been levied by the Dukes of Burgundy. To obtain this, prohibitions against fishing were again threatened in 1549, whereupon the States offered a gratuity of tenpence on the last of herring for the current season only.* The offer was at once rejected, the Queen demanding "not a gratuity, but a tax." Holland then doubled its offer† on the 29th of August, 1550, and last-money was accordingly levied from the fishermen of the province to the amount of one florin per last of herring caught, Zealand having before granted two, and the men of Flanders consented to equip convoying ships at their own expense. The tax was granted again in the next year, when a prohibition against fishing was issued notwithstanding, to which, however, little observance seems to have been paid.‡

The armed protection thus obtained by the States at the fishermen's expense was very ineffectual. The Imperial convoying ships appear, indeed, to have been utterly inadequate to their task. They could neither cover the whole of the herring fleet, nor be of any use to the busses sailing home with their cargoes; they could not even keep the sea in rough weather, but had frequently to make for the nearest port and leave the fishermen to their destinies. The States, therefore, towards the beginning of the fishing season of 1552, begged the Queen to give up convoying and get safe conducts for the busses from the King of France.§ A similar request was made in 1553,‖ when the shipowners

* *Res. Holland*, 1549, p. 288.
† *Idem.* 1550, pp. 372–380.
‡ *Res. Holland*, 1551, pp. 415, 431 ; Wagenaar, *Vad. Hist.* v. p. 368.
§ *Ibid.* 1552, p. 454 ; *Cf.* Wagenaar, *Vad. Hist.* v. p. 377.
‖ *Ibid.* 1553, pp. 484, 504.

even offered to sail without any protection from Government, and arm some of their vessels for war, so they might be freed from last-money. But the offer was rejected. The Imperial Government was ready, if needed, to send out some worn-out ships of war after the herring busses, and would not give up the tax, part of the produce of which may be confidently supposed to have gone to the Imperial coffers instead of being employed for the purpose it was granted for. Accordingly, the last-money, which had been granted by the States at two florins per last of herring in 1552,* was demanded to the amount of three for 1553 ; and when refused by the States, a prohibition to sail without convoy was once more resorted to on the 30th of May, in order to enforce acquiescence.† The quarrel on the subject between the States and the Queen Governess rose higher as the fishing season approached,‡ but was brought to an accord ; for a few days before the sailing term, the Queen's consent to the shipowners sailing at their own peril, and equipping their vessels for armed resistance in case of need, was notified to the States.§

A placard issued July 30th, 1553, and "ampliated," on July 5th of the next year, determines the number of cannon, pikes, swords, and the quantity of ammunition to be carried on board each fishing vessel, subject to inspection before sailing. The extent of the armament was in virtue of these placards (4ᵉ *Mem.-boek v. Dam.* fol. 117, 232) to be proportioned to each vessel's size, the largest mentioned being forty lasts ; and the amount of warlike preparation

---

* 4ᵉ *Memoriaelboek* v. *Dam*, p. 260.
† *Ibid.* p. 91, verso.
‡ *Res. Holland*, June 14th, 1553, p. 506.
§ *Ibid.* July 19th, p. 512.

prescribed is such as to constitute a heavy charge upon vessels of such a capacity.

It would be tedious to pursue the further course of these money quarrels between Sovereign and subjects, which, as said above, lasted intermittently as long as the House of Austria held sway in the Dutch provinces. The depressed condition of the fisheries under these circumstances is testified to, not indeed by any statistics, but by several legislative acts. Desertion was of frequent occurrence among the seamen hired for service in the herring fishery, as appears from several edicts against it. The business was subject to immense risks of war, and crews were difficult to hire, and apt to disband when hired, as their duty on the armed busses was more of a soldier's than a fisherman's, and "shooting" and "fighting" are mentioned in several placards as a part of their customary work. Shipowners were often tempted to sell their boats and fishing gear abroad, as appears from prohibitions against such sales;[*] and, while forced by Government to keep their vessels in the concern, were during a series of years repeatedly annoyed by prohibitions against sailing without a Government convoy, which appears to have been seldom or never forthcoming in due time. Frequent grants of money made by the States to shipowners or their representatives, in order to enable them to cover losses and repair damages, likewise testify to the trade's depressed condition as a result of the Sovereign's unceasing wars. Not only did these wars expose the fishermen to constant danger, and occasion frequent extortions of grants from them; the fact of the Sovereign being at war with one half of Europe also gave rise to prohibitions against exporting fish, which

---

[*] Placards of July 22nd and Sept. 12th, 1553; 4ᵉ *Mem.-bock*, v. *Dam*, fol. 112, 126, verso.

of course depressed the markets and occasioned bitter remonstrances at the hands of the parties concerned. Working regulations on fisheries must in these evil days have greatly contributed to the trades' depression ; for being, one and all, calculated to warrant the excellence of the fisheries' produce with a view to secure the foreign markets at the cost of severe restrictions upon the industry's liberty, their favourable effect of course was lost in times when many markets were closed, and their only result was to clog the fisherman and preclude him from taking instant advantage of such favourable conjunctions as might occur.

Such working rules were indeed issued with an unsparing hand both under Charles V.'s and his son's government. It has been shown that under the placard of 1519 herring was allowed to be caught and cured before St. James's Day ; and the beginning of the season seems to have been left to the fisherman's discretion.

A prohibition to fish for herring before St. James's, or the 25th of July, seems to have been first thought of in the year 1526, when it was adopted by the States of Holland upon the advice of all the towns concerned in the fishery, Amsterdam alone excepted.* But this enactment was at once complained of on the plea that, not being applicable to the French fishermen, it would put the Dutch at a disadvantage against them. A sharp debate occurred on the subject in a meeting of delegates from Holland, Zealand, Friesland and Flanders, on March 12th, 1526, when by way of a sharp taunt, the Flemings were upbraided with having sold early herring at a low price, which imputation they at once declined in indignant terms. The Northern delegates persisted in the new rule ; and the matter was

* *Res. Holland, in Aert v. d. Goes' Register*, p. 35.

laid before Our Gracious Lady Margaret of Savoy, then Governess of the Netherlands, in the name of the Emperor She, however, declined to enforce the new prohibition in the province of Flanders, upon which the towns of Delft and Schiedam likewise refused to observe it, which the other fishing towns of Holland and Zealand were content to do by way of an experiment.* The question was again moved in May, 1528, between the delegates of Holland, Zealand, Brabant, and Flanders ;† but no agreement was come to, and herring fishing appears to have gone on both before and after St. James's, until the Emperor prohibited the former by a placard dated June 24th, 1536, ‡ and thereby sanctioned the principle that no early herring was to be caught or sold by Dutchmen, which has since been religiously observed as a fundamental fishery law. It should be noted that initial dates for herring fishery have been frequently shifted. About the period now spoken of, a Burgundian law prohibited herring to be salted, i.e. to be caught, before August 24th. A period of liberty as to the date came next; it was fixed at July 25th, in 1536, and shifted more than once in latter years, until definitely appointed on June 24th. *Variations in the annual migrations of the herring shoals* must have occasioned these several alterations of laws.

Besides the edicts just now referred to, police regulations for fishing vessels were issued by Charles V. on August 4th, 1545, and July 9th, 1546, and renewed by his son Philip on the same day of the year 1564. This edict, which was afterwards re-edited by the States, in the King's

---

* *Res. Holland, in Aert van d. Goes' Register*, pp. 38, 39.
† *Ibid.* p. 80.
‡ *Tweede Memoriaelboek's Hof's van Hollant*, fol. 43.

name, on April 26th, 1578, and March 9th, 1580,* contains dispositions against the stealing or destroying of nets, &c., which prove the fishermen, three centuries and a half ago, to have been similarly addicted, in the way of petty piracy, as they appear to have been until the late International Convention. Besides penalties against such piracy, sailing orders to hoist certain signals by day and night while the nets are overboard, and to straighten the helm for fear of getting caught in them, and regulations as to the treatment of fishing gear lost at sea, are found in these statutes. Whoever finds a "fleet," or set of nets, afloat and unowned, and hauls it aboard, is enjoined to carry aloft as many empty herring baskets as there are brails on the nets found; and with these baskets in his rigging, as a sign that he has another man's nets on board, the finder is obliged to sail till their owner has claimed them, in default of which he is to hand them over to the nearest magistrate on coming into port. It is easier to issue laws of this nature than to enforce them; and the several renovations of the placards in question make it very probable that Dutch fishermen were in the course of the sixteenth century by no means averse to make free with the property of friend and foe when occasion offered, or destroy it if coming across their own. It would indeed appear that fishermen, who live by appropriating the unowned and masterless treasures of the sea, are easily brought to stretch the principle a point or two, and appropriate objects which have distinct masters

---

* *Groot Placaetboek*, i. pp. 684–91. The placards of 1546, 1564 and 1578 have been registered by the Court of Holland, and are to be found in their memorial books (1st *van Dam*, fol. 198; 3rd *Ernst*, fol. 173; 7th *Ibid.* fol. 236). It appears from the exordium of the placard of 1580 that both this and that of 1564 were renovations of another dated August 4th, 1545.

and owners; whence the North Sea has for centuries been the theatre of a *bellum omnium contra omnes*, which the legislation of all countries has till now never succeeded in thoroughly restraining. The constant presence of convoying ships with the busses did not prevent abuses of the above nature; nor was this end attained by a more stringent measure enacted in most of the placards just named, viz. the skippers' obligation, when home from a voyage, to have three or four men out of their crews examined upon oath by the competent magistrate as to damage done to others or suffered at their hands, or other breach of statute committed.

Besides police and working rules, taxes were frequently applied to the herring fishery by the Austrian lords of the land. Last-money, which we have seen exacted by a proceeding little short of actual compulsion towards the end of the first half of the sixteenth century, and which was then reluctantly granted, "in the hope of its being for the last time this year,"* became, on the contrary, a perpetual tax, the amount of which was determined annually, and varied accordingly as the Government's wants were greater or lesser, or the occasion for convoying ships more or less pressing. The tax, however, never exceeded two florins (or "pounds of twenty pence") till the end of the century. To this tax, originally a retribution for convoy, an excise duty on herring was added in 1571,† amounting to twopence on the barrel, to be paid by the last seller. A third tax, the exact nature of which I have not been able to ascertain, is mentioned about 1555 by the name of tithe or tenth penny ("*tiende penning*")

---

* *Res. Holland*, 1550, p. 172 and following.
† *Ibid.* 1571, p. 512.

of all herring.* The levying of this tax was deferred to William of Orange, appointed Stadtholder, or Lord Lieutenant, of Holland, Zealand, and Utrecht, when King Philip left the country after the peace of Cateau Cambresis, in the spring of 1559. If the youthful Lord Lieutenant ever levied this tithe at all, he certainly did so with exemplary leniency. Upon taking charge of the Provinces' affairs he found the tax considerably in arrear, as appears from a resolution of the States of Holland dated June 6th, 1559,† by which they begged to know the herring fishery's returns for the years 1553 and 1557, in order to determine the amount due as tithe for the said years. The Prince answered their request by a prayer to suspend the recovering of the tax till his Highness's return from France, and it was still due in 1561,‡ nor have I found any positive evidence of its having ever been recovered at all.

A very different method of drawing money out of the fisheries was pursued by the Spanish governors. The Duke of Alva, who was sent to the Netherlands in 1567 with orders to put down heresy and generally break the country to the iron Spanish rule, first obtained a loan of 28,000 fl. from the States in 1571,§ by a menace of withdrawing the fishermen's convoy if the money were not forthcoming. The exaction was the worse, as the inefficiency of Government convoying ships was as bitterly complained of about this time as twenty years before, and the Commissioners of the herring fishery, of whom more anon, were obliged to equip men-of-war for their safety at

---

* Wagenaar, *Vad. Hist.* v. p. 386. mentions this tax to have been first exacted in 1553; but is not at all sure about the matter, and abstains from giving particulars.

† *Res. Holland*, 1559, p. 289.

‡ *Ibid.* 1561, p. 483.   § *Ibid.* 1571, p. 569.

their own expense in 1570, and sued for a loan from the States in 1571 in order to do the same during the fishing season of that year.*

Fresh taxes to the fisheries' detriment were exacted under the terrible Duke's successor in 1575, when a twentieth penny, or 5 per cent. duty, was ordered to be levied on all fresh fish brought to market in the towns and townships of Holland, and a new excise duty of sixpence per ton of salt fish was moreover established, to be paid by the buyer during the four months succeeding the 1st of March.†

Whatever may have been the fisheries' condition in these times of violent warfare and constant danger, it is evident that they were never entirely stopped, though it may be readily assumed that many fishing vessels and crews left the nearly unprotected trade and joined the bold privateers, who, under the name of "Watergeuzen," took a prominent share in the military events of the time. Still, requests of the fisheries for either subsidy or protection are of annual occurrence even in this period, as proofs of the fisheries' continuation; and it is indeed a strong instance of the trade's vitality that it was never completely given up in years when fishing vessels were constantly beset by many enemies, and never obtained anything like efficient protection.

The year 1575 marks the beginning of a new era for the sea fisheries of Holland and Zealand. The sovereigns of the house of Austria and their several lieutenants had generally considered fishermen and shipowners as subjects from whom considerable sums might be extracted under promises of protection which never was efficiently given. No sooner, on the contrary, did the Prince of Orange take

* *Res. Holland*, 1571, p. 555.
† *Ibid.* 1575, pp. 88, 108, 113, 123.

the provinces' government into his own hands after the revolution's first successes, but the fisheries came in for Government's most earnest solicitude, and were treated as so important an industry deserved. Up to the said year, the point at issue between Government and fishermen had been, who should obtain most from the other and do least for him. The situation at once became the reverse when a national government was virtually established, and a ready willingness to do their utmost for the trade's benefit prevailed on both sides.

This altered state of things was first clearly seen when, towards the beginning of the herring season of 1575, William of Orange called a general meeting of the fisheries' delegates, and earnestly represented to them the expediency of sustaining their trade by their own energy at any cost, as the state of the country's affairs for the moment left no possibility of effectual Government assistance.

A body representative of those concerned in the herring fishery, which in 1575 was recognised by the Prince as a semi-official institution, had in truth borne such character long before. The herring shipowners' habit of appointing some of themselves to forward their common outward interests appears indeed to have been about as ancient as the trade itself, inasmuch as "the common merchants" of certain towns of Holland are mentioned as grantees of privileges extending to the fishery, in the edict of Albert King of Sweden (1368), which has been mentioned above. An organised body of local fishery committees, however, does not appear to have existed before the middle of the sixteenth century, when such an organisation seems to have been the result of constant need of common defence against both enemies abroad and Government exactions at home. A committee of the herring fishery is first mentioned

THE HISTORY OF DUTCH SEA FISHERIES. 31

in 1548, as having conferred with a Government officer on the ways of furthering the herring fishery's interest.* In 1556,† the same Board, or Corporation, gave a receipt for moneys granted by the States for the trade's benefit; it was then composed of the Burgomasters of the several towns and townships where herring ships were owned, viz. Delft, Rotterdam, Schiedam, Brielle, Enkhuizen, Wormer, Jisp and Grootebroek. About this period requests for subsidy and convoy to the herring ships are generally mentioned as having been preferred by "the fishery," "the common fishery," or "those of the fishery;" and the variations in the name by which the corporation was designed at the time confirm the supposition that its existence as a recognised public authority cannot date from a period much anterior.

At any rate, they held considerable official power and responsibility at the time mentioned. The delegates of Delft, Enkhuizen, Brielle, Rotterdam and Schiedam in 1558 agreed to an "accord"‡ by which the fishing boats of the coast villages were bound, in return for the enjoyment of warlike protection, to pay into the hands of the Delegates' Commissioners such a sum per ton of fresh herring sold either at home or in England, as should be appointed by the delegates aforesaid; and this agreement was ratified and registered by the Court of Holland. By another accord, dated September 26th, 1558,§ and registered by the same authority, the "Deputies of the Herring Fishery" agreed to have every tenth fishing buss equipped for war; the expense of such armaments to be borne by the ten

* *Res. Holland*, 1548, p. 288.
† *Ibid.* 1556, p. 92.
‡ *Eerste Memoriaelbock. B. Ernst*, fol. 136.
§ *Ibid.* fol. 133, verso.

vessels together, forming what is, in very un-nautical style, denominated a *band* (bende). The arrangement must have been short-lived, if ever executed at all; but it testifies to the public authority of those who made it on behalf of the rest. Again, in 1562, a loan of 10,000 florins was granted to " Deputies of the Herring Trade" by the States of Holland and West Friesland.* They were therefore at the said period a recognised public body qualified to act in the name of all concerned in the trade. A much more extensive range of official qualification was opened to them after the proceedings between them and the Prince of Orange, which, as said above, took place in 1575.

The Herring Commissioners' attitude in this conference is a strong evidence both of their extensive acting powers and the considerable resources of their constituencies, in spite of bad times. The Prince having explained to them the impossibility of any considerable financial aid out of the public exchequer, the delegates, with a readiness strongly contrasting to the reluctant grants formerly wrung from the States and the fishing towns, voted a supply of three thousand Carolus florins for the first month of the fishing season, and two thousand more for each of the three months to follow, the said charges to be borne by the shipowners according to a fair repartition.† Twelve convoying ships of war were to be equipped out of this money, and further funds, in case of insufficiency, to be found out of the customhouse duties (licenten) on herring. But the Commissioners' task did not stop at the granting of money. They were now for the first time to have a fair share in the disposal of it. A committee was to be appointed by the States and the fishers' delegates jointly, for the organisation of the

* *Res. Holland*, 1562, pp. 689, 694-696.
† *Ibid*. 1575, p. 549

convoying service, the appointment of officers to command the ships of war, and the regulation of all further matters thereunto pertaining.* This agreement between the Prince and the parties concerned was readily ratified by the States on July 5th, 1575,† and the Herring Commissioners were further empowered to levy such last-money on the herring busses as they should see fit, for the gradual reimbursement of the sums advanced; i.e. properly, to distribute the charges of their safety among shipowners as they should judge equitable. Last-money was accordingly decreed to be levied at thirty pence per last of herring in the year 1576,‡ not by the States' collectors, but by officials appointed by the Herring Deputies in each of the fishing towns. Thus the tax, formerly a loathed and hard-grudged Government exaction, took the shape of a contribution willingly granted by the parties concerned towards their mutual protection and safety; and fishing shipowners, as soon as the management of their joint interests was put into their own hands, formed themselves into an extensive corporation and at once proceeded to take the measures most urgently required. It is a fact worth mentioning, as an instance of the national energy of former times, that the whole of the men concerned in one of the principal industries thus organised their business, and readily assumed heavy pecuniary obligations to keep it going, at a moment when every nerve of the nation was strained in self-defence against an overwhelming enemy, and the very heaviest financial sacrifices had to be demanded by Government to keep up a war, the duration and event of which no one could at the time foresee.

* *Res. Holland*, 1575, pp. 550, 551.
† *Ibid.* p. 588.
‡ *Ibid.* 1576, p. 89.

The Herring Committee's official attributes were soon further extended. They had been appointed administrators of their own tax in 1575; they had judicial functions granted to them two years later.

By a placard of May 3rd, 1577,* the States, as in the King's name (who as yet was the legal Sovereign), enacted severe penalties against selling herring or fish † caught by Dutchmen elsewhere than upon Dutch markets, and exchanging them for salt or barrels with foreign fishermen at sea. A resolution of the States of Holland, dated July 12th,‡ appointed the Fisheries Delegates ("*die van de Visscherije*") to enforce this statute and proceed against all who should infringe it, the fines pronounced to be for the common fisheries' benefit, as a means of ensuring the Committee's utmost vigilance.

Legislation on herring fishery had now gradually become rather extensive. But it was disseminated in divers laws and placards, the observance of which must have been fraught with considerable difficulty, as the method of publishing laws was at this period very defective. This circumstance probably led to something like a codification of the fishery statutes, which took place in the year 1582, after the formal defection of the Northern Provinces and their constitution as a free State. This statute, in which all former ones were resumed, may therefore be considered as the first instance of legislation on fishery under the Dutch Republic.

* *Groot Placaetboek*, vol. ii. p. 2145. The statute was re-inforced on April 26th, 1578, and registered in the 7th *Mem. Boek. B. Ernst*, fol. 234, verso.

† The word *fish* is not used in the ancient Dutch fishing vocabulary for *herring*. "Fish" means other fish, generally cod.

‡ *Res. Holland*, 1577, p. 415.

PART II.

SEA FISHERIES UNDER THE DUTCH REPUBLIC.

THE history of the Republic of the United Netherlands embraces the period of Holland's utmost political greatness. It is likewise in this period that the Dutch sea fisheries reached their culminating point, at which they exceeded those of most foreign nations; while in the latter days of the Republic the nation's glory and the trade's prosperity were both swept away by the effect of one common cause.

In accordance with the tremendous development of the fisheries, and of the herring trade especially, during the first century of the Republic's existence, both literature and legislation relative to them are plentiful in the course of this period, and a better idea of the trade's importance may be formed than before, when laws, indeed, were frequently made, but facts on record are few. These several circumstances make the republican period a peculiarly interesting part of the fisheries' history.

It is not till this period that some knowledge can be obtained of the different branches of fishery, one of which (the whaling trade) did not exist before, while as to another (the cod business) only a few indications exist during former centuries. The several branches of the fishing business have throughout the Republic been separate concerns, or nearly so. They were carried on under circumstances so different, that laws held necessary for one were never thought of for others. It is therefore advisable to divide this part of their history into several chapters, relative to, 1, the "grand" or cure-herring fishery; 2, whaling;

3, cod fishery; and 4, the minor industry of catching fresh fish of different kinds, both in the North Sea and Zuider Zee.

Differences with other nations about the right to fish in certain parts of the sea have been frequent during the period which will be treated in the annexed pages, when as yet there were no generally adopted rules of international law. As these differences were of vital interest to a nation whose fishing vessels once frequented the shores of several States, a brief account of them will be given in a separate chapter.

CHAPTER I.

Grand Fishery.

THE distinctive points about the cured-herring fishery under the Republic are the following :—

1st. It was exercised in the second half of the year, chiefly about the coasts of England and Scotland.

2nd. It was carried on in keeled vessels known by the general denomination of busses (*buizen*), the size of which afforded room to cure the herring on board as soon as caught, and thus produce the excellent and easily exportable article for which Holland has long been famous throughout the world.

3rd. It was, by reason of the immense market open to its produce, at one time very far ahead of all other branches of fishery as regards actual importance, and its preservation was one of the chief objects of the Government's solicitude, whence the history of fishery legislation is chiefly that of regulations on herring fishery.

It has been said at the conclusion of the first part of this work, that something like a codification of the laws on

THE HISTORY OF DUTCH SEA FISHERIES. 37

herring fishery was aimed at in the very first year of the Republic's existence. As these statutes have been in vigour, with slight alterations, for two centuries and more, and their influence on the fishery's destinies has been very considerable, it is necessary to expose their tenor at some length.

Part of the fishing code alluded to was indeed anterior to the Republic, being contained in several placards dated March 9th, 1580,* and issued in King Philip's name, though his actual authority had then ceased to prevail in the country, and he was no party to the laws issued, for form's sake, as under his authority. Besides the police regulations referred to at the conclusion of Part I., these so-called Royal placards contain certain rules to be observed in the hiring of sailors for service in fishing vessels, and the relations between them and the ships' masters or "steersmen." The prohibition to carry Dutch herring abroad or dispose of it at sea to foreign fishermen is likewise repeated in one of these Acts. The most interesting part of them is, however, the fixation of the season for "salting herring in barrels," between June 1st and January ult., being a derogation to former placards prohibiting the trade before St. James's Day, which seem to have ere this fallen into oblivion. To preserve the ancient reputation of the Dutch brand-herring was once more the object of this enactment. "Whereas," says the placard, "it has come to Our knowledge that some *for their singular profit* do catch the herring before its season and time, ere they be good and right natural to eat, and salt them in barrels and sell them in the market, though such herrings be quite untimely and often prejudicious to the consumer thereof, thereby causing in

* *Groot Placaetboek v. Hollandt en Westvriesland*, vol. i. pp. 684–691, 696–707, 715–717, 748–751.

these countries not only, but also and in particular in other lands, whereunto herring is carried and diverted, a great disgust, dishonour and contempt of herring, so that the taste for good and timely herring is likewise spoiled, the latter being thereby made unwilling and often remaining unsold along with the bad, to the loss of the merchants, and consequently to the prejudice of the fishery, which is one of the principal mines of our common countries' welfare ; against which sundry abuses wishing promptly to provide, We do well and expressly prohibit," &c. It is a constant and prominent feature of Dutch fishery legislation that people are always forbidden to do what they saw fit to do " for their singular profit."

Legislators never, until twenty-five years ago, could realise the notion that, upon the whole, the fisherman is the best judge of his own interests. Constant infractions of the herring laws, instead of bringing the governing powers and their advisers to acknowledge that to break the law must upon the whole be more profitable than to observe it, only caused them frequently to renew the different Acts, and enact still heavier penalties against transgressors who were uniformly considered as reckless and unprincipled men ready to sacrifice the common interest to the success of their own misdoings. It was considered laudable to seek profit by catching herring, provided the profit should only be looked for where Government pointed it out. All other profit-seeking was a heinous offence.

The same anxiety to maintain the reputation of the Dutch cured herring abroad, which speaks from the above-quoted considerations, also dictated another part of the herring legislation of 1580, viz. the prohibitions against tampering with brands. It has been said in the first part of this work that the branding of herring barrels was ever

THE HISTORY OF DUTCH SEA FISHERIES. 39

since 1519 subject to control by assayers ("*keurmeesters*") appointed for the purpose in each town; and the brand thus constituted an official certificate of the article's excellence. In order to preserve this character, and likewise to protect the Dutch fishermen against foreign competition, it was in 1580 prohibited under severe penalties, firstly, to privately mark barrels containing spawn-sick and other defective herring with counterfeits of the controlled brands, or even with fancy marks,* and next, to pack herring caught by foreigners in barrels properly branded before. The use and even the importing of foreign or unrefined salt † was also prohibited by this Act, and the prohibition was even extended to "small salt" made or refined in the country, which it was forbidden either to sell or use, unless to foreigners and for the purpose of exportation.

But these regulations were not deemed sufficient. The brand inspector's control, which till now only served to warrant the quality of *barrels*, appears not always to have been sufficiently close; and the deputies of the herring-fishing towns found upon inquiry that the quality of both herring and barrels exported under the official brand was sometimes deficient "because of the small control hitherto exercised thereon." Wherefore, "having often been collegially assembled at Delft and ripely communicated on the matter," they drew up a regulation "touching the making, assaying and branding of herring barrels, the time of catching, salting, handling, and packing of herring," which

---

* Literally, "with ornamented bye-marks or otherwise."
† "Salt not sodden of salt." The "moor-salt," or "zelle" highly recommended in the placard of 1519, appears to have been utterly out of use towards the end of the 16th century, as it is not even mentioned in the laws of 1580.

was arrested by the States of Holland on April 27th, 1582,* and is the first instance of Republican herring legislation. The principal provisions of this Act, which has for more than two centuries been the base of all working regulations upon the herring trade, are the following :—

Besides the cooper's private mark, already prescribed by the placard of 1519, a town-brand, which in the said year was admitted in such towns as should see fit to use it, is now ordered to be established in every town where barrels are made. All barrels, whether whole, half, quarter (kinnetgens), or eighth part, are to be marked with this town-brand (here called *tonnebrand*) previous to their being carried out of the town. The cooper apposes his own brand, but the town-brand is added by municipal officers or *branders*, under the assayer's supervision. These branders are forbidden ever to let their tools and marking-irons go out of their hands, or send them to the cooper's by their wives, children, or servants. They are enjoined, before branding each barrel, to examine it well and roll it over three or four times containing a certain quantity of clean water, and refuse it if found to leak, or to be worm-eaten, made of light wood, or otherwise defective. No branding of barrels is allowed between sunset and sunrise, and when the brander comes to the cooper's to perform his business, the latter, his wife and journeymen are not to be present at the operation, but keep within call either in the house or a street's width from it, in case the brander should want to show them any defectivity in the barrels. The number of staves to each barrel is to be twelve or thirteen as a minimum, and the dimensions of barrels, staves and hoops,† as

* *Groot Placaetboek*, vol. i. pp. 718-727.

† A standard measure of herring barrels appears to have been kept at Dordrecht. According to van der Lely's *Recueil* (p. 15) the

well as the places where to appose the cooper's and the town-brand, are accurately determined by the law. Branders are allowed to exercise the coopering trade on their own behalf, but they are in this case to have their article examined and branded either by a colleague or by the assayer or "keurmeester" himself. The barrels carried to sea by fishermen are to be either new, or provided with fresh hoops and assayed and branded afresh since last used. The packing of herring and piling up of barrels is ordered to take place either in the public street or with doors open, so as to enable all and sundry to control the execution of the aforesaid dispositions as regards the quality of the barrels used.*

The nature of the salt to be used by fishermen at sea is regulated in detail. Gross salt, if used at all, is to be previously examined by the assayer, and, for full herring caught after St. James's, Bartholomew's, or Elevation day, " small salt sodden from salt " is the only sort allowed. No salt is to be sold, bought, or taken on board, unless accompanied by a certificate as to its quality, delivered at the place of fabrication.

As to the fishery itself, the most important disposition of this Act is the fixation of the fishing season for cured-herring between July 1st and December ult. of each year. The former, or opening date, which had been appointed at June 1st two years before, was again shifted to St. John's

---

Herring College in 1593 resolved to have the assayers' measures adjusted to this standard, and a general "equalization" of all barrels was ordered to take place in 1624.

* It was commonly done in public ; whence probably the name of "Haringpakkery" still applied to one of the broadest quays of Amsterdam.

(or the 24th of June) in 1588 * as an evidence of the uncertainty about, and probably the variations of, the true fit herring-season. It cannot be doubted that by these successive enactments fishermen have often been prevented from exercising their trade at times when it might have been done with a fair result. To bind a business to certain dates and seasons is at all times a dangerous practice in legislation ; but whenever nature shows the fit season for such an industry to be variable, all restrictions ought to be abolished at once. The mere fact that an alteration of laws of this nature is found necessary should be a reason to repeal them altogether ; for there can in that case be no certainty that the new law is better than the old.

The treatment, or mode of handling† herring when caught, is accurately prescribed in the State's placard of 1582. Besides a reiteration of former prohibitions against disposing of herring either abroad or at sea, the masters of herring-busses are enjoined on their responsibility, and under considerable penalties, to see that the fish be laid in the barrels in regular layers, four in length, from bottom to bottom. The packing of bad herring together with good is severely prohibited, and it should be noticed that the sale of the very worst ‡ article was allowed, provided it should be classed and owned as such when sold.

* See also a placard dated March 17th, 1593, *Gr. Placaetboek*, vol. i. pp. 726-29, where the date is likewise fixed at " St. John's Day in midsummer."

† " Havenen," a word actually used only in the sense of "damaging."

‡ " Yelen-, nachtschamel-, kuytsieck-, melk-sieck-, *stanck ofte want haring*." The latter words were substituted in 1584 for the original term : *sterke haring*. The one means " stinking," the other " bad " or " strong," in the sense of " strong butter." " Kuytsieck " and " melk-sieck " are the words indicating extreme ripeness of the spawn

In order to ensure the observation of these statutes, each fishing captain is enjoined as heretofore to have his private mark apposed to each barrel before letting it out of his vessel, and have this mark and his name entered in a register kept by the town magistrate. Obligatory inspection of the *fish*, if for exportation, is now for the first time added to assay of the *barrels ;* the inspector's duty being to prevent herring of different qualities being packed in one fust, and to see to the quality of the salt used. It is prohibited, as formerly, to wash, clean, pack or otherwise manipulate foreign herring. The present law is ordered to be annually promulgated afresh in every fishing town, on the 1st of March, at which date most herring captains are stated to be at home ; and all such alterations and fresh statutes on the subject as may be found necessary are ordered to be drawn up by the Deputies of the towns where the herring trade is exercised, and promulgated after the States' approval. The Herring Deputies or Commissioners' functions, which till now involved the police of the trade and the administration of its common financial interests, are thereby completed with what is, in fact, legislative power ; for it will appear further that their draft statutes were always approved without any alterations by the proper Legislature, i.e. the States-Provincial or General, as the case might be.

It will be seen from this brief account of what may perhaps, though improperly, be styled "the herring-fishery code of 1580–82," that its chief object was to uphold the reputation which herring of Dutch brand then already enjoyed in all foreign markets ; its next, to keep the staple

---

and milt ; "nachtschamel" I take to stand for "overnight" or herring not cured immediately after the catch.

market of the article in the country, and have it exported from the Dutch emporiums only.

The first-named and chief pre-occupation of the successive Dutch governments had indeed been apparent, besides laws, from several facts on record previous to the Republic's establishment. In 1552 it was reported that citizens of Antwerp had presumed to tamper with the town brand of Dordrecht, erasing it from certain herring-barrels and substituting another mark for it, "notwithstanding the brand of Dordt is older and more authentic, and known all over Germany, France and other countries." Dordrecht laid the matter before the States of Holland, who thought it of sufficient importance to send their Advocate (whose functions had some analogy with those of a Secretary of State) to Brussels on purpose to obtain redress.* In the next years regular lawsuits were carried on against the authorities of Malines, Ghent, Flushing and Nieuwpoort respectively, for having repacked herring from Holland in other barrels,† thereby enhancing their Zealand and Flemish marks or brands with the excellence of the Hollands produce, and perhaps using the empty barrels marked with the Hollands brand to pass off foreign fish of inferior quality. Again, in 1582, the States of Holland intervened in a lawsuit then pending between certain citizens of Spires and Worms, in the heart of Germany, about the quality of herrings bought and sold between them, merely because the herring in question bore a Dutch brand.‡

The importance of the salt-herring fishery and trade

* *Res. Holl.* 1552, pp. 482-3.
† *Res. Holl.* 1554, p. 584; 1555, p. 697; 1561, pp. 480, 517; 1565, p. 33.
‡ *Res. Holland* 1582, pp. 241, 248.

about this period is testified to by many more credentials. In 1581, the States thought it worth their while to despatch an embassy to Bremen,* in order to obtain the removal of certain edicts there issued, prejudicial to the Dutch herring trade's interest ; and let it be remembered that the Provinces were at this very time occupied by so very momentous a plan as the abjuration of their Sovereign the King of Spain, and their constitution as a free republic in the face of the world. It is likewise a fact not to be overlooked that at this most critical juncture of their history, while weighed down on all sides by cares innumerable of war, finance, and politics, the Province of Holland never once let her herring-fishermen lack convoy, when imminent danger from the enemy at sea did not force them to prohibit the fishery altogether.

The fishers fully responded to their government's care and energy ; for though many of their busses were taken year by year, either by the enemy's cruisers or by Dunkirk privateers, they never lost heart, but still continued the trade, under protection generally insufficient, and in the face of the enormous financial liabilities laid upon them by their disasters, and borne by them in common, under their self-appointed commissioners' administration. The name of Grand Fishery,† which in 1580 and afterwards was generally applied to the cured-herring concern to indicate its being "the chief industry of the country and principal gold-mine to its inhabitants," is indeed justified at the period now spoken of, by the splendid pluck and untiring tenacity displayed by the men who exercised it, under circumstances which reduced to insignificance many industries less directly exposed to the war's calamities than theirs.

* *Res. Holland* 1581, pp. 579, 732, 766 ; 1582, pp. 240-1.
† "*Groote Visscherye.*"

The war, indeed, took manifold effect upon the herring-fishery. Besides losses at sea and taxes ashore, the trade had to bear the consequences of a prohibition to export victuals, fish included, which was one of the most unpopular measures adopted by the Earl of Leicester during his short-lived and infelicitous administration of the United Provinces. The interdiction was indeed, at the Herring Commissioners' request, repealed in 1586 as regarded exportation to neutral States ; * and traders managed to get their produce carried to Germany by a circuit, the Rhine being closed by the town of Nijmegen having embraced the enemy's cause,† and refusing to let any merchandise pass out of the revolted provinces, even upon the States' urgent request. Still the prohibition was maintained as against exportation to the enemy's dominions, and sometimes enforced by the exporters being obliged, upon their ships' return, to show an attest mentioning the place where the herrings had been sold.‡ It is a curious example of the political status of the day, that an Englishman sent to govern the Republic should have enforced a measure which closed the important markets of Belgium against the herring traders of the country, while the States were at the same time making considerable money sacrifices in the latter's behalf.

Among these sacrifices it is now time to mention the immunity of excise duty on salt used in curing herrings at sea, which was conceded to the Grand Fishery as a special boon by the Prince of Orange, and ratified by the States-General soon afterwards. This privilege is first mentioned

* *Res. Holl.* 1586, p. 308.
† *Ibid.* 1585, p. 245 ; 1584, p. 538.
‡ *Ibid.* 1585, p. 808.

in 1586 ;* it has been maintained ever since and exists to the present day, as will be seen in another part of this work. It was extended to the whole of the Republic as emanating from the central legislative power; but the province of Holland very soon bought the privilege off, for their province, by an agreement with the College of the Grand Fishery, in virtue of which the fishermen paid the excise duty, and a consideration of fl. 6000 a-year was granted to the College out of the provincial treasury.†

The duty in Holland then amounted to fl. 14 per hundredweight of fine white salt; whence the quantity of salt annually used by the sea-fisheries of the province would appear to have been something less than 43,000 pounds. It would not, however, be safe to attach much importance to this average calculation ; for compared to the far superior quantities of salt now used free of excise by the Dutch sea-fisheries, it does not correspond to the probable extent of the trade in the province of Holland at the period now spoken of. Many considerations, which it would be highly interesting to trace at leisure, may have led the Fishery College to sell their immunity for an inequivalent sum.

Besides the Spanish fleets, the great bane of the Dutch sea-fisheries at this time were the privateers from Dunkirk, who may be said throughout the Republic's history to have been to herring fishers what the dog-fish is to the herring. Constant complaints were made of busses taken and destroyed by these audacious filibusters, against whose superior strength and seamanship such convoy as the States could

* *Res. States-General* 1586, June 12th and November 4th, 1587 September 4th.

† *Res. Holl.* 1588, pp. 133, 231 ; 1589. p. 459 ; 1593, p. 407 ; 1595, p. 69, &c.

afford was insufficient. The plan of self-help, which had been pressed upon the fisheries by Charles the Fifth's lieutenants, was now once more adopted; and by a States of Holland placard, dated May 14th, 1596,* busses were forbidden to sail unless either under convoy or "in admiralship" i.e., in squadron of twenty at the least. In the latter case each of the vessels was to carry a certain quantity of artillery and ammunition, and the whole squadron to be commanded by an "Admiral" appointed by the captains out of their number. This expedient was especially recommended by the promise of a gratification to the fishing commander who should capture or sink a vessel of the enemy's. It does not appear that the premium was much contended for, as the paying of ransom, or safeguard-money, was at the time resorted to by numerous fishermen,† until the passports delivered were denounced by the enemy in 1599.‡ A special committee of ship-owners and Government officials had meanwhile been appointed § to draw a plan for the fisheries' perpetual preservation; but there is no result of their deliberations on record, and in the end, as the prevailing financial distress made it impossible to provide sufficient convoy by Government men-of-war, the States granted an extraordinary subsidy of fl. 20,000 to the fisheries' commissioners in 1600,‖ out of which they were to find their own convoy. The grant was repeated for a long series of years, when fishermen accordingly sailed under cover of convoyers equipped at their own expense. These vessels, afterwards called "Direction-ships," (*Directie-*

---

* *Groot Plac. Boek*, i. 711.
† *Res. Holland* 1598, pp. 135, 193.
‡ *Ibid.* 1599, pp. 27, 623.
§ *Ibid.* 1598, pp. 128, 193.
‖ *Ibid.* 1600, p. 71.

schepen)* to signify their nature as belonging to the Fisheries' directors, were nevertheless commanded by officers appointed by the Stadtholder and under oath of fidelity to the States-General. A pusillanimous plan for pacifying the Dunkirk Vikings, by issuing letters of safe-conduct under the States' seal to such enemies as should reciprocally let the United Provinces' vessels fish unmolested, "in the hope," as the States of Holland candidly aver, "that fewer pirates will this year put to sea from the ports of Flanders," † was indeed tried a few years afterwards, but there is no evidence of its having had anything like success. And this, indeed, seems highly improbable; for there was not much promise in an attempt to make the Dunkirkers give up piracy by offering them a permission to fish within range of the guns of the States' men-of-war.

The fishery laws were in the meantime strenuously maintained, although under considerable difficulties. It was not easy to enforce the prohibitions against carrying herring caught by Dutch fishermen directly abroad; and moreover, the inevitable "gain-seeking" people, who "for their singular profit" did not fear to break the law, managed to smuggle herring not lawfully packed and branded through the United Provinces, and elude the authorities' vigilance. Notwithstanding the yearly reminder to the herring-skippers, the placards, in a word, got out of observation "by the slowness and the passing of years," and were frequently re-enacted in the first years of the seventeenth century.‡

* *Cf. de Jonge, Geschiedenis van het Nederl. Zeewezen*, i. pp. 257–8. This institution is also mentioned in Meynert Semeyns'" *Beschryvinge over de Haring visscherye in Hollandt*," but with the lack of precision usual in that otherwise precious contemporary author.

† *Res. Holland* 1606, p. 783.

‡ Viz., the years 1604, 1606, 1607, 1612, 16 5, 1620, 1621, 1632, *Groot Plac. Boek*, i. p. 733, and following.

They were, besides, altered in some points, among which some importance may be attributed to the shifting of the salt-herring fisheries closing-day to January ult., the express prohibition against curing salt-herring ashore, the prohibition to cure herring with other salt than Spanish or Portuguese, and the institution of divers brands, each to be solely exported to certain towns or countries. The leading idea of these several enactments is an extreme anxiety, not only to have the foreign markets constantly supplied with a good article, but also to have that article packed and otherwise made up in the fashion customary in the several markets. For instance, a "Rouen brand" was consecrated to exportation to France, and there was also a "Cologne brand." The principle of having distinct brands for herring caught at different parts of the season, which we have seen established in 1519 by the prescription of a "St. James's brand," was much extended in the early years of the seventeenth century, when a "Lady Day" (Vrouwe brand), an "Elevation Day" (Kruis brand), and a Bartholomew brand were, if not first used, at least first mentioned in the herring laws.* Each of these brands was to have the peculiar look customary in the several markets; and to this effect very detailed prescriptions were given as to the number of hoops to be applied to the barrels marked with each brand. In short, having undertaken in many points to regulate the fisherman's business, legislation by degrees took the dealer's, broker's, and expeditioner's likewise into her own hands, and the merchant's activity and acuteness were superseded by Government rules. Constant changes in the different markets' requirements of course led to fre-

* Brands stating the time of capture were then the only distinctives. The quality-brands stating herring to be "full," "matties," or "ylen," are of much posterior invention.

quent alterations of these enactments, and the branding and packing legislation of the period now spoken of is, as a consequence, rather intricate.

But of the several ampliations to the herring fishing laws in the first quarter of the seventeenth century, those relative to the practice of "sale-hunting" are the most important. This peculiar trade has originated in the Dutch fisheries' particular situation. Being obliged to fish far from their own shores, the busses would have lost much precious time if they had been obliged to sail home as soon as their cargo was completed, and land their fish before catching more. They would, moreover, in most cases have lost the advantage of landing herring very early in the season, and being first in the market, which was, and is, of great importance, as freshly salted or "new" herring has always been very much appreciated, and paid for at several times the price of fish caught or sold later in the year.* To secure the

---

* In fact, a frantic eagerness to be first in the market has always been an interesting characteristic of the Dutch herring trade in the early season; so much so, that it may be doubted whether the very real advantage of selling the first barrels in any given market was often worth the outlay of money and trouble made to secure it. Throughout the Republic's time, slow coaches and slower canal boats were the only conveyances; the Dutch never were great horsemen, and journeys on foot were not disdained even by those endowed with worldly goods. But on the day when the first "ventjagers" arrived at Rotterdam, or Vlaardingen, no speed was deemed sufficient to carry the first barrels of "new" herring to the inland towns. Dealers kept light curricles and fleet horses on purpose, and the minute a few barrels were unshipped and assayed, a furious race to the Hague, Amsterdam, &c., began. Each of the vehicles could carry a few barrels only, and the profit of the thing perhaps did not generally cover the expense. But to be first in the market anywhere was always a point of honour with the Dutch herring-dealer; and the day when the first herring arrived, and the barrels were posted across country in chaises, with foaming teams and streaming flags, was a day of general

advantage of the early market, fast-sailing vessels, called "*ventjagers*" or "sale-hunters," used to accompany the herring-fleet, buy up the first herring caught and cured, and carry it home with the utmost speed, leaving the busses to fish on at leisure. This trade, if not attended to, might of course have afforded ample facilities to elude the prohibition against selling herring elsewhere than in the Dutch emporiums, and "sale-hunting" was therefore, soon after the fishing laws before quoted came into vigour, an object of the legislator's peculiar supervision and solicitude.

From the fact that no particular legislation on the subject existed before, it appears that the custom of sale-hunters following the busses did not come into use before the beginning of the seventeenth century. "*Ventjagers*" are indeed mentioned as early as the year 1556, but from a placard of January 11th of that year * it is evident that at that time they did not go beyond the rivers' mouths, and the wording of the first law relative to sale-hunting *at sea*, (dated 1604), plainly shows the practice to have been then very recently adopted. The first enactments on the subject are chiefly calculated to prevent the laws on catching, curing, landing, and branding herring to be eluded by

---

rejoicing. Even to the present time, when herring brought home by the first "hunter" is prosaically sent inland by rail, some of the traditional festivities are kept up. Dealers in fish sport bunting from their house-tops ; " New Herring " is cried through every city, and an old-fashioned one-horse chaise on immense wheels, decked with the national colours, may be seen to race to the King's palace at the Hague, in order to supply the royal table with the very first barrel of herring. The whole of this pageantry, however, is now little more than a remembrance of the time when " New Herring " actually meant an influx of millions into the country, and a shower of gold upon thousands of its inhabitants.

* *Vierde Memoriaalboek's Hofs van Hollant, van Mr. J. van Dam*, fol. 37 ; *Vijfde, ibid.* fol. 201.

"sale-hunters." They prescribe that every skipper who sails after the fleet for the purpose of buying up herring shall be provided with a license under the seal of, and delivered by, the "magistrate and treasurers of the fishery," i.e., the local fishery boards. Every such skipper is, before sailing, to take oath not to buy any salt-herring but from Dutch steersmen, and to have every lot he takes on board covered by a certificate from the seller, stating the latter's name and his vessel's, his domicile and the quantity of fish transferred. Sale-hunters are besides, like skippers, prohibited from carrying their ware abroad.

Sale-hunting appears at the outset to have been allowed during the whole of the season; though of course the business could only pay as long as high prices lasted. A restriction as to time was first put upon it, and a "hunting-time" (jaagtijd) established in 1632, the closing date after which it should not be lawful to transfer herring at sea, being then fixed at July 15th. The object of the enactment evidently was to prevent an overstocking of the market at a period when prices naturally declined, the first eager demand for early herring being satisfied. But the practice of "hunting" sometimes occasioned a glut at the very outset of a favourable season, or, as a placard of the time has it, "so threw the herring-market prostrate * that neither fishermen nor dealer could make a profit upon it." This evil was, in later times, prevented by the *hunting-monopoly*, i.e. the prohibition to fishermen to sail home during "hunting-time" unless with a full cargo. *This monopoly never legally existed under the Dutch Republic; it has been a creation of the present century*, or may possibly have been established as a College bye-law late in the eighteenth century; and those who in the course of the dis-

* "*Sulcks onder de voet wort geworpen.*"

cussions on Herring Law Repeal have given it in part the credit of the fishery's former greatness, argued from a statement utterly erroneous. The old Dutch herring laws, never for the hunters' benefit, restricted herring carriage by fishers; when a glut occurred *they prohibited hunting*, and such prohibitions are frequent enough.* As a fact, the industry was either permitted or prohibited, upon the College's annual advice, as the state of the market seemed to require abundant or slower supplies. Opinions were generally divided on the subject in the College; Rotterdam, Schiedam and Brielle generally moving to allow sale-hunters to sail, and Delft and Enkhuizen opposing them. Delegates from these five towns have for a long period composed the College, and the point whether three cities could overrule two was frequently contested *à propos* of the hunting question, and generally decided by the majority having their mind.

The said College about this time showed considerable activity. Besides the extensive administration of the convoying ships, and the collecting of the shipowners' contributions out of which they were equipped, they were constantly advising or petitioning the States for such legislative measures as the times seemed to give occasion for, and accordingly had their eye always upon the herring-fishery trade and market in the most extensive sense. Not content with these functions, "they of the Grand Fishery" constituted themselves as guardians of the laws enacted upon their advice. Every town where herring-ships were owned had a fishery board of its own: and Delft, Rotterdam, Amsterdam, Brielle, Schiedam, Hoorn and Enkhuizen, and

---

* See the placards on the subject of the years 1604, 1606, 1607, 1612, 1614, 1615, 1621, 1632, *Gr. Pl. Boek* I., pp. 731-748; *v. d. Lely. Recueil*, pp. 20, sqq.

THE HISTORY OF DUTCH SEA FISHERIES. 55

probably more towns not particularly mentioned, were by means of these local boards constantly on the look-out for each other's trespasses, which, as soon as discovered, were reported to the central College residing at Delft, who took steps for the better enforcement of the law. Thus in 1604* it was discovered that skippers from Enkhuizen sometimes acted against the fishing laws, and the magistrates of the said city were compelled, upon the remonstrances of one of the Burgomasters of Rotterdam and of " them of the Grand Fishery " to issue an order for the observance of the existing rules by fishermen hailing from the Enkhuizen port. On the other hand, some of the fishing towns took upon themselves considerable responsibilities in the way of mitigating the laws when found too severe. On the 15th of December 1609,† the local boards of Delft, Rotterdam, Schiedam, Brielle and Enkhuizen met at the first-named town, and agreed, on their own authority, upon a "mild execution" of the statutes against selling herring at sea, provided such herring should not have been caught before the lawful season. This striking instance of open tampering with the law is strongly illustrative of the very ill-defined and swaying conditions under which public power was held in the Republic. Still more strongly does it testify to the fact that, even in the first outset of systematic fishing legislation, its flaws and nuisances were realised by those concerned, who knew their immediate interest even where the law precluded them from following it up.

The Central Fishery College's influence manifested itself afresh in 1606, by a prohibition against exporting herring-barrels, whole or half-staves, nets and cross-gear,‡ which prohibition was suggested by " those of the

* *Res. Holland*, 1604, p. 158.
† *Res. Holland*, 1609, p. 1089.   ‡ *Kruyswant*.

Fishery" to the States of Holland, and by them applied for to the States-General, who at once enacted it to be a law for the whole of the Republic.* Nor was the College's vigilance against transgressions of the herring laws confined to stopping them at home. When any were detected abroad, diplomatic intervention was resorted to upon their advice, and sometimes successfully. As an instance of this, an "accord," of the nature of what would now be called a commercial treaty, was concluded between the States-General and the Senate of Hamburg on May 22nd, 1609,† by which the latter city bound itself over not to let any herring caught before St. John's be sold in its market. This treaty, about the observation of which considerable difficulties arose a century afterwards, was urged by the States, upon the College's advice, who had detected the sale of early herring at Hamburg, in dangerous concurrence with the Dutch exporters, who were bound by law not to fish before St. John's.‡

The year 1609 was a momentous one for the Dutch Grand Fishery, for more reasons than the treaty with Hamburg. It was in this year that James the First of England, by the famous "proclamation touching fishing," menaced the trade with a blow which, if not averted,

* *Res. Holland*, 1606, p. 934 ; *Gr. Placaetboek I.* p. 755.

† *Res. Holl.* 1609, p. 918. A copy of the document is inserted in *Ned. Zaarboeken*, 1752, p. 483.

‡ Treaties, or contracts of a similar nature seem to have existed between the city of Cologne and those of Rotterdam, Delft, and Schiedam, at even an earlier period, by which the former bound itself not to admit any herring unless branded under the Hollands' regulations. In 1754 the Dutch Consul at Cologne reported that herring from Zealand was admitted there against the treaties, "whereas no other herring than from Holland had been seen there since more than two hundred years."

might have prevented its further development, and the rivalry between England and the Netherlands as regards sea-fishery first came to an open outbreak. The several phases of this rivalry, down to its end in the war of 1652, are of considerable moment in the Dutch fisheries' history; but as they belong to an order of events entirely separate from the trade's home regulations, it is preferable to treat of them in a separate chapter.

As regards home legislation, the now following years offer little or no matter of interest, and are only marked by a series of renovations of the placards before mentioned, occasionally varied by alterations of little importance. The only novelty in any way suggestive of the state of the business, besides the placards on sale-hunting already alluded to, is an Act of May 12th, 1620,* by which it is prohibited to fish for herring among the cliffs of Shetland, Ireland and Norway; not in order to avoid collisions with the inhabitants of those countries, but merely, as appears from the entire tenor of the statute, because the herring caught in the said waters was said to be of inferior quality and unfit for curing. By this edict, besides, a very notable extension of the Herring Fishery College's functions is sanctioned for the first time, viz., their being invested with judicial power. Any person sentenced by the common magistrate for catching herring in the prohibited waters, or salting, barrelling, or selling herring so caught, is granted the right of appealing to the college, who shall examine the matter in their next session, and finally decide it by a judgment from which there shall be no further appeal. The college is thus appointed to be a court of appeal in some fishery cases, and its attributions as such were in the course of times extended to most other

* *Groot Placaetboek* I. p. 752.

contraventions against the fishery laws, besides those against the particular statute now mentioned. Nor were the judicial functions of this board confined to cases of breach of common law. According to a manuscript "Recueil of the Grand Fishery," or register of notes concerning it, kept, or owned, about 1753, by one Mr. J. v. d. Lely and preserved in the Royal Netherlands Library,* they have "from all old times" vindicated for themselves the right of disciplinary jurisdiction against all misdemeanours ("wandivoiren") committed by the officers and men serving both in busses and convoying ships. This competence was officially confirmed in their hands, and probably much extended, by a Resolution of the States of

---

* I have no positive clue to this v. d. Lely's social position. His title of "Mr." shows him to have been a graduate-at-law. The *Recueil* under his name frequently quotes the record-books of the Fishery College, and its author appears to have been otherwise possessed of extensive information on the fishery subject. It is by no means improbable that v. d. Lely may have been secretary to the College, a post of considerable importance in the republic's later years. At any rate, such information as his *Recueil* imparts may, if not contradicted by other evidence, be accounted conclusive. Unfortunately the *Recueil* is drawn up in a very succinct style, so as often to leave some doubt about the meaning of the words and abbreviations. It has evidently been composed as a private register to aid the memory of the author as deeply concerned in fishery matters, and has never been published. The original record-books of the Fishery College appear unfortunately to have been lost; and without them no very precise idea of that body's constitution and attributions can be formed. There is extant another "*Recueil van de Groote Vissclicryc*," also manuscript, owned, or written, by Mr. J. van der Craght, and now in Mr. Nyhoff's private collection. I have, upon inspection, found both manuscripts to be literally of the same tenor, and have therefore quoted the one bearing the latest date. V. d. Craght's is dated 1745. Both look like copies of some original bearing a still earlier date.

Holland dated December 20th, 1625*, which indeed constitutes the College a supreme court of justice in fishery matters, with very extensive attributions. All misdemeanours of the seamen and officers in the convoying vessels, who it will be remembered were in the country's service and under oath to the States, were by this Act attributed to the College of the Fisheries' Deputies and expressly withdrawn from the ordinary military courts for naval matters, i.e., the Admiralty Boards. Proceedings against convoying commanders guilty of "shameful running away out of the sea," and "omitting all devoir against the enemy," as well as common breach of discipline cases, were at the time now treated of committed to the college's jurisdiction. Their sentences were decisive and without appeal. Like all other fishing laws, the statute in question was enacted upon the college's own presentation, or rather was enacted by them and ratified by the States of Holland.

"Devoir" was indeed required from both convoying men-of-war and fishing vessels at the time when the college was thus qualified to enforce it; for in no period of the republic's naval history did the Dunkirkers cause as much prejudice to the fishing interest. In 1625 the town of Enkhuizen alone is reported to have lost a hundred busses to them.† Naval battles *in forma* were fought between them and the herring fleet and convoyers; and numerous instances of busses being taken by ten together, and convoying ships overcome by "the enemy," are balanced by accounts of the latter having lost both ships and men.‡

* *Res. Holland*, 1625, p. 604. *Recueil v. d. Lely*, p. 8.
† *Gevers Deynoot de magno sive halecum piscatu Belgico*, p. 41.
‡ *Res. Holland*, 1627, pp. 240, 248, 252, and many others in the next years.

This irregular warfare was not carried on without considerable outlays of money. Sums averaging up to thirty thousand florins were annually granted to the Fishery College for the warlike armament of the busses; and subsidies very much larger were granted to the Admiralty Boards to provide the necessary convoying ships. In 1627 the latter subsidy was carried to one million,* to be furnished by the several provinces, each for a part proportioned to its interest in the business, and twenty-four men-of-war were sent to protect the busses in the said year. Indeed, during a series of years the main part of the States of Holland's Acts relative to the herring fishery consists of money grants to the College and the Admiralties, and exhortations to the latter boards to be prompt in equipping the necessary vessels. The difficulties with England about the herring fishery in the North Sea, and the insecurity arising from the British Sovereign's manifestly hostile intention to Dutchmen fishing on his shores, of course made matters still worse for the trade. It is indeed a marvel that it should, in spite of so many difficulties, have attained a high degree of development. Yet such was the case, as appears from Meynert Semeyns' curious little book already quoted, and which, written in 1639,† gives a very high idea of the state of the business at the time, even if due allowance is made for a tendency to exaggeration natural in the author as a citizen of Enkhuizen, then one of the most important among the herring-fishing towns.

With Semeyns it is a point beyond dispute that Providence has specially destined the Netherlands to be the centre of the world's herring fishery. "The Dutch," he

---

* *Res. Holland*, pp. 164, 166, 247.

† Meynert Semeyns, Corte beschryvinge over de Haring visscherye in Hollandt.

says, "catch more herrings, and prepare them better, than any other nation ever will; and the Lord has, through the instrument of the herring, made Holland an exchange and staple-market for the whole of Europe. The herring keeps Dutch trade going, and Dutch trade sets the world's afloat," whence the author states Dutch herrings to be the mainspring of the world's trade and traffic. No other nation, he says, ever tried this industry but to their detriment; and as an instance of this, he relates the fact that herring caught by Englishmen at the same time and place with Dutch fishermen had been found bad and corrupt at the market of "Danswyck" (Dantzig?), while the Dutch produce was eagerly bought there. Besides such general statements, which at any rate are additional proof that herring was at the time a considerable article of exportation, the author gives some valuable details about the way in which the fishery was carried on in his days. The first cast of the nets is made at St. John's (June 24th) about the Shetlands, Fairhill and Buchan-Ness,* and the fishing continued in those waters till St. James', or the 25th of July. From St. James' to Elevation Day (September 14th) Buchan-Ness or "Sevenjot"† was still the herring-fishers place of resort; while in the autumn they sought more southerly seas, and fished in the so-called "deep water" off Yarmouth till St. Catherine's Day (September 25th). But these were general rules; precise sailing orders to the fleet were yearly agreed upon by the college of the herring

* "Hitland, Phayril, ende Boekenes." The name of the latter locality seems to correspond with that of Buchan-Ness.

† As to the place designated by "Sevenjot," I do not wish to hazard a guess. Luzac (*Holl. Rijkdom II.*, p. 261) spells "Jeveniot," and the name is given as "Sevenaths" in the periodical called *Nederlandsche Hermes* for Dec. 1826, p. 14.

fishery at their annual meeting at Delft, some time before the opening of the season. This often-mentioned corporation, denominated by Semeyns, "the Lords of the Grand Fishery," is stated by him to be composed of two delegates from the magistrates "of such towns as are notably concerned in the business." But this is inexact; for several towns and villages owning herring-ships were more than once refused a seat in the college, whose members appear to have had a full share of the exclusive spirit common to all who held power of any kind in the Republic. The college's power over all concerned in the herring trade was very large, especially as the licenses without which no buss could sail were delivered under the Grand Fishery's seal, although by the intervention of the local fishery boards; whereby the college were possessed of the means to enforce their rules upon the ships of towns not represented. It is therefore a matter of easy comprehension that a vote in the college was strongly desired by every fishing town, whereas the towns already represented there used to resist intruders with equal perseverance. Amsterdam and Hoorn, for instance, demanded admission of their delegates to the college in 1628,[*] but were repelled, and not admitted even when the States had appointed a special committee to bring the rival parties to an agreement; although it appears from a very obscure entry on page 2 of v. d. Lely's 'Recueil,' that Amsterdam would, in order to obtain a seat in the college, have consented to bear her share in the common charges, but have none in the subsidies, which were to be divided as before among the other towns. In 1636, Dordrecht in her turn sued for a seat in the college, but also met with systematic opposition. Monnikendam was likewise rejected in 1701, but

[*] *Res. Holland*, 1628, p. 556; 1629, pp. 665, 757.

Enkhuizen generously consented to deliver licenses to fishing captains from this town, which was thereby enabled to send herring busses to sea on its own account. Besides the fishing towns of the Maas, Enkhuizen appears for a long time to have been an influential member of the college, in which the preponderance of each town was, according to Semeyns, determined by the number of vessels hailing from it. Still, as the author avers, the greater member has no right "to introduce any novelties into the trade," and especially to permit the sailing of "sale-hunters," without the lesser's consent. It has been shown above that, if such a bye-law or tradition ever existed in the bosom of the college, it was often transgressed, and that Delft and Enkhuizen were overruled by the other three towns, as regards the admission of sale-hunters. Still, as a general rule, Semeyns' statement may be true enough; for a reluctance to admit "novelties" of any description has always been the college's prevailing disposition, much to the prejudice of the trade they were called upon to promote.

As regards the herring fishery's extension at this period, no precise statement can be made out with any degree of credit; but it certainly was very considerable. Walter Raleigh has certainly committed exaggeration by averring in his 'Observations' touching trade and commerce,[*] that 3000 ships and 50,000 people from Holland were yearly employed in the herring fishery upon the British coast; and other English writers of the period have given lower estimates. De la Court, in his famous essay, 'Heilzame Politique Gronden en Maximen,' evaluates the fleet at 1000 busses; but he wrote at a period when the Grand Fishery's halcyon days were avowedly over. A writer in

[*] Muller, *Mare clausum*, pp. 72, sqq.

"den Koopman" (vol. i. p. 235) states 1500 busses to have sailed in 1610 and 2000 in 1620, and doubtingly adds that 3000 are said to have sailed a few years later. According to Semeyns, Enkhuizen alone had 700 afloat in 1639 or thereabouts; and this certainly was not undervaluing the resources of a city whose glory and renown are the author's continuous boast. The towns on the Maas were then and afterwards ahead of Enkhuizen as regards the development of their herring shipping. Taking all together, I should be inclined to tax any one with exaggerration who values the number of Dutch salt-herring busses above 2000 at the time of the fishery's greatest expansion. Holland and Zealand are the only provinces which under the Republic owned herring-busses; and Zealand's share in them was very small. Considering that foreign trade, agriculture, and several manufacturing· industries have always occupied the majority of the population of Holland, and that some eight or ten towns at most were more or less concerned in the fishery, two thousand herring ships would appear to be a maximum which can scarcely have been exceeded; and it certainly is a matter of wonder that such a number should ever have been attained. A herring buss in Semeyns' time cost fl.3150, hull and standing rigging; and the "equipment," by which name the author designs tackle, nets, salt, barrels, and crew's hire and food, in the course of a season came to fl.4380 more. Each buss commonly made three voyages between St. John's and December, at the end of which the whole inventory was used up, and nothing remained but the vessel's hull, and that generally in a very deteriorated condition. The sum annually invested in the herring-fishery during its greatest expansion must, by the above considerations, have amounted to something like fl.15,000,000, an immense outlay indeed, considering the value of money at the time. The expenses of the trade appear to have augmented fast, notwithstanding the prohibition against exporting fishing materials. In 1669 a herring ship was estimated at fl.4550, and its equipment at fl.5500.* In 1768 the hull was calculated at fl.9000, and the equipment at fl.6000 for two voyages, and fl.8000 for three.† As for the trade's returns, each buss is stated in Semeyns' time to have brought ashore on an average forty last of herring in a season. The herring-prices at the time are not known; but such sums as 37 and 43 millions, stated to have been the fishery's annual revenue by several foreign authors,‡ are certainly strong exaggerations.

It is not certain how long this golden period of the Grand Fishery lasted. Statistics were not then in use, and, as regards the herring fishery, did not begin to be published till the trade's decay had very decidedly set in. The College, whose business it was to swear in every herring-skipper and appose their seal to the license without which none were allowed to sail, will probably have kept some record of the number who sailed in each year. But their books and accounts, if any, are no longer extant; nor do any of the authors on the subject give any chronological details as to the duration of the trade's greatest prosperity. As for legislation, some slight additions to the placards before spoken of, and many resolutions of both the States-General and those of Holland, about convoying-ships to be sent out and subsidies to be granted, compose the whole of it on record during the subsequent years; but these give no clue to the fishery's annual condition or progress.

* P. de la Court, *Heilzame Politique Maximen.*
† *Den Koopman,* i. p. 354.
‡ *Ibid.* i. p. 235.

Such sums as fl.100,000, borrowed by the Grand Fishery College in 1647,* and fl.187,958, exhibited by the Admiralty of Rotterdam in 1641 as convoying expenses,† do indeed show that, if the requirements for the herring fishery's safety were heavy both on the hands of the State and the parties concerned, the latter were able to meet, and Government found it worth while to cover them. The first serious check to the trade's expansion appears to have been the first war between the Republic and England in 1652 ; and from that year downward, for more than 60 years. War, Convoy and Prohibition are the words in which the Grand Fishery's history might not improperly be resumed. The Dutch fisherman's most redoubted foes under the Republic were the English man-of-war and the French privateer; and during the greater part of the period between 1652 and 1713 the Republic was at war either with England or France, or both.

Some time before the war of 1652, complaints of Dutch fishing vessels being taken or plundered by English were frequent, and peculiar activity in the equipment of convoying ships was accordingly recommended by the States to the Admiralty boards. Tromp's encounter with Blake off Dover, in May, 1652, having determined the formal opening of hostilities, the herring-fleet were the first sufferers, and a considerable number of busses, together with eleven convoyers, were taken by Blake in July. The States of Holland at first seriously considered the advisability of calling home the rest of the fleet, and stopping the fishery till better times ; but the measure was ultimately rejected, and twenty-four fishing vessels were armed as convoying ships

---

* *Res. Holland,* 1647, p. 164.
† *Ibid.* 1641, p. 146.

instead, besides six regular men-of-war.* Some English herring-boats having been taken by the Dutch, Holland at first tried to move the States-General to release them, and issue further orders for respecting the British fishermen, in the hope of meeting with similar forbearance on the enemy's hands. But as the English on the contrary made a thorough use of the rights of war, orders to do their fishermen the utmost possible damage were issued, and several more of their boats were accordingly taken in 1652 by Dutch armed fishing vessels.† But the grand tournament of naval skill and daring, of which the North Sea was the theatre during the war of 1652–4, left no room for much casting of nets. Though in the year 1653 the Herring College applied for protection with even more than usual persistency, the States, then obliged to strain their utmost means towards the equipment of the squadrons which fought under Tromp, Evertsen, de Witt, and de Ruyter, could afford no men-of-war for convoy throughout the season, and were obliged to grant "commissions" to some fishing skippers, which documents, although ostensibly delivered to promote the fishery's protection, appear indeed to have been nothing short of *lettres de marque*.‡ Such covering could, of course, be of no avail against the British fleets, and it is accordingly averred that in 1653, the herring fleet, then still consisting of some two thousand vessels, was kept at home,§ not indeed by Government order such as was in the said year issued to the whaling fleet, but by the ship-owners' prudence, who saw the impossibility of fishing in anything like safety.

* *Res. Holland*, 1652, pp. 343, 387.
† *Res. Holl.* pp. 364, sqq. *Holl. Mercurius*, 1652, p. 86.
‡ *Res. Holl.* 1653, pp. 462, 538.
§ Aitzema, *Zaken v. Staat en Oorlog*, v. iii. p. 810.

The Treaty of Westminster, in April 1654, put a term to the misery inflicted upon the United Provinces by this disastrous war; and in the same year the fishing was recommenced, but still under difficulties, as appears from several complaints of violence, suffered from English men-of-war in the next years.* A general renovation, in 1656, by the States of Holland of the placards of 1582 on the Grand Fishery is the principal event on record during the short interval of comparative quiet which succeeded the Peace of Westminster. Nearly the whole of this placard of 1656† is a literal reproduction of the existing laws; but a few additions, now enacted for the first time, point out in some degree the fishery's already altered condition. The fact of convoying ships equipped by the Herring College being always with the fleet is now, for the first time, officially apparent from a clause which enjoins the "captains of the Grand Fishery" (i.e. the commanders of the above-mentioned direction-ships) to arrest any fishing skipper guilty of either selling herring to foreigners or attempting to carry it directly abroad, and send him home to be tried. Besides this precaution against trespassers, a general aggravation of the penalties, consecrated by the placard of 1656, may be considered as an indication of the pressure exercised by the law upon the trade at large, and the consequent frequency of infraction. A custom of selling herrings unassayed and unbranded, or, as termed in the new placard, "as it lies, or upon trial" ‡ is made the object

* *Res. Holland*, 1656, p. 990 and others.
† *Groot Placaetboek*, vol. viii. p. 1242.
‡ "Aen 't hoepje te tasten, of zoo die leyd." The former words are obscure, and may perhaps be relative to some peculiar mode of sale of unassayed herrings, viz., by touching the hoops of the barrel as a sign of agreement followed by immediate transfer. But as "tasten" in the Dutch of the period was, I believe, sometimes used for "to

of a special prohibition, no other sale than "*op Pak en Keur*" (i.e. after the prescribed packing and assay, and upon the quality determined by the brand) being permitted. Another clause, prohibiting to pack salt, spices, or other goods in herring barrels under cover of the brand, is indicative of fraudulent habits among fishermen and herring dealers ; and this supposition derives additional strength from the official fixation, as appendices to the law of 1656, of a series of very detailed forms of the several oaths to be taken by herring skippers and sale-hunters both on sailing and returning, which oaths provide for every variety of infraction of the law which a person of either description might have committed or might be tempted to commit. Even these stringent measures did not prevent frequent breaches of the law, which, as soon as May 1658, determined a special re-enactment of the prohibition to sell herring caught before St. John's.* Another renovation of the clauses against selling herrings at sea was thought necessary in 1663.† It is more than probable, from such indications as these, that the wrong effects of several of the laws in vigour, and the prejudice they did to the trade, had by this time been realised by most of those immediately concerned. A very far-sighted and able writer, P. de la Court, has delivered an opinion to the same effect in his "Heilzame Politique Gronden en Maximen" (edit. 1669). "Several placards on the herring fishery," he says, "have been made ere now ; the which

---

taste," it is probable that a trial of the ware by the buyer was substituted for the official brand. The custom is already referred to in a resolution of the States of Holland of the year 1651 (*Res. Holland*, 255).

Res. Holl. 1658, p. 178.   *Groot Placactboek* ii. 2501.
Ibid. 1663, p. 172 ; 1664, p. 110.   *Groot Plb.* ii. 2898.

tend greatly to the advantage of the foreign Fishermen, who are not constrained to obey them."

Being unable efficiently to enforce their self-made rules at sea, the Herring College resorted to the greater stringency in the execution of such part of them as lay within the control of their officers ashore; and the towns whose delegates were excluded from the college were of course the first sufferers by this severity. The laws were not only executed with great severity, but actually overstepped by the college. Thus, in 1659, Hoorn, which it will be remembered had no seat in the college, complained of her ship's masters being obliged, before sailing, to get a licence (acte van consent) from the Grand Fishery, which document was only delivered upon the applicant taking oath not to fish before July 8th.* This date was posterior by a fortnight to the lawful opening of the fishing season, and it is not clear in virtue of what alleged competency of their own the college established a "*keure*" or bye-law derogating from the law of the realm in so vital a point. The author of Van der Lely's Register, who certainly wrote at a much later period, does not appear to have been precisely informed about the matter, and simply states that, "in 1659," the opening date was at one time delayed till some day in July," † without adding whence the college derived a title to such delay. At any rate, Hoorn, being excluded from the college, alleged the proceeding to be unlawful as applied to her own busses, and laid the matter before the States of Holland. A conference was called between delegates from the college on one hand and Hoorn on the other; and as a conse-

* *Res. Holland*, 1659, p. 199.
† "In 1659, wierd het eens vers (choven) tot in July, maar't Jaar daaraan hersteld."—*Recueil*, p. 14.

quence the lawful date of June 24th was restored in the next year, and not thenceforward departed from.

In 1663 another difference occurred, still more strongly illustrative of the efforts made by many to escape the college's rule. One Francis Denick, a citizen of one of the herring towns on the Maas, obtained the citizenship of Veere, in Zealand, in order to avoid the statute of Holland which prescribed all herring caught by Holland fishermen to be brought to one of the markets of that province. Though now a citizen of Zealand, Denick continued to send his busses to sea from the Maas, and the college therefore persisted in applying the law of Holland to their skippers and cargoes. Upon the owner's petition the States of Zealand instructed their delegates to the States-General to remonstrate with those of Holland; and a debate on the Denick question accordingly took place in the latter's assembly, in which the Zealanders advocated their new made citizen's rights, but without any success, Holland maintaining the supremacy of the college and the validity of the provincial statutes of 1582 and 1656 over all ships sailing from any of the Holland ports, whatever province the owner might belong to. "The question made much noise, but led to no result," as Van der Lely mentions in his 'Recueil.'*

The short period of peace with England, as said above, brought the Grand Fishery only comparative quiet and

* *Recueil v. d. Lely*, p. 14. *Res. Holl.* 1663, pp. 336, 352, 609. It will be remembered that the several Provinces were their own legislators, and that only such statutes as were promulgated by the States-General took effect in the whole of the republic. As there was no codification, and laws were often laid down in very unprecise terms, collisions between provinces on points of legislation were very frequent throughout the Republic's existence.

security. The war with Sweden (1656-60) did not directly affect the herring fishery, as hostilities were carried on in the Baltic, far from the herring seas. It appears, however, that English privateers, sailing in English vessels under Swedish commission, in the summer of 1659, took occasion from this war to annoy the Dutch herring fleet; and the Republic's ambassador was ordered to intercede with the British Government to obtain the cessation of this abuse.* Fresh complaints of violence suffered from the English occurred in October 1660, and Charles the Second's displeasure being soon after aroused by negotiations between the Republic and France, by which the States aimed at a reciprocal guarantee of free fishery all over the sea, the Dutch ambassador to the British Court was not successful in his endeavours to obtain redress of his country's fishing grievances.† The conclusion of the eventful alliance with France on April 27th, 1662, by which the fishery were promised the desired reciprocal protection, and the short-lived treaty between the States and England, of September 14 of the same year, could not long shield the Dutch herring trade against the inevitable consequences of the profound divergence between Charles the Second's political notions and de Witt's government by an aristocracy. In the course of 1664 both rival countries captured several of each other's vessels; and on January 26th, 1665, even before England had openly declared that war which already existed *de facto*, the States-General for the first time prohibited all ships from sailing from the United Provinces, whether for trade or fishery.‡ England at the time proffered passports or "*actes de sureté*" to the Dutch

* *Res. Holl.* 1659, p. 261.
† *Ibid.* 1660, p. 749; 1661, p. 181.
‡ *Groot Placaetboek.* iii. 291.

fishermen against payment of safeguard-money, but the States of Holland, "considering that this might be of very dangerous consequence, as making the inhabitants of these countries indirectly tributary to the King of England," prohibited the taking out of such passports, and on February 3rd insisted afresh on a strict observation of the prohibition to sail.* The treasurer of the Herring Fishery at Maassluis even incurred the States' severe censure for having procured British passports for the shipowners of his city; he was strictly enjoined not to make use of the documents bought and paid for, and only escaped punishment upon consideration of his having acted "more from inadvertency than malice."† Wishing, however, if possible, to divert the evils of war from their fishermen on equal and honourable terms, the States-General ordered one of their naval commanders to offer England a safeguard for her fisheries on terms of reciprocity; and a letter to that effect was accordingly sent from the Dutch flagship to the magistrate of Yarmouth.‡ No answer being received, the herring fishery remained forbidden in the years 1665 and 1666, in the course of which the prohibition was re-enacted more than once, and prohibitions against importing foreign herring and salt-fish were enacted to prevent the enemy's profiting by the stand-still of the trade in Holland.§ A proposition to

---

* *Res. Holl.* 1665, pp. 59, 78.

† *Ibid.* p. 78. It will be remembered that every town where herring busses were owned, even though not represented in the College, at this time and afterwards had a local fishery board of its own, and a "*Penningmeester*," or treasurer, appointed to manage the local fishing interests. The Treasurers of Enkhuizen, Rotterdam, Schiedam, Brielle, and Delft, were usually the delegates of those towns to the College.

‡ *Hollandsche Mercurius*, 1665, p. 143.

§ *Groot Plac. Boek.* iii. 293, 295. *Res. Holl.*, 1666, pp. 101, 310.

re-open the fisheries was not made in the States of Holland, till July 1st, 1667, some days after de Ruyter's splendid success up the Thames ; and when peace had been concluded at Breda on July ult., and the herring fleet could sail in safety, the best part of the herring season, being the third during the war, was over and lost.

There is no evidence to show on what scale and with what success herring fishery was exercised in the years 1667-1672. But even admitting these years to have been favourable, the trade can scarcely have had time to repair the immense losses undergone during the foregoing war, from ships taken or kept inactive during the sailing prohibition, and able sailors turned out of the business and killed in the country's service. The only indication of the altered state of the business is a debate which occurred in the States of Holland [*] in March, 1669, on the expediency of re-enacting the penalties against selling fishing-vessels and gear to foreigners, and taking service on foreign herring vessels ; which debate, however, does not appear to have led to any definite result. The formidable war of 1672, which eventually brought the Republic to the verge of destruction, occasioned a fresh prohibition from sailing on mercantile or fishing expeditions, which again preceded the war's actual outbreak by some days, being first proclaimed on March 19th, 1672. It was indeed repealed on September 15th of the same year, but re-enacted in the next, towards the opening of the fishing season ; and it lasted even after peace had been concluded with England in February, 1674, as the continuation of war with France still left little chance of fishing in safety. Mutual grants of free fishing were indeed conceded by France and the States on September 15th, 1675, and June 22nd, 1677, but on both occasions repealed soon after-

[*] *Res. Holl.* 1669, pp. 63, 102.

wards;* and the liberties taken by French and Zealand privateers with the reciprocal enemies' fishing vessels for some time proved an impediment to the protracted negotiations carried on at Nijmegen for the conclusion of peace with France. Warfare between fishermen and Dunkirk privateers lasted till late in 1678, and not till the conclusion of the peace of Nijmegen, in August of the said year, could the herring fishery be recommenced in safety. For six consecutive seasons the trade had been either interdicted or virtually impossible except on a small scale. No indications have unfortunately been preserved as to the extent to which it was carried on in 1678 and the next years, but even without precise knowledge of the facts there can be no doubt that a twenty-five years' period of nearly constant naval warfare must have occasioned a lasting decline. The very considerable amount of capital which, as shown above, was invested in the trade before 1652, cannot but have been partly withdrawn from it in consequence of the long and repeated periods of entire inactivity brought over the fishery by the several wars.

It is apparent from many circumstances on record that the trade's inward organization has suffered considerably from the consequences of the war. Although sustained by annual subsidies, generally to the amount of fl.30,000, and in some years more, besides the annual consideration of fl.6,000 paid to the Grand Fishery as redemption-money for the exemption from duties on salt, the treasury of the Grand Fishery College was in constant distress from 1670 downwards, and their administration appears to have been often in a disordered condition.

* *Groot Plac. Boek.* iii. 292, 298, 305 ; *Holl. Mercurius*, 1677, p. 230 *sqq.*; *Resol. St. Gen.* Sept. 2, 1675, June 3rd and 22, 1677 ; *Res. Holl.* 1677, p. 381.

From a very succinct list of the college's annual balances, to be found on p. 45 of v. d. Lely's 'Recueil,' it is evident that yearly arrears, ranging from fl.21,000 to fl.30,000, occurred between 1670 and 1679, and that in 1672-75 and 1677-78, no proper accounts have been kept. The quality of the fisheries' produce appears at the same time to have been in decline, as a proof that even by the most vigorous control and detailed legislation it is impossible to warrant the excellence of any article against the effect of the dealer's cupidity. In July, 1683, Dantzig merchants complained that the Dutch brand-herring brought to staple in their market was frequently either found unsaleable or sent back to the seller from the inland German towns in consequence of the fish being bad, the barrels half filled with salt, &c. Complaints of a similar nature were sent to Dutch herring dealers by their correspondents at Stettin; and the States of Holland, besides admonishing the college to better enforce the statutes, resolved to write to the magistrates of the said German towns and beg them, in case of any further complaints, to note the marks on the barrels returned, and communicate them to the States, in order to facilitate the detection and punishment of the culprit fishing steersman, cooper, or brander.* Again, in November, 1687, complaints on the quality of herring exported to Sweden were laid before the States by the Dutch Ambassador at Stockholm, who represented that, if such dealings continued, Dutch herring was in danger of losing the Swedish markets to the Scotch produce.†

A short return of relative prosperity appears to have dawned upon the herring fishery after the peace of Nijmegen. At least, no other statistics being extant, such

* *Res. Holl.* 1683, pp. 256, 260, 309.
† *Ibid.* 25 Nov. 1687.

a conclusion may be drawn from v. d. Lely's 'Recueil,' in which (p. 45) it is recorded that from 1679 to 1689 the deficits on the Herring College's accounts were replaced by surpluses. The subsidies granted to them by the States in these years uniformly amounted to 30,000 florins; and as their income besides these subsidies was mainly derived from last-money, the revenue from which was proportioned to the quantities of herring caught, the condition of the College's treasury must in some measure have reflected the trade's prosperity and adversity. Deficits on the books accordingly recommenced in 1690, a short time after the beginning of the war against France. This war was indeed chiefly carried on ashore and in the Mediterranean; but for Dutch fishermen war against France meant destruction by Dunkirk privateers. To keep these at bay was accordingly one of the principal aims of the English and Dutch fleets in the course of the war; but the impossibility of sheltering the fisheries from them was once more proved, though liberal grants of convoying ships were made to the Fishery College by the States of Holland. These, as of old, proved insufficient against the omnipresent Dunkirkers, and a prohibition to sail was therefore once more resorted to in 1691. Having been promulgated in the first days of the year, the prohibition was indeed withdrawn, at the College's request, on June 23rd, being the day before the opening of the herring season;* but on November 6th, before the season's end, the fishery was again prohibited and only permitted in the next years on condition of the busses' steersmen delivering one-fifth of their crews to the Admiralty Boards under which they resorted, to be employed on the Republic's squadrons. Holland at the same time interdicted the ransoming of busses captured by

* *Res. Holl.* 1691, p. 347. *Gr. Plac. Boek.* iv. 235, 237.

the Dunkirkers,* in order, if possible, to discourage them by withholding the price of their exploits ; and it may be assumed that in these circumstances the Grand Fishery fared very miserably even during the short periods of the war when it was not subject to an actual prohibition. A declaration proclaiming the mutual freedom of the fisheries was agreed upon between the Dutch and French delegates towards the close of the negotiations which in September, 1697, led to the peace of Rijswijk ; but the results of a six years' war, in the course of which neither the efforts of the allied English and Dutch fleets, nor Jean Bart's taking regular service under the French colours, could quell the Dunkirkers' audacious invasions, told heavily upon the herring fishery at the end of the seventeenth century. The " extraordinary " subsidy of 30,000 florins, which during the war had been withdrawn and replaced by Government convoy, was granted again on November 5th, 1701, upon the Grand Fishery's representation to the States of Holland, to the effect that they had got deeply indebted during the war, in consequence of many busses and several of the College's own convoyers having been taken by the enemy.†

Nor was the end of their trials then at hand. The war for the Spanish succession again brought the Republic and France into the field as foes in 1702 ; and even before war was declared by the States (May 8th) they once more, on March 30th, laid an interdiction on all sea fishery.‡ Now, as in 1691, the interdiction was withdrawn on June 23rd, the day before the opening of the herring season ; and this time the Grand Fishery was, in consideration of its supreme importance for the country's most vital interest, exempted

* *Res. Holl.* June 22, Aug. 22, 25.
† *Groot Placaetboek*, v. p. 1562.
‡ *Ibid.* v. p. 376.

from the obligation to send one-fifth of the crews to serve under the Republic's colours,* to which all other branches of fishery were indiscriminately subjected. In the course of the war, frequent deliberations on convoy by men-of-war to be granted to the fisheries, at their urgent and repeated request, again form the main part of the States' records concerning them. An idea of the convoyers' efficiency may be formed from an account of an engagement between four of them and four heavy French men-of-war, in which, on June 26th, 1703, the Dutch convoyers were either sunk or taken, and part of the herring fleet burnt by the French in the Shetland seas.† A fresh renovation in 1707 of the existing laws against exporting herring barrels or nets,‡ and a "warning," proclaimed in August, 1708, against herring fishers taking passports from the enemy "whereby the foe is much strengthened and our other subjects are exposed to serious prejudice,"§ are further sinister testimonies to the Grand Fishery's sufferings by this war, which were only terminated by the peace of Utrecht in April, 1713.

An era of peace now dawned upon the Republic. But her herring fishery was broken down by the series of wars and disasters, of which the last pages contain a very rapid account. It is in the nature of sea fishery as a trade to require an uninterrupted rotation of capital; for, besides the stock sunk in ships being subject to deterioration, the considerable floating capital annually expended in equipment cannot of course lie idle, and must be withdrawn from the trade if an interruption of any length occurs. To keep a fishing vessel idle for a season is to incur a clear loss;

---

* *Groot Placaetbock*, v. p. 377.
† *Europische Mercurius*, 1703, ii. p. 107.
‡ *Groot Placaetbock*, v. 1566.
§ *Ibid.* v. 1573.

and the only way in which to avoid this loss is, if possible, to sell her, and buy a new ship when better times are come. Wherefore, a fishery which during sixty years was scarcely ever exercised without danger, which was several times prohibited for years together, and from which it was constantly forbidden to sell out, may by a safe deduction be assumed to have been brought down to a low level at the end of such a period, not to speak of losses of ships to the enemy. I have not found any statistics or positive records as to the Grand Fishery's condition immediately after the peace of Utrecht ; but it may be safely assumed to have at the time presented but a shadow of its former greatness. And now the full weight of the legislative restrictions imposed upon it contributed to keep it down. Being intricated in a net of regulations intended to warrant the quality of its produce, it could not compete with foreigners, who managed under a more liberal system to produce an article equally marketable, if not equally good. Being tied to one first-hand staple market, viz. the Dutch emporiums, it could not regain in the foreign markets that privileged position which it had of course lost during the years of its actual stoppage and stand-still. The fishing laws have perhaps contributed to the herring trade's greatness, but they have certainly prevented it from rising when prostrated by the force of events. As a very convincing proof of this the herring negotiations with Hamburg may be cited, which are the principal centre of the present narrative's interest, in the period to which it has now advanced.

It will be remembered that a treaty had been concluded in 1609 between the Republic and Hamburg, in virtue of which either party was to exclude herring of whatever origin from its markets if not certified to have been caught after St. John's, or June 24th, and cured on board.

THE HISTORY OF DUTCH SEA FISHERIES.

Holland had obtained this agreement as a shelter against competition by Scotch fishermen, whose laws left them at liberty to fish at an earlier date, and whose coasts lay so near the herring seas as to enable them to cure their fish ashore. As "new" or first herring was sometimes paid tenfold prices, it was of great consequence to be first in the market; and this privilege Holland hoped to secure by binding Hamburg over to apply the Dutch law to foreign herring.

In the course of the seventeenth century, however, Hamburg's execution of the treaty seems to have been such as from time to time to occasion recrimination on the Dutch side. In 1668, a plan formed by some citizens of Hamburg to fish for herring very early in the season and pack the fish in Dutch barrels was detected by the Fishery College and protested against by the States of Holland.* In the first years of the eighteenth century, the British herring fisheries having meanwhile acquired considerable development, Hamburg was eagerly sought as a market for Scotch herring. Hamburg dealers were, on their side, peculiarly anxious to have their market stocked early, and often complained of having to put off their expeditions to the inland of Germany, till herring caught on or after the 24th of June and cured at sea could be brought to their market.† There were two ways of gratifying this eagerness for early herring: firstly, to fish before June 24th, and secondly, to sail to Hamburg straight from the fishery. Dutch fishermen were of course precluded from the former method, and as their law forbade them to carry their herring elsewhere than to their own ports to be assayed and branded, they were likewise obliged to refrain from the latter, and thereby placed at a very great disadvantage.

* *Res. Holl.* 1668, p. 173.
† *Ibid.* 1715, p. 724.

Matters became still worse for them when Hamburg began to take liberties with the treaty of 1609, and admit Scotch herring without the certificate required by the treaty with the Republic, which infraction seems to have been pretty habitual in the first years of the eighteenth century. The British Ambassador at Hamburg appears to have employed himself in favour of these imports, and the Senate for some time closed their eyes on them, whereby Holland was in danger of losing the considerable advantage inherent to having no early rivals in the Hamburg herring market.

The Republic's Ambassador at Hamburg in 1715 detected what was going on. He straightway reported matters to the States-General, and upon their instructions insisted with the Hamburg Government upon the strict observation of the treaty of 1609. England, he urged, in virtue of her treaties with Hamburg, was not entitled to any more favourable treatment than the Republic, or to have her herring admitted under conditions refused to Dutch and other herring upon the terms of the treaty. This was true enough, and indeed made out a strong case for the Republic; but she spoilt it by adding another argument based upon her adversary's interest as interpreted by herself. The States instructed their diplomatic agent to represent that the Dutch regulations imposed by treaty upon the Hamburg market had been observed there for a century, and found beneficial for that market as well as for the trade in Holland. Being averse to let Dutchmen manage their own interests in the herring concern, the States could not see that Hamburgers were perhaps the best judges of theirs. After some exchange of memorials, Hamburg on October 25th, 1715, pledged herself henceforward strictly to observe the treaty. But even admitting this pledge to have been quite sincere, it was impossible to fulfil it against the combined interests of Hamburg dealers and English fishermen, the latter backed more or less openly by their Government's ambassador; and, in consequence, complaints about Scotch herring being admitted without a certificate were heard in 1716 even louder than in the preceding year.

Here, now, was a tangible indication of the Dutch regulation system's wrongs and of the danger of maintaining it. Evidence had already been, and about this time was still further obtained to the system's inadequacy always and everywhere to warrant the excellence of the Dutch brand-herring, and it was now clearly shown that, so far from shielding the Dutch fisheries against foreign competition, it left them at the competitor's mercy by preventing them from using the only expedient by which concurrency could be upheld, viz. doing as the foreigners did. It is a remarkable instance of the force of habit and long conviction, that no one among the Republic's legislators seems in 1715 and following years to have realized this most evident truth. They were imbued with the notion so strongly expressed by Semeyns of old, viz. that Providence intended Holland to supply the world with herring; and in virtue of this notion they did their utmost to enforce the supremacy of their laws, but neglected such measures as might have actually maintained their superiority in the market. In the long list of States' Resolutions registered on the Hamburg question no mention is made, till it was too late, of any proposal either to relinquish the system of the herring laws or adapt it to circumstances. The Dutch Ambassador's reports on the subject were invariably laid before a Committee of the Herring Towns Delegates to the States of Holland, who had been trained to a stalwart and uncompromising belief in the herring laws' impeccability; and upon their constant advice the year 1716 was wasted in futile representations to Hamburg, to the effect that admitting early herring in the market was tantamount to ruining Hamburg trade. Hamburg traders by their conduct manifested a contrary opinion; but to such evidence Dutch legislators were blind, being accustomed since long years to consider the trade's regulation as their exclusive business, and their supreme wisdom as the only safe guide for all parties concerned.

The course of events strikingly belied this policy of self-importance and obduracy. While the Dutch Ambassador was memorialising the Government of Hamburg upon his principals' instructions, his colleague of England succeeded in concluding a convention relative to the importation of British herring in Hamburg, which, when a copy of it had after some fruitless efforts been obtained and sent to the Hague, was there judged irreconcilable with the treaty of 1609, and gave rise to fresh protests on the Dutch side, and high-toned rejoinders from the Hamburg senate, in the course of the spring of 1719. As a conclusion the States acquiesced in the convention between England and Hamburg, "readily believing the latter city to have had good reason for concluding it," but at the same time instructed their ambassador to strictly supervise the application of the treaty of 1609 to British herring as well as to Dutch. It may be doubted whether this control was exercised with adequate vigilance, or whether it was possible so to exercise it. At any rate for the next ten years the matter seems to have occasioned no further difficulties.

In 1722, Dutch dealers indeed complained of their herring being re-packed by their Hamburg correspondents, and considered the expediency of transferring their staple importations to Bremen, whereupon the governor of the rival port of Altona tried to secure the staple market for his place, and conferred with the Dutch Ambassador at Copenhagen on the subject.* But there is no evidence of this plan having led to any result, and Hamburg in the next years retained the transit trade of Dutch herring bound for the greater part of Germany.

In the course of the year 1731, the Republic's Embassy at Hamburg being then held by J. J. Mauricius, a diplomatist of great vigilance and activity, a series of complaints about Scotch early herring being sold there without a certificate reached the States-General; and it appeared from the ambassador's despatches that the Dutch brands were gradually disappearing from the market. Mauricius at the same time sent over a copy of a new convention between Great Britain and Bremen, dated October 17th, 1731, which opened the latter market for Scotch herring without any restriction. With Bremen the Republic had no treaty, so to prevent the loss of that city's market for early herring there was nothing to be done but leave the Dutch at liberty to concur on equal terms with the Scotch fishermen; but this measure was never thought of. Hamburg, on the contrary, was still bound by the treaty of 1609, and with that city a fresh exchange of memorials and remonstrances was opened, the result of which, in 1732, was another promise from the Senate that the treaty of 1609 should be strictly adhered to. Similar difficulties arose in 1737, and led to an identical result, viz. the receipt by the Dutch Ambassador, for the third time, of an "extractus protocolli" to the effect that the Hamburg Senate was disposed to observe the treaty of 1609. And while transmitting this document to his patrons, Mauricius ventured to express his opinion "that they of the Grand

* *Res. Holl.* 1722, pp. 398, 531; 1723, p. 29.

Fishery had better do their utmost to keep the Hamburgers in their present favourable mood."

There was but one way of following this sensible advice, viz., to take measures in order to stock the Hamburg market in time, and not keep the dealers waiting for Dutch herring till the time required for lawful catching, packing and branding of the fish had elapsed. But the college as yet would not be brought to give up their habits of leisurely observing the placards to the letter; and of course the Hamburgers, treaty or no treaty, went on dealing in early Scotch herring, to the Dutch exporters' incalculable prejudice. In 1750, the then Dutch Ambassador Buys once more reported considerable imports of Scotch herring without a certificate, and in the course of the next two years, upon the States-General's instructions, delivered several remonstrances to the Senate and was answered by the usual "extractus protocolli," containing promises, the fulfilment of which never came. The Republic, time after time, let herself be silenced by these stale promises, and still kept up her worn-out belief that the treaty of 1609 was for Hamburg's good, and could conveniently be observed there. At last, in July, 1752, it appeared from one of Buys' despatches that a cargo of English herring had been sold at Hamburg without a certificate *before Dutch herring had been heard of by anybody upon the market*. And now, after some forty years' steady perseverance in a rotten system, and fruitless and futile efforts to enforce that system upon others whose interest was opposed to it, the College at last, upon Buys' most pressing advice, made one single tardy concession which, if made in time, might perhaps have prevented all the difficulties just now related. They asked, and of course obtained, the States' permission to send herring to Hamburg direct from the North Sea. This was

a breach of some width in the system; for it was a derogation from the laws made to uphold the herring markets of Holland; and besides, herring brought straight to Hamburg was of course to go without the sacred brand of the Dutch assayers. For these reasons there was much opposition to the plan. The delegates from Enkhuizen foresaw "the most ruinous consequences" if it were to be adopted; and by way of a transaction the exports of herring to Hamburg direct from the fishery were restricted to three vessels' cargoes in 1753 and the next year. The step was taken, but the States hung back from taking it thoroughly, and still did things by halves. Nor were these restrictions abandoned when the measure, such as it was, proved a brilliant financial success. In 1753 two Dutch sale-hunters brought the first herring to Hamburg and sold it, *although unbranded*, at fl.1562, and fl.814 a last severally, whereas the first English herring-ship, having reached the same port a few hours later, made only fl.543 for the same quantity.*
But even this could not convince the ultra-conservative Dutch legislators of the expediency of trying the experiment on a larger scale. Having so far belied the provisions of the opposition in the Herring College, the experiment was indeed repeated in the next years, but always with a very few ships. Although of course involving a tacit admission of the existing legislation's noxiousness, these exceptional expeditions were to the very last treated as an irregularity contrary to the law, and strictly limited in consequence. If, having succeeded with three ships, Holland had next sent thirty and aspired to send three hundred from the North Sea to Hamburg, there is reason to believe that great profits might, as of old, have been made in that market; for the eagerness for "new" Dutch herring was

* *Ned. Jaarboeken*, 1753, p. 1226.

now proved to be unabated. As it was, a few vessels only were sent, a few shipowners made handsome profits, and the trade's decline was not for a moment retarded by the event of 1753. The market was not entirely lost; in 1768 Hamburg and Bremen were still markets for Dutch brand-herring.* But the shower of gold which used to be poured down upon the Dutchmen who landed the first herring was now, if not transferred to, at least shared by, others. Hamburg had grown accustomed to see British vessels first in the market, and even when competition was brought on a square footing in 1753, Holland could not regain what was lost.

The herring fishery's general history now takes us forty years back, after the above disgression relative to the Hamburg affairs.

Some renovations and ampliations of the placards against exporting herring barrels, staves, nets, and fishing implements in general, which were enacted in 1719 and 1725,† first show that even after the peace of Utrecht the fishery's extension was not such as to open a sufficient inland market for the industry of those who fabricated fishing materials. No such renovations were required at the time when Holland wanted all the barrels and nets she could produce; and if the supply now exceeded the demand, the herring legislation certainly was one of the causes. The trades of coopering and net-making might, in virtue of the renown of Dutch barrels and nets, have survived the fishery's greatness if the former's produce had now been allowed to be exported. But such a departure from the established rules was against the legislators' views, and the prohibition once made in order to

* *Den. Koopman*, i. p. 237.
† *Groot Placactboek*, v. 1580, and vi. 1433.

prevent a scarcity of fishing materials, was maintained at a time when its only possible effect was to make the auxiliary trade share the decay of the principal one. It certainly did at times prevent coopers from selling off their stock, as is proved by the following facts. On January 9th, 1722, a change was made in the lawful dimensions of the herring barrels as established in 1582. As, however, a considerable stock of staves, hoops, &c., made under the old regulation was still upon the cooper's hands, and unexportable under the placard of 1719, branders and assayers were, by Resolution of the States of Holland, empowered to brand such barrels until June 1st, 1722. And to prevent the branding at a later date of barrels made upon the old model, it was further enacted on June 2nd, 1723, that each brand apposed to a barrel should henceforth mention the year of its branding.*

Despite these sundry provisions against the depreciation of the Dutch brand, herring bearing that mark of excellence was more than once, at this very period, shown to be of inferior quality. In 1721, the magistrates of Stettin † or "Old Stettin" (Oudstetijn) again remonstrated with the States of Holland, about their brand-herring's quality and packing, and were put off with assurances that the Dutch laws on packing &c., were maintained with the utmost possible severity. At the same time the Stettiners were invited, as they and the Dantzigers had been before, to co-operate towards the maintenance of the Dutch laws by transmitting to the States the branded stave of each herring barrel which should have occasioned complaints as to the quality of its contents, in order to have the guilty steersman or brander detected and punished. There is no

* *Groot Placaetboek*, vi. pp. 1431-2.
† *Res. Holl.* 1721, pp. 578, 618.

instance on record of the Stettiners having acceded to the invitation; but in 1727 they again found reason to complain of Dutch herring being bad.* It would not be worth while to mention such incidents as these, if they did not stand as curious samples of the Dutch legislator's candid belief, against all evidence to the contrary, that his work was perfect and could not but be admired and seconded by all who had dealings with the Grand Fishery's produce.

While Holland tried, by such means as these, to maintain some of her herring fishery's ancient splendour, foreign competition rose and prospered in proportion to its decline. It will be superfluous in this place to digress upon the rise in the business in Great Britain at the time.† Nor was Great Britain the only concurrent. In 1727, a privileged fishing company was chartered at Nieuwpoort, in the Austrian Netherlands, against whose competition measures had accordingly to be taken. These measures were once more based on the customary belief that the existing system, if thoroughly enforced, sufficed to put foreign competition down. Instead of taking steps to place the Dutch on an equal footing with them, the Herring College, fully convinced that without Dutch sailors a foreign society could do nothing, sued for and obtained a renovation, by the States General, of the prohibitions against taking service on board a foreign fishing vessel, and the penalties against breach of this law were aggravated by the semi-barbarous enactment that the families of such fishermen as should be abroad in foreign service should be removed from their dwelling-places and be entitled to no

---

* *Res. Holl.* 1727, p. 5.
† *Europische Mercurius*, 1720, i. p. 279.

succour from the public poor-houses.* But no laws, however severe, could withhold the vital elements of the Dutch fishery from taking refuge abroad in their present state of decline, as is shown by an extensive correspondence carried on in 1727 and 1728 about a Dutch vessel arrested for smuggling nets, &c., to Nieuwpoort.† The Nieuwpoort business does not appear to have been prosperous, but Dutch competition certainly was no party to the scantiness of its success ; for, in 1736, its further encouragement was considered by the Belgian authorities, mainly upon the plea *that Dutch herring was not imported into the Austrian Netherlands in sufficient quantities* to supply the fast-day requirements of the Catholic population.‡ And this, again, is not a matter of wonder, for the Grand Fishery was by this time reduced to about one-tenth of what it was a century earlier. In a Paper contributed to the often-mentioned periodical " den Koopman," in 1768,§ it is stated that only 219 herring-ships and 31 sale-hunters sailed in 1736. This precise statement, being the first instance of herring statistics during the trade's decline, is sufficient proof of what it had been brought to in the course of a century, by frequent naval wars, and by its inability to compete with foreigners at a time when peace allowed the fishing interests to be actively pursued abroad.

The renewed war with France in 1743 does not appear to have greatly affected the Dutch herring fishery. Beyond a renewal of the subsidy of fl. 30,000 formerly granted for convoying purposes,‖ and which had not been sued for

---

* See *Res. Holl.* 1727, pp. 844, 994, 1012, 1042.
† *Ibid.* 1727, pp. 1029, 1031 ; 1728, pp. 53, 281, 325.
‡ *Ibid.* 1736, p. 666.
§ " *Den Koopman*," vol. i. p. 236.
‖ *Res. Holl.* 1744, pp. 380, 391.

between 1715 and 1743,* and a further resolution of July 7th, by which one ship of war was detached to protect the herring fleet, no trace of the war's effects upon the trade are visible in such documents as form the basis of the present narrative. The institution of a fishing company in Sweden, reported by the Dutch ambassador in 1745, did not elicit any particular measure from the States. Matters became different when, in 1750, Great Britain took steps for promoting her herring fisheries on a very extensive scale, by chartering a company with a capital of half a million sterling and the promise of considerable premiums. Such protection as this could not but reflect on the Dutch concurrents; and from the day on which Engl.nd definitely adopted the policy of encouraging her fishery out of the public pocket, the Dutch shipowners' cry was for having the same expedient resorted to. In 1749, the Grand Fishery had spirit enough left to decline a subsidy of fl.50,000 in consideration of the Treasury's exhausted state;† but when England in the next year set an example of paying fishermen out of the public purse, no such generosity further occurred, and Dutch fishers likewise began to look to the Exchequer for the profits which the sea no longer yielded. Direct premiums were not indeed resorted to at once. Protection was first applied to the once Grand Fishery in the shape of exemption from taxes. On the 6th of May, 1650, Holland granted an immunity of the several provincial excise duties for articles used in victualling herring-ships; and as both the number and the amount of these duties were considerable, the privilege was worthy of note. Three days afterwards, the States-General allowed an exemption of

* *Recueil v. d. Lely* p. 43.
† *Res. Holl.* 1749, p. 274.

export duty on Dutch herring, which duty then amounted to fl.2-10 (i.e. two florins and a half) per last on St. James' brand-herring, and to fl.4 on the Cologne (also called St. Bartholomew's or Elevation Brand) and the great Rouen brand.* Both exemptions were granted to last three years, and were renewed every three years till the end of the Republic. At the same time the placards against exporting herring barrels and gear and taking service on board foreign fishing-vessels were once more renewed,† and this furbishing up of old and worn armour was believed to be sufficient precaution against the now stimulated concurrency of English fishermen. The trade fared ill in 1750, notwithstanding its new privileges. A paragraph by a contemporaneous writer states the condition of the Grand Fishery to have been such, that "most busses sailed money overboard, some returned neither gain nor loss,‡ and a very few brought a small clear profit." As for the number of herring-ships sailed, it will be found in Appendix A to this work, for this and the following years, and will show the quondam Grand Fishery's now reduced and still further declining condition. The table is taken from the Committee's Report of 1854, who compiled it from the contemporary yearly statistics to be found in the "Ned. Jaarboeken." The figures are certainly exact, or very nearly so, and are the first regular herring statistics ever compiled in the country.

Further encouragement was obtained by the salt-herring fishery in 1758, when France, as a reward for the fidelity

---

* *Groot Placaetboek*, vii. p. 1592. A supplementary exemption from a peculiar duty on salt, known as "round-measure duty," was granted for herring-ships in 1754 (*Gr. Pl. Boek*, viii. p. 1077-1080).

† *Groot Placaetboek*, vii. pp. 1593-4.

‡ "*Speelden Kamp*," see *Ned. Jaarboeken*, 1750, p. 723.

with which the Republic kept neutral in the Seven Years' War, opened her frontiers for Dutch herring, which had long been forbidden the country. The neutrality did not tend to the Republic's political glory, and its fruit did not yield the fishery much profit; for it will be seen from Appendix A that the decrease in the number of herring-ships was peculiarly rapid in the years following 1758. Even the opening of such a market, from which English herring was excluded,* did not act as a stimulus on the once Grand Fishery, whose energy, as a natural result of two centuries' paternal regulations, was now at as low an ebb as the Republic's in general. The privilege was contemptuously withdrawn by France in 1763, after the war's termination; and as a proof that it had not been taken advantage of while it lasted, its withdrawal, instead of further injuring the herring fishery, was actually followed by a slight increase of it in the next two years (see Appendix A).

Fiscal immunities proving inefficient to restrain the fisheries' decline, direct premiums were now resorted to. Such a premium seems to have been first granted by the city of Flushing in 1754, to the amount of fl.30 for each herring-ship sailing from the said port, and for a period of

* So strictly was this exclusion maintained that the French ambassador at the Hague in the course of 1758 took steps to prevent English herring being sent to France together with Dutch, or packed in the same barrels. A placard dated July 24th and expressly prohibiting to mix up foreign herring with Dutch (*Gr. Pl. Bock* viii. 1261) was issued by the States merely to content France's apprehension, which power does not seem to have placed much trust in the famous Dutch fishing laws, which implicated a similar prohibition since two centuries. This disgraceful moment in the fisheries' history is fully described in Wagenaar's *Vad. Hist.* xxii. p. 456; xxiii. p. 77, and *Ned. Jaars.* 1758, p. 1045. See *Res. Holland*, 1758, pp. 601, 874, 988.

seven years.* A premium double the amount was allowed to fishing boats from Burch in Zealand, in 1758, out of the provincial treasury ; and some inhabitants of Veere having applied for a similar bounty, the premium system was extended to all Zealand fishermen in 1759.† Holland adopted it some years afterwards.

Some fresh difficulties with Hamburg are on record in the following years. English and Dutch herring at this time were still concurrents in the Hamburg market, both under certificate as to their having been caught after St. John's Day ; and as a few Dutch sale-hunters were annually sent to Hamburg straight from the fishery, competition between them was now on a fair footing. But others began now to obtain unlawful advantage. In 1769, England and the Republic ordered their ambassadors jointly to remonstrate against the proceedings of the Danes, who managed to smuggle forbidden herring into Hamburg under certificates mentioning not the date of their catching, but the one on which the Danish trader had taken them on board.‡ Worse enemies than these appeared in the Hamburg market in 1773. A Prussian fishing company, incorporated at Embden some time before, toward the opening of the season of that year, boldly announced its intention to bring herring to Hamburg a week before the lawful term ; and it was the Prussian *chargé d'affaires'* boast, that the ancient city would not dare to refuse these cargoes, treaty or no treaty. He was mistaken in the first instance ; for an Embden vessel, having fished as early as June 18th, was refused admittance by the Hamburg authorities, although coming into the port a day after the first lawful Dutch cargo. The King of Prussia in the next year, quite in the

* *Ned. Jaarb.* 1754, pp. 92, sqq.
† *Notulen Staten* v. *Zeeland*, 13, 20, 21, 24, Sept.
‡ *Res. Holl.* 1769, p. 701. *Res. Stat. Gen.*, April 21st

spirit of Frederick the Great's downright politics, ordered the sovereign magistrate of the Free City of Hamburg to admit early herring from Embden at whatever period such herring might have been caught ; and when the order was protested against, vouchsafed no answer. Hamburg excused herself to the Republic "as being unable to withstand a powerful neighbour ;" and the States, who at this period of their government were as a rule very anxious to keep out of harm's way at any price, did not venture any opposition. The herring treaty of 1609 being thus virtually annulled, there was now, if ever, good reason for Holland to allow her fishermen to fish as early as the Embdeners ; the more so, as the Dutch ambassador Hop had recently, in 1770, strongly impressed upon his Government the stringent necessity of being early in the market at whatever cost, since the first herring, whether good or bad, English, Dutch or Danish, was sold there at fabulous prices. But once more the States were deaf to the most urgent expostulations, and though every shadow of observance of the treaty of 1609 was now withdrawn, still kept their St. John's rule upright.* It would indeed appear from such facts as these, that some notion at the time prevailed to the effect that it was better to catch herring after St. John's and find no market for it, than to catch it earlier and sell it at good prices. The system was maintained with the more obduracy in proportion as its powerlessness to do any good to the fishery became more strikingly apparent on all sides.

The Grand Fishery was now indeed beset on all sides. Denmark, in 1767, chartered a herring fishery, and, in 1774, prohibited all importation of foreign fish. Austria did her utmost to promote the fisheries of Nieuwpoort and Ostend.

* *Res. Holl.* 1770, p. 1272 ; 1773, p. 485 ; 1774, p. 496; 1775, pp. 155, 193. *Res. St. Gen.* 1775, p. 419.

England persevered in encouraging hers by considerable bounties. Prussia, besides making free with competitors in the summary way described above, in 1775 prohibited Dutch herring to be imported in July, August, and September of each year.* The trade in Holland and Zealand, as the often-quoted writer in "den Koopman" picturesquely states,† had, "despite all unceasing offerings up of sighing prayers and zealous heaven-solicitations, aye, notwithstanding all public supplications in the Reformed Churches of these countries by so many up-lifted hands and hearts, come to diminish from year to year, a matter of wonder as regards the one, and of sorrow with respect to the other." Besides leaving the trade at liberty and repealing the herring statutes, which measure was never thought of by an enlightened and paternal government, there was but one remedy as yet untried, viz., direct bounties to fishermen out of the tax-payers' pockets, besides the fiscal immunities they were already possessed of. This last resource of all protective legislation, which as shown above had been adopted in Zealand before, was accordingly sued for in Holland, in May 1775, by "those interested in the herring fishery at Delfthaven, Rotterdam, Schiedam, Vlaardingen, Maassluis, and in the north quarter at Enkhuizen de Rijp and Noordend, being the whole of those concerned in the trade in Holland and West Vriesland."‡ No less a premium than fl. 600 for

* *Res. Holl.* 1775, p. 445 ; 1777, p. 326 ; *Res. St. Gen.* 1775, p. 277.
† "*Den Koopman*," i. p. 235.
‡ It is to be noted that, according to this enumeration, the herring trade had before this been entirely abandoned at Hoorn and Brielle, where it was formerly exercised to some extent. The towns named in the text petitioned as severally concerned in the common interest, and not as members of the College, in which several of them were not incorporated.

each buss was asked for, besides a bounty on exportation of herring at fl.1 per ton, and a recommendation *ex officio*, that the inhabitants of all poor-houses, and similar establishments, should be fed on herring at least twice a week. The College of the Grand Fishery examined the request, and of course seconded it, "because the business could not be kept going without notable assistance." The College besides reminded the States that, having in 1748 refused a proffered subsidy when not required, they were entitled to it now they could not do without it. They omitted to state that the subsidy rejected in 1748, had been formerly accepted readily enough whenever there was occasion for it, and that the said subsidy was widely different from the premium now sued for ; the former being a grant to the central direction of the fisheries to meet convoying expenses, and the latter a direct payment to each skipper out of the provincial treasury, to be obtained in full peace, and upon no other consideration than the fact of his having sailed for herring. The States of Holland, however, granted the new bounty by Placard of May 19th, 1775.* Upon mature consideration, related in the intolerably tedious style of the period, they allowed fl.500 to the proprietor of each herring ship which should sail in the course of the next two years. The other measures sued for, viz., the exportation bounty and the order to the poorhouse boards to feed their poor on herring, were both declined.

It was expected that in the course of the two years for which the bounty had been allowed, the herring trade, thus encouraged, should beat foreign competition out of the field and regain its former greatness. And as a fact, now they were sure of a bounty, the number of busses increased

---

* *Res. Holl.* 421, 464. *Groot Placactboek* ix. 1303.

from 158 in 1775, to 179 in 1776. But they were now fishing more for the premium than for herring, and accordingly, when after the lapse of two years the bounty was reduced to fl. 400, in order to maintain equality with the amount allowed to whaling vessels, the number of busses sailing decreased faster than ever, as shown by Appendix A. In 1780 it came down to 151, or about as low a figure as had occurred before bounties were granted.

The war declared by England to the Republic on December 20th of that year inflicted another heavy visitation upon the herring trade, although at the war's outset the fleet, then not yet returned from the Deepwater, escaped destruction by a hairbreadth. The moment the declaration of war was known at the Hague, a fast-sailing sloop was sent to warn the busses; and though closely chased by British cruisers, the vessels all got safe home, where their return was commemorated by a day of public prayer and thanksgiving, and the coining of a medal.* But there was no durable occasion to rejoice. The Republic had scarce men-of-war enough to cover her coasts; convoy was therefore out of the question, and on January 26th, 1781, a general sailing prohibition, improperly styled "embargo," was laid on all Dutch merchant and fishing vessels, and not repealed even upon the fisherman's most urgent request. A negotiation which the Dutch ambassador at Brussels was directed to open with his British colleague, with a view to the parties' engaging to leave each other's fishermen unmolested,† led to no result. Herring was now, perhaps for the first time, actually *imported* into the Republic from Denmark, and the Danish Herring Company kept an agent at Amsterdam, who tried,

* *Ned. Jaarb.* 1781, p. 250.
† *Res. St. Gen.* 1781, p. 333.

though in vain, to obtain an immunity of import duty for his principal's article.* No herring busses sailed during the season of 1781, and this time, as a further derogation from the herring laws, the States-General saw the expediency of allowing shipowners to sell their vessels abroad, under a promise of buying them back in better times, and subject to the advice of the Admiralty Board on the Maas for each special case.†

In 1782 it appears some Dutch busses went about their trade, and fished unmolested under the British men-of-war's guns,‡ but this was a mere act of toleration, as passports were only exchanged in 1783,§ pending the negotiations which on August 28th of that year led to the signing of peace preliminaries. No less than six hundred passports were applied for at the time by the local fishery boards in several Dutch fishing towns; but only 120 busses, besides a few trawls of the coast fishery, appear to have sailed. The trade was recommenced on a somewhat larger scale, but as yet without a premium, in 1784. In the next year, "those concerned in the herring trade of Holland and West Vriesland" once more sued for a bounty of fl. 700 or 800 for each buss, which was granted in 1786 to the amount of fl. 700 for each ship that had sailed in the preceding year. At the same time the Admiralty of the Maas having reported that William Cunningham, Receiver-General in Ireland, had tried to induce a skipper from Vlaardingen to establish himself on the Irish Coast, the prohibition against engaging in foreign fishing concerns was renewed once

---

* *Res. St. Genl.* 1781, pp. 647, 734; *Res. Holl.* 1781, p. 778.

† *Res. Holl.* 1781, p. 1286; 1782, pp. 85, 121; *Res. St. Gen.* 1782, p. 1388.

‡ *Ned. Jaarb.* 1782, pp. 566, 663; *Vervolg op Wagenaar*, pp. 4, 376.

§ *Res. St. Gen.* 546, 560.

more by Placard of May 3rd, 1786.* In 1788 the bounty system was regulated on a footing intended to be durable, a premium of fl.500 per herring buss being granted by a States of Holland's Publication dated April 17th, to be repeated annually for twelve years.† The measure once more called forth a slight increase of the trade towards the Republic's end, although the number of 200 busses was never reached. Fishing laws were maintained to the end. A renovation of the edict against sending herring to the Weser and Elbe unless cured, packed, and branded according to the law,‡ which law had been last re-enacted in 1715, at the outset of the difficulties with Hamburg, is the last act of legislation on herring fisheries under the Republic.

CHAPTER II.

WHALE FISHING.

THE *origines* of both Dutch and English whaling coincide with the beginning of the second decade of the seventeenth century.

Spitzbergen having been discovered by Van Heemskerk in 1596, and by British mariners the next year, reports about the seas off this island being very full of whales, soon began to spread, and set ship-owners' imagination and spirit of enterprise working in both countries. Still, in Holland, some time yet elapsed before any one ventured in a trade so entirely new. One Captain Huygen van Linschoten, in 1601, published an account of his voyage to the Arctic seas, accomplished in the years 1594-5; and he

* *Res. Holl.* 1786, p. 2952. Gr. *Plac. Bock.* ix. p. 1310.
† *Groot Plac. Bock.* ix., p. 1313.
‡ *Ibid.* ix. p. 1315.

described the whales, their tameness and multitude, and added, "A goodly fishery might be made upon these animals, if people would turn their thoughts that way."* But in the next years nobody did. The novelty and risk of the thing probably deterred single-handed enterprise; and subscriptions towards a whaling company are not reported to have been collected until the year 1611. The two first Dutch whalers sailed to Spitzbergen in 1612, but failed utterly: firstly, in consequence of outrages committed upon the ships by English concurrents, and, secondly, from lack of experience how to manage the business. Having sailed in quest of the whale, the Dutch found securing and killing him a very different sport from their accustomed business of netting the herring and hooking the cod, and were unsuccessful till the fashion of hiring harpooners from the Bay of Biscay came into use, when the trade at once proved a promising business. Frenchmen from Biscay, and from St. Jean de Luz especially, had practised whaling at a more remote period, when a peculiar kind of whale was found off their own coasts. They seem to have afterwards followed the animals to Greenland and acquired a degree of training which fitted them to teach the Dutch the art of whaling, in which the latter soon became such adepts as to find plenty of skilful harpooners in their own country.

The command of a whaling expedition was at first divided. The navigation department belonged to the ship's master; but when in sight of the fish he abdicated, and the harpooner took the direction of the further proceedings upon himself. By his orders boats were manned, fish attacked or left alone, and when killed towed alongside and left in the water till they "rose," so as to enable the

* P. 7.

men to stand on them, which period was the fit one for slicing or "flensing" the blubber. As the harpooning and blubber-carving business was the most important in the eyes of the ship-owners, the harpooner of course was a great personage on board, and his authority seems at first to have exceeded that of the skipper or "commandeur."*

Spitzbergen, as said before, was the cradle of the whaling industry. Its seas were then alive with whales; and, moreover, its geographical position and the nature of its coasts afforded the trade peculiar advantages.† In consequence the shores of the newly-discovered island were soon the theatre of contentions between British and Dutch whalers, as both nations claimed to be its first discoverers. A collision between the rivals in 1612 (see Chap. V.) led to the chartering of the Dutch Arctic Company (*Noordsche Compagnie*).

This company appears at first to have borne a merely private character. Subscriptions towards it, as said above, were raised as early as 1611. In 1612 they made their first and unlucky whaling attempt, after which the States made it their business to succour them. This was first done in 1613, by a prohibition to all Dutchmen fit for whaling service to take such service abroad,‡ in order to prevent a scarcity of men trained to the business. In the same

---

* *Zorgdrager*, Bloeyende Opkomst der aloude en hedendaagsche Groenlandsche Visschery, p. 99. The author speaks of but one harpooner, but of course the vessels carrying five or six whaling boats had several men to perform this part of the service. The personage mentioned by Zorgdrager is probably the chief harpooner, who in the first years of the trade was always a "Biscayer." Several harpooners are mentioned in the lists of some whaling crews which have been preserved.

† *Zorgdrager*, Bloeyende Opkomst, etc., p. 160.

‡ *Res. St. Gen.*, March 23rd, 1613.

year the company sued for a charter from the States, which was granted them on January 27th, 1614, and in virtue of which they set up as monopolists, after the manner of the East India Company, then already extant.

Their charter of monopoly, though applied for to last ten years, was at first granted for three only.* It conferred on them the exclusive right " to trade and fish from these United Netherlands, on or to the coasts of the lands between Nova Zembla and Fretum Davidis," including Spitzbergen, Beeren-Eiland, Greenland, etc. Partners in the company were to be entitled "not only to the profits of their money in proportion to the sums they shall have ventured, but also to all such further advantages as shall arise to the company within the aforesaid time, whether pertaining to the administration of the said company and equipage, or otherwise." On April 4th, 1614, towards the beginning of the whaling season, the States-General decreed that the company's ships should sail under convoy, and pay last-money; and in the next years one or more of the States' men-of-war generally sailed with the whaling fleet. The object of these warlike expeditions, and of the company's own armaments, was twofold. Besides catching whales, they meant to discover new countries, and as a fact, made several discoveries of islands in the Arctic seas. Their charter, as shown above, included such islands in their fishing monopoly, which circumstance of course stimulated their exploring ardour. The principle that the discoverer had a right to profit by his discovery, was applied by the Republic with remarkable fairness. In 1618 the States of Holland granted their worst enemies,

---

* *Groot Plac. Bock.* i. 670. The document is also to be found in Aitzema, *Saccken van Staat en Oorlogh*, vol. ii., p. 356; *Zorgdrager ll.*, p. 173; *Wagenaar Vad. Hist.* vol. x. p. 68.

the Dunkirkers, the right to fish off a small island discovered by some of them, provided they should sail thither under Dutch colours, and contribute towards the expenses of the common defence, *i.e.* pay last-money.* The foreign discoverer's rights were thus respected at the price of a breach of the company's monopoly.

The ardour for discoveries on the company's side was great. They even seriously attempted the north-east passage, and towards the opening of the whaling season of 1615 resolved to send some ships to China, or "Cathay," by that route, and applied to the States-General for permission, if obliged to return by the Indian seas, to water and victual their ships in the colonies then comprised in the East India Company's monopoly.† The whaling ships and their convoyers seem from the very first to have sailed in a sort of squadron; for it is registered that on April 29th, 1614, the States-General drew up an instruction for "the commander of the ships, both of war and others, destined to the Northern islands whether for the purpose of whaling or making discoveries." Their occasion for convoy and armament was constant and pressing; for besides repeated difficulties and conflicts with British whalers, they in 1616 had to provide against apprehended violence from the King of Denmark, who in the said year set up a claim to the exclusive right of fishing on the shores of Greenland. Both these matters will be treated of in another chapter. The States-General in the course of the year 1616 granted the Arctic Company no less than five convoying men-of-war, and, moreover, lent them artillery to arm their own whaling vessels.‡

* *Res. Holl.* 9th April, 1618, p. 591.
† *Res. St. Gen.*, 2nd April, 1615.
‡ *Ibid.* April 13, 28; May 11, 12; June 2, 1616. See ch.

Fishing operations were in the meantime commenced on a large scale, and a permanent establishment was set on foot on Amsterdam Island, near Spitzbergen, including warehouses and accommodation for boiling blubber and making barrels. This factory, called *Smeerenburg* (or Oil-city), in course of time formed a village, which in 1636 was fortified and provided with guns and ammunition. Smeerenburg of course decayed with the Arctic Company, but its remains were still to be found in 1768,* long after the first prosperous days of the trade had ceased.

A very thriving business was at first done by the company, notwithstanding frequent collisions with foreign, and especially with British, concurrents. In the very year of their chartering they sent out eighteen whalers, and the number increased greatly in following years. The Spitzbergen shore waters in these times were extremely redundant with whales; the shores were accordingly in a few years covered with blubber boilers and warehouses, and swarmed with whalers from several countries. The company's charter was prolonged in 1617 for the space of four years, the area monopolised this time including the island of Mauritius or Jan Mayen, discovered since 1614; and such was the number of fish caught by their skippers, that the whaling vessels did not suffice to carry home the blubber, oil, and whalebone, and several ships were chartered year after year solely for this end,† sometimes bringing to Amsterdam in one summer two freights of a thousand quarters of train oil each.

In spite of this extraordinary prosperity of the trade, discord arose between the Arctic Company's partners in 1621, towards the expiration of their charter. There were

* *Den Koopman*, i. p. 239 ; cf. *Zorgdrager*, p. 191.
† *Zorgdrager*, p. 180.

several chambers, or separate boards, in the company, viz. one at Amsterdam, one in the towns on the Maas, one in North Holland (or the "North Quarter"), and one in Zealand; and these had agreed to a repartition of convoying, and other general expenses between them. In 1621, the charter being about to expire, a change in this repartition was desired by some, and opposed by others; and as very high disputes arose on the subject, a simple renovation of the charter under these circumstances was impossible. The rival parties laid their differences before the States of Holland, who, on January 14th, 1622, appointed a committee to inquire into the matter and effect a reconciliation. These umpires proposed to leave the repartition as it was, viz., a quarter of the common expenses for each chamber. But to this the parties did not agree; the "small company," by which name the chamber for Zealand, though not then a separate body, seems to have been designated, pretending to pay less. There were, moreover, differences about the right to establish blubber boilers, &c., on some parts of the available coasts, to which rights both Holland and Zealand pretended. The upshot of the matter was the separation of the Zealand chamber from the company, and their establishment as a separate corporation. On May 28th, 1622, the States-General issued a placard assuring the Zealand company the right of whaling on the coasts of Mauritius or Jan Mayen's Land, and enjoining both parties not to trouble each other's establishments there, as the island was large enough for both. Upon this provisional charter the fishery was carried on in the course of the year, but the contending parties in the same year came to a definite agreement, in virtue of which, on December 22nd, the charter of 1617 was renewed for twelve years, for the benefit of both the companies of Holland and Zealand, whose rights to the whole available whaling area, Jan Mayen included, were by this Act made equal.*

It may be mentioned here that in the early days of the whaling trade a rival concern sought to obstruct its progress. When in 1621, the Arctic Company applied for their usual convoy, their request met with some opposition in the States, on the plea "that it had as yet to be established whether the public at large should profit by the whaling business, whereas any measure taken for their protection was sure to hasten the ultimate ruin of the ancient and respectable industries of manufacturing and dealing in rape-seed oil."†

But such arguments as this prevented neither the granting of the demanded convoy nor the trade's general prosperity. A very tempting account of the latter, about and after the time now spoken of, has been handed down to posterity by an author before quoted, Zorgdrager, who, however, wrote about 1720, and was then a retired whaling commander, and may, both as an old man and an old sailor, have been inclined to magnify the splendours of yore and the exploits of his predecessors on the deep.

Dutch vessels, he says,‡ used in the whaling season to lie alongside of each other in Smeerenburg Bay, so close together that boats could barely pass between them, and tow aboard the oil barrels manufactured and filled ashore. The vessels were moored safely, three or four miles from the high sea, in an excellent roadstead, having an anchor

---

* *Groot Plac. Bock.* i. p. 674 ; *Res. Holl.* 1622, pp. 627, 641 ; Zorgdrager, p. 181 *sqq.*

† *Res. Holl.* 1621, p. 403 ; *Res. St. Gen.* April 28th and 30th, and May 15th, 1621.

‡ Pp. 174, 191.

seaward, and fastened by ropes to large whale's ribs set up on shore as mooring stocks.* From this station the fishing business was done at ease, without unmooring the vessels, by boats cruising in the bay, which was uncommonly full of fish. The ships were manned double, one half of the crews being constantly employed in killing whales and towing them ashore, and the other in cutting the blubber, preparing the train oil, and rolling the full barrels into the water, whence they were floated to the ships and hauled on board. A fleet of merchant vessels from Amsterdam, Rotterdam, Hoorn and other ports was constantly to be found alongshore, the vessels from each town lying close to their own blubber-boiling establishments to ship cargo ; and a vast stock of blubber, oil, whalebone and whaling implements was constantly to be found in the Smeerenburg warehouses, to which dealers in all the commodities of life had begun to repair, making existence in the Arctic Sea a tolerably comfortable one. Rolls, hot from the baker's, were even to be had every morning in the height of the whaling season.

The company's halcyon days did not, however, last many years. In 1633, the expiration of their charter being again at hand, they, in spite of their monopoly, complained of ill-usage by foreign competitors and the backward state of the business, and further protectory measures were taken in their behalf. It had been shown to the States that, " By the act of certain unquiet persons, envious of the welfare of these United Countries," sailors were frequently tempted forth from the company's service, and got to exercise their abilities abroad. Wherefore in the true spirit of the times, when Governments were always ready

* Such posts have been brought home as curiosities, and may still be seen here and there in the Dutch pasture grounds, where they are used as scratching poles for cattle.

for the interest of a privileged few to prevent the people at large from seeking their gain where they best might, it was enacted that "No man living in the United Provinces should navigate to Greenland, &c., in the whaling trade, or after any sea-monsters, either from this or other countries, except it be in the Arctic or Greenland Company's service;" and heavy penalties were at the same time edicted against hiring out vessels or sailors to foreign whalers and participating in foreign whaling concerns. Dutch whaling vessels and implements were then indeed in some demand abroad. A month after the date of the placard just mentioned, the King of Denmark applied to the States-General for an exception in favour of one of his subjects, who used to procure whaling sloops and gear from Holland. The Royal letter was submitted to the Arctic Company, and I have not found whether the request was granted or not.*

The Arctic Company's charter being now once more about to expire, some enterprising inhabitants of the province of Friesland determined to try competition; and the delegates of Friesland to the States-General sought, in June, 1633, to prevent another prorogation of the Company's monopoly. But the delegates of Holland contrived to have this instance put off, and the Frisons found themselves excluded as before. Far from acquiescing, the whaling season being meanwhile advanced, they sent three ships north, and the states of Friesland, as sovereigns in the province, in the next year granted their subjects a license to exercise the whaling trade for twenty years, provided they should be entered as shareholders in a Frison whaling company chartered by the same Act (dated November 22nd, 1634). This charter was based upon the consideration that

* *Res. Holl.* 1633, p. 471.

it was "unlawful and contrary to the Union for one province to preclude another from traffic in the free sea," and the Arctic Company's monopoly had therefore no title to be respected. But the participators in the Frison Company nevertheless found it expedient to apply for the States-General's approbation on their charter, to prevent "misunderstandings and actual collisions" (*dadelijkheden*) between the whalers of both provinces. The Holland Arctic Company's Charter had meantime been prolonged for eight years, by a fresh privilege dated October 25th, 1633; but in spite of the monopoly thus maintained the States-General issued orders for Hollands whalers not to molest the Frisons. The latter accordingly fished, in virtue of their own charter, and, as it were, on sufferance from the States-General ; while at the same time the Arctic Company averred the Frison charter to be void, as in collision with their monopoly. This ambiguous state of things, a result of the very ill-defined rights of sovereignty in the Republic of the United Provinces, of course gave rise to frequent disputes between the rival parties, to terminate the which the States of Holland once more offered their mediation, and had a series of meetings held between delegates from the Zealand, Holland, and Frison whaling companies before a committee of the States, in the course of the years 1635 and 1636. As the result of these deliberations, an accord was agreed upon on July 25th of the latter year. To this agreement or "treaty" (which was simply a private contract concluded before a notary) the companies of Holland and Zealand combined were one party, and that of Friesland was the other, and the latter was allowed to share the whaling monopoly.[*]

A repartition of common profits and expenses was

[*] *Zorgdrager*, p. 188 ; *Aitzema*, ii. p. 359 ; *Gr. Plac. Boek*, ii. 3018.

agreed to in proportion as three for Friesland to twenty-four for Holland and Zealand combined ; and Friesland was secured the range of the other companies' whaling area, provided they should not place their establishments nearer to each other than was reasonable. A general assembly of shareholders was to be held thrice a year, in which Holland was to have six votes, Zealand two, and Friesland one, and all parties agreed to trade only to and from the United Provinces, and keep secret, and exploit for the common advantage any new discoveries or inventions to be made by any of them. The Frisons soon afterwards established a blubber-boilery of their own at Smeerenburg, from the ruins of which part of the shore was called the "*Harlinger* Traankokery*" till late in the eighteenth century.

Notwithstanding this extension both of their capital and working power, matters went backward with the Arctic (or Greenland) Companies after the renewal of their monopoly in 1633. Several very unfavourable seasons, in which the state of the ice occasioned the loss of many vessels, contributed to their decline ; but Zorgdrager, who certainly was a competent judge of the matter, mainly attributed it to their improvident way of fishing. When the great whaling establishments near Spitzbergen were first constructed, the company seems to have counted on a perpetual affluence of whales to the same spots. But as this animal procreates slowly, and has, moreover, a propensity to migrate when much chased and annoyed, sport became rare after a few years of abundance and reckless destruction of them. The train-oil and whalebone mine had been

* Harlingen is a town in the province of Friesland, and one of its burgomasters, named Hilbrand Dirksz, was one of the first participators in the Frison whaling concern.

much overworked, and consequently became exhausted ;*
and the Spitzbergen whales, formerly described as
"innocent creatures," who unsuspectingly came and disported within a short distance from the ships lying off
Smeerenburg, in time became cunning enough to avoid
them, and retreat into the more northerly ice regions.
They were, indeed, pursued from place to place, but the
greater distance from Smeerenburg made the landing of the
prey more and more difficult. Whalers were at last obliged
to "flens" or carve the blubber and whalebone while
out at sea, and carry home blubber instead of oil, whereby
the extensive Smeerenburg boiling establishments and the
thriving trade of the oil-ships had to be gradually abandoned, involving, of course, considerable loss of capital.
This caused the ardour for whaling to slacken, and thereby
prevented the founding of new establishments on other
places, which was, besides, made very difficult by the fact
of other nations having by this time taken possession of
most of the available whaling area, and each excluding others
from the shores of his own domain, to which, as stated by
Zorgdrager, no foreign boat was admitted unless the harpoon
were previously taken out of the "mik" or stand used in
shooting or throwing it. The pretensions of Denmark
relative to the exclusive right to some parts of the whaling
sea will be spoken of in another chapter.

The company's charter once more expiring in 1641, the
state of their affairs was such as to prevent their suing for
another renewal of it. Still, whaling experiments in parts
till then unvisited seemed full of promise, and the trade was
accordingly commenced at once by men from several provinces and towns, as soon as the discontinuance of the

---

* Wagenaar, *Vaderl. Hist.* x. p. 68.

monopoly left competition free.* Not being bound to any particular place or establishment, nor burdened with a considerable capital sunk in buildings, boilers, forts, &c., whalers from Amsterdam, Rotterdam, Zaandam, Rijp and many other towns began to sail after the whales wherever they could be found, and generally brought home sufficient cargoes of blubber and whalebone. The killing of walrus and seals was likewise practised with some success after the Arctic or Greenland Company's dissolution, which took place in 1645; and the trade, which had at first been fostered by the company's monopoly, thus acquired renewed vigour after its extinction.† It should, however, be added, that quarrels and even actual deeds of violence between Dutch whalers occurred frequently in the first years after the expiration of the monopoly.‡

A trade so very dependent on climatic circumstances could scarcely yield anything like constant profit; and it is accordingly described as being "more of a lottery than a trade," by most of the authors who have written about it. A series of accounts of ships wrecked and crews miraculously saved from death by cold and starvation sufficiently corroborate this statement, and are corroborated in their turn by several placards issued at different periods by the States of Holland to secure the owner's rights to vessels abandoned in the ice in various parts of the Arctic Sea. These accidents gradually became more frequent as the whales retreated into or under the more northern ice; a period of their migrations which coincides with a considerable change in the method of fishing. During the prosperity of the Arctic Company, when whales, as related above,

* *Zorgdrager*, p. 195.
† *Den Koopman*, vol. i. p. 239.
‡ *Res. Holl.* 1644, pp. 576-578; 1645, p. 108; 1651, p. 279.

flocked round the coasts of Spitzbergen, whaling was a harmless and easy, though very profitable, summer sport, and such danger as it involved was amply recompensed by pleasant life at Smeerenburg. As the fish retreated seaward, things became less pleasant both for the shipowner and the whaling crew; but the real hardships of the trade, as writers of the period express it, did not commence for either till the whales began to hide away in the ice, and "sea fishery" was forcibly superseded by "ice fishery." Worn-out merchant-vessels were at first used, or "risked," in this perilous trade; but the number of casualties increasing, shipowners gradually found it worth their while to provide new and very strongly built vessels,* and this circumstance caused fresh capital to be invested in the trade. In a word, as a writer in the commercial review 'Den Koopman'† shows, the whaling trade revived when it became a less easy one, and ceased to be in the hands of a few monopolists.

Another circumstance must have contributed to this phenomenon. Whereas the herring fishery was from the very beginning regulated by law down to minute details, whalers were always left at liberty to fish where and how they judged best. They were, indeed, no less than the herring trade an object of Government solicitude, as appears, besides frequent grants of convoy, from the above-mentioned prohibitions to export whaling ships and implements and take service in foreign whaling ships. They were, on the other hand, occasionally ordered to stop their trade in times of war, and were not exempt from the financial burdens imposed upon the fisheries in general. The latter were indeed the chief cause of the only restrictive measure

* *Zorgdrager*, p. 204.
† He wrote in 1768.

ever put upon their trade, viz. a placard of May 25th, 1652, by which whalers were enjoined to carry the whole of their blubber, oil, and whalebone home and sell them in the Dutch markets " for the conservation of the custom-house duties and the market tax."* Besides this edict, which probably was never enforced with much vigilance, no working regulations were ever applied to them. There was no fishing season determined for them by law, and no rules for branding their produce. Government, however paternally minded towards them as well as others, never undertook to teach them their business. They were protected, not directed; guarded, not led. They accordingly managed to mind their own business with generally satisfactory results, and keep their trade going when others, fettered down by a multitude of working rules, saw theirs go to ruin.

This important difference in the Government policy towards the two fisheries is fully explained by the different nature of the trades. One of the leading features of herring legislation under the Republic was to prevent unripe, or too early herring being caught; and as the whale's existence is not limited to one season, no such measures were required for the Arctic fishery. Next, train-oil and whalebone are not subject to amelioration by any peculiar process, such as the curage of herring; whence Dutch train never excelled, or was fancied to excel, that of other nations, and there was no occasion for branding it, or for any of the several obstructions to trade which result from such a process. Thirdly, the annual migrations of the herring shoals have always taken place at a date recurring with a considerable degree of regularity every year, and their progress through the North Sea is traced upon a constant route, whence

* *Groot Placaetboek*, i. p. 683.

herring fishermen could be told when and where to sail without exposing them to utter discomfiture; whereas the whaler, by reason of the shifting ways of his sport, could never have done well without entire liberty of action. Thus, until the era of Bounties set in, whalers never looked for gain but to their own enterprise, spirit, and labour; while herring-fishers were forbidden to seek it elsewhere than in the observation of laws. The latter were regulated over, and by degrees lost their energy; whalers were free, and preserved theirs long after the herring trade's decay. These are the reasons why there never was a whaling legislation properly speaking; and certainly the principal reasons why the prosperity of the whaling trade survived that of the Grand Fishery, although the produce of the former obtained no Government warrant as to its excellence, and whalers were by the nature of their trade exposed to far greater risks of accident. On the other hand, as regards risks by war, the Grand Fishery were worse off, being obliged to exercise their trade in seas constantly swept by the enemy's squadrons, and in the centre of warlike operations. Moreover, Dunkirk privateers seldom roved as far as Greenland or Spitzbergen, and the whaling fleets were only exposed to their depredations while sailing north or returning home. The latter circumstance, besides legislation, accounts for the fact of the Grand Fishery having decayed long before the Arctic, or as it was generally called in the 17th century, the Greenland business.

The war with England of 1652–1654, which occasioned the beginning of the Grand Fishery's decay, was also prejudicial to the Greenland trade. In April of the former year, before hostilities had actually begun, Holland resolved not only to permit the said trade for the next season, but even, if possible, to prevent its being thwarted by lack of able seamen.* In July, the advisability of calling the whaling fleet home to prevent the vessels being taken was strongly considered, but for the moment the States of Holland only warned them to keep together "in form of Admiralties" (or squadrons) for their safety.† In December, a request of some whaling shipowners for restitution of the expense of a vessel of war equipped by them to protect their other ships, was favourably advised on by Holland,‡ from which fact it is evident that the trade was actually kept going during the summer of 1652. On March 25th of the next year, however, the States-General prohibited it,§ not only in order to keep the vessels safe in port, but mainly because Government wanted the sailors, and perhaps some of the ships, for warlike ends. Seamen who have learned their business under the Northern lights have always been found very valuable for any service; and the prohibition to sail was therefore enhanced by a reinforcement of the former edict against hiring out seamen into foreign service, and especially into the whaling business abroad.‖

For the same reason, while the States' fleet operated in Sweden in 1659, the whaling prohibition was repeated by placard dated April 4th. It was indeed repealed soon afterwards (May 2nd); but "navigation to Greenland" was then permitted only on condition that the shipowners and captains concerned in the trade should put fifteen hundred able sailors at the disposal of the Boards of Admiralty or buy them off for fl.15 per head.¶

* *Res. Holland*, 1652, p. 172.
† *Ibid.* 1652, pp. 343, 387.
‡ *Ibid.* 1652, p. 659.
§ *Groot Placactboek*, ii. p. 505.
‖ *Ibid.* p. 302.
¶ *Ibid.* pp. 507–510.

The repeated wars of course took some effect upon the Greenland trade's prosperity; and it appears that about this time whaling ships were sometimes sold to foreigners, or freighted to sail under their flags. The prohibition against this proceeding issued in 1633, for the Arctic Company's benefit had of course become void upon that body's dissolution; and a fresh prohibition against letting Dutch vessels go into foreign whaling service was therefore enacted on March 10th, 1661, and renewed on December 14th, 1663.* Both this edict and the penalties against Dutchmen taking whaling service abroad were strictly maintained. In 1662, the magistrates of Emden interceded in favour of one Klaas Dirks Meunsz of Edam, who had served as commander in a whaling vessel from Emden; but instead of acceding to their wish, Holland ordered the prosecution against the culprit to be maintained without any consideration, and on March 20th of the next year re-enacted the placard, adding expressly that Emden should be considered as a foreign town.†

The war against England in 1665 brought a fresh prohibition over the whaling business,‡ when as a consequence "certain gain-seeking persons" once more sold their vessels abroad, to the effect that the laws against such sales, and against exporting whaling implements, were re-enacted in the course of the spring of the said year.§ Still the danger to the trade did not appear to be very imminent, as the English naval force was at this period required on other service than that of pursuing whalers to Greenland. Several Dutch shipowners there-

* Gr. Pl. B. ii. pp. 2639, 3087.
† Res. Holl. 1662, p. 523; 1663, p. 114.
‡ Placard dated Jan. 24th, 1665; Gr. Pl. B. iii. p. 291.
§ Gr. Pl. B. iii. 292-293.

fore prepared to try their luck in the Polar Seas as soon as the Republic's naval preparations had come to a close, "deeming the prohibition might as well be withdrawn after the country's fleet had sailed;" but they were reminded of the placard of January by another dated March, 1665, besides which, on the 25th of April, the States went the length of cancelling all contracts between sailors and shipmasters or shipowners for the Greenland trade. The whaling prohibition was moreover renewed in December, 1665, and February, 1666; and there was no whaling, as far as can be traced, during the whole of the war. No sooner had peace been concluded (July ult. 1667) than Dutch whalers set about their business with renewed energy, to stimulate which an amnesty was granted in 1669 to all whaling commanders and sailors who had, against the placard, taken service abroad during the late war. Moreover, Holland in 1670 decreed differential duties against the importation of foreign whalebone and blubber,* while the prohibitions against selling whaling implements to foreigners were re-enacted more than once. Zorgdrager's statistics of the trade, which begin at the year 1670, mention 148 vessels to have sailed in that year and mastered 792 whales (see Appendix B).

The disastrous war of 1672 soon put another forcible stop to the proceedings. All whaling expeditions were expressly prohibited as early as February, 1672;† and while the other fisheries were at one time re-opened during the war, the prohibition against whaling lasted for three years without an interruption. But the suspense does not appear to have done much prejudice, as the trade was recommenced in 1675, with a number of vessels scarcely

* *Res. Holl.* 1669, p. 120; 1670, pp. 434, 534, 552.
† *Gr. Pl. B.* iii. p. 298.

inferior to what it was before the war. And now a vestige of working regulations was for the first time imposed upon the trade, but for reasons widely different from those prevailing with the herring fishery. In order to ensure their sailing together, i.e., in squadron or "Admiralty," Holland decreed that no whaling vessels should sail before April 28th, and the order was repeated in several subsequent years.*

The only object of this measure was of course to promote the safety of the Greenland fleet. It was taken at the request of a body representative of the whalers' common interest, which now appears for the first time as a duly organised corporation.

A representation of the whaling interest did, indeed, exist some years earlier. In 1665, two whaling ship-owners named William Bastiaansz and A. den Hertog, sued for an exemption from taxes for all whaling vessels, and in return offered to supply the Republic's fleet with 1200 sailors; and the offer was made in the name of, and upon authorisation by, "the community of those concerned in the Greenland trade." † Request and offer were both declined, but the event appears to have occasioned a closer organisation of those concerned in the whaling trade, and the appointment of a definitive Committee, analogous to the College of the Grand Fishery. In 1675 this Committee was already invested with defined powers, and qualified to act on behalf of all without especially naming its constituents, as appears from the fixation of a sailing date by the States in the said year, upon the request of the community of those interested in the whaling business at and about Greenland," and not of one or more individuals as repre-

* *Res. Holl.* 1675, April 4th ; 1677, March 27th.
† *Ibid.* 1665, May 6th and 12th.

senting that community. This variance in the denomination, and the fact that no such requests made by some in behalf of all are on record in earlier years, justify the supposition that an organisation of the trade had not taken place since the downfall of the Arctic Company, and that such an organisation, and the appointment of a perpetual representative body, was effected between 1665 and 1675. At any rate, the Committee, or central representative body of whaling shipowners, never had anything like the attributions of the Herring College, and they never seem to have acted in any other capacity than as the spokesmen of their constituents presenting requests to the States, and the draftsmen of such bye-laws as seemed advisable for the common weal. The vast power with which the Herring Deputies were invested was a result of the herring legislation; and no such power was held by the Whaling Committee, who had no laws to enforce, no licences to deliver, and no skippers to swear in. In their quality as draftsmen of bye-laws, the "Commissioners of the Greenland trade" in 1677 issued an order, or regulation concerning the salvage of ships wrecked, and goods lost in the northern seas. They sued for the States of Holland's approbation upon the document, which, however, was not granted till January 22nd, 1695.* The order was, however, printed in 1677, and although as yet unapproved by the proper legislator, was observed not only by whalers from the United Provinces, but also by those of Hamburg, Bremen, and Emden.† The above-named William Bastiaansz was again

---

* *Res. Holl.* 1677, p. 87 ; *Gr. Pl. Bock*, iv. p. 1355.

† The approbation was granted in 1695, because applied for anew by the Committee who had in the course of eighteen years "on some few occasions (*soo nu en dan*) experienced difficulties in the execution," whence their authority appears as a rule to have been unquestioned.

the first signer of this bye-law, and thence appears at the time to have been President of the Board of Whaling Commissioners. The principal dispositions of the order are as follows : When a vessel is wrecked, and her crew leave her, the first ship they meet is obliged to take them on board, and is entitled in her turn to transmit half of the men saved to the next vessel she hails. Such victuals as may be brought on board by the wrecked crew shall be consumed by themselves ; if they have none, they shall be fed out of Christian charity, and be obliged in return to do a common sailor's work.

If the crew do not leave the wrecked vessel, her commander shall be free either to accept or refuse salvage by others, as long as he remains in or near his ship. Whosoever finds a ship abandoned, shall be free to take her cargo and whaling gear on board, and on coming home be entitled to one half of the goods saved, the other half to be given up to the owner, without any further claim upon him for salvage-money, freight, &c.

Sailors, whether serving on monthly-wage or share in the returns (*Maentgelders of Parteniers*) shall be entitled to nothing out of the value or cargo of a whaling vessel abandoned by them. If they have remained near her and aided in the salvage, they shall be entitled to their wages, &c., to the amount of one-fourth of the value of the goods saved, and have no pretension whatever on the other three parts.

A vessel's crew having killed a whale and been prevented from appropriating it, remains entitled to the fish as long

---

Hamburg, Bremen, and Emden, were accustomed, as regards whaling, to sail in the Republic's wake ; i.e. join their fleets to hers and sail under a common convoy. *cf. Zorgdrager* p. 178.

as any of her crew shall have remained near the body. If abandoned, the fish becomes the property of the first occupant, unless it should have been killed near shore, and made fast to an anchor or buoy bearing some mark of the vessel by whose crew the fish was caught, in which case the finder has no right to the body.

The period between the years 1675 and 1685 was one of considerable prosperity for the Greenland trade, as appears from the statistics contained in Appendix B,* which also shows the extreme vicissitude of whaling luck. It will be remarked in consulting this table, that years of very prosperous fishery were usually followed by a considerable increase in the number of vessels sailed, as a proof of the unabated energy and interest with which this trade was carried on. Being no longer a monopoly, and being, besides, free from legislative working rules, there was a "considerable ardour for Greenland," as stated by a writer in 'den Koopman.'† The trade was indeed a lottery; but many tried their chance in it, often with favourable results. Five or six fish caught in a season were then considered a fair success, as stated by Zorgdrager; and the

---

* As this table is now given for the first time in its present shape, I feel bound to state the origin of its contents. The entries from 1670 down to 1719 are taken from Zorgdrager's book, quoted above. Between 1719 and 1738, the decennial totals are taken from Mr. Brandligt's '*Geschiedkundige Beschouwing van de Walvisch-visscherij.*' The annual returns between 1737 and 1750 are collected from the periodical called '*Europische Mercuur*,' and the rest is drawn from the table printed as Appendix XVI. to the report of the Commission on Sea Fisheries, 1854, which table appears to have been compiled out of the '*Nederlandsche Jaarboeken.*' The figures now given are tolerably reliable, for whenever statements as to one and the same year are found in more than one of the works quoted, they always coincide, or very nearly so.

† Vol. iv. p. 222.

number was often considerably exceeded. So great was the ardour for whaling, that when a fresh prohibition to sail was issued by the States-General in 1691 * on account of the French war, a couple of ships belonging to Dutchmen were sent to Greenland from Hamburg and Bremen, and the experiment was repeated in the next years on a scale very much larger, although the prohibition was maintained during the next six years, and the States-General had expressly stipulated all contracts between master and sailors for whaling expeditions to be void, "setting all such sailors and seafaring persons, none excepted, on their free feet, to pass into the country's service." † The trade was not lawfully re-opened till April 1st, 1697, under provision that the vessels should sail in squadron, and under a sufficient convoy, the expense of which was to be repartitioned among those concerned in the business.‡

The war for the Spanish succession once more occasioned a considerable demand for able sailors in the Republic's squadrons, wherefore all navigation from Dutch ports was once more prohibited on March 31st, 1702, and re-opened on June 23rd on condition that each ship should give up one fifth of her crew or pay 15 florins per head of them to the Admiralty officers.§ The Grand Fishery was exempted from the latter charge, but the Greenland trade was not, the difference being made on account of the superior skill of the sailors trained to the latter business. The trade rose to a high pitch in the same year, notwithstanding the crews'

* *Gr. Pl. Boek*, iv. p. 236.
† *Ibid.* p. 240 (Nov. 1691).
‡ *Res. St. Genl.*, April 1st, 1697 ; *Gr. Pl. B.* v. p. 376–7. *Res. Holl.* March 29th, 1697.
§ *Res. Holl.* 1702, p. 441.

decimation,* and though the expense of convoy equipped by themselves appears to have burdened them considerably. On August 18th, 1702, the States of Holland considered the request of "certain persons styling themselves the Commissioners of the Greenland Fishery," who having procured convoyers and demanded of the shipowners a retribution of 300 florins per whaling vessel to cover the costs, had met with opposition at the hands of several shipowners, who wanted the contribution for each ship to be proportioned to the quantity of train-oil brought home in her.† The contribution was either paid very irregularly, or denied outright, whence in 1704 it was two years in arrear, and part of it irrecoverable, so as to necessitate the intervention of the regular legislative authorities. On July 17th of the said year the States of Holland declared the Commissioners entitled to recover the arrears by execution.‡ As a fact, the Committee's authority, having not been hitherto expressly sanctioned by law, was at the time very ill obeyed ; and this led to a Resolution of the States-General dated March 24th, 1706, § by which the Commissioners of the Greenland Fishery were authorized and qualified "to issue the necessary orders for the Groenland fleet, for the next season, and especially to establish a convenient Admiralship, determine a sailing day and rendezvous, and enact such secret orders as shall be found advisable for the conservation and well-being of the fleet;"

* It appears that whaling vessels were frequently manned with foreigners. On March 3rd, 1713, the States-General granted a request made by the Greenland Fishery Committee to be allowed *as usual* to draw sailors from Jutland for their crews, although a contagious disease was then prevalent there (*Gr. Pl. B.* v. 1579).
† *Res. Holl.* 1702, p. 441.
‡ *Ibid.* 1704, p. 419.
§ *Gr. Pl. B.* iv. p. 1564.

which orders all whaling commanders were enjoined to obey strictly, under a penalty of 300 florins, to be recovered out of their pay and available goods and chattels. This power, though at first granted to the Committee for one season only, was continued in the next years.*

A change of some importance was introduced into the whalers' proceedings about this time. They had, from the exhaustion of the Spitzbergen seas down to the season now spoken of, fished chiefly about Greenland, and restrained their operations to the seas once included in the Arctic Company's monopoly, of which "Fretum Davidis" was the western limit. It now became customary to look for whales in Davis' Straits also. It is not certain when this part of the northern seas was first visited by Dutch whalers. Zorgdrager, who was quite at home in the details of the business, does not particularly mention the Straits fishery in his valuable work, of which the first edition was published in 1720. Still, in the said year whaling in the Straits had already acquired some extension; for an immunity from last-money granted to the Greenland fishery in 1687, was then expressly extended to those who navigated to the Straits "whither a considerable part of the ships are now bound." † The same fact is evident from a States-General Resolution dated November 18th, 1720,‡ by which penalties are enacted against offering violence to the natives of the Straits shores. It appears from this edict that the first exploits of Dutchmen in the Straits were anything but glorious, and that robbery and ill-treatment of Esquimaux

---

* *Res. Holl.* March 23rd, 1707 ; Feb. 18th, 1708, &c. The subject was generally re-considered by the States in the course of February of each year.

† *Res. Holl.* 1720, p. 197, 306 ; *Res. St. Gen. ibid.* p. 786.

‡ *Gr. Plac. Bock*, v. p. 1581.

by them were matters of daily occurrence. Their behaviour, in a word, was that of pirates, and as such accordingly, the above-quoted Resolution prescribes those guilty of further acts of this nature to be proceeded against.

A writer in 'den Koopman'* states the Straits fishery to have become considerable after the year 1714, and a separate statistical table relative to that branch of the trade, added by Mr. Brandligt to his above-quoted pamphlet, begins at the year 1719. Zorgdrager's not especially mentioning the Straits fishery is not contradictory to these statements, for his book was written some years before it was published. The period when Dutch whalers first began to visit the Straits may, upon these several authorities, be stated to be not much anterior to the year 1720.

In the next years, besides statistics, no facts of any importance relative to the whale fishery are on record. In 1724 a whaling company was chartered in England; † but their competition does not appear to have severely prejudiced the Dutch, as the years 1719-1728 were, according to Brandligt's statistics, a period of very considerable prosperity for the Straits trade especially. In 1731, the Dutch Ambassador to England reported on a contrivance to shoot harpoons out of a musquetoon, or portable cannon, by which the instrument was thrown fifty feet, or thrice the distance the best harpooner could cast it, and without setting the line on fire; but though the Dutch diplomatist had seen the instrument alluded to in a London wharf, and spoke of it in highly commendatory terms, there is no evidence of its having been adopted.‡ In 1739 and the next years, Denmark's pretensions to exclusive fishing

* Vol. i., p. 239.
† 'Europische Mercuur,' 1724, vol. ii. p. 32.
‡ Res. Holl. 1731, p. 172.

rights in the Northern seas, which will be treated of in another chapter, caused the Dutch whalers some uneasiness. A few of their vessels were actually taken by the Danes, and they had for some years to sail under convoy by Government men-of-war. Still these events did not materially affect the trade; for the number of ships sailed to Greenland, which were especially the object of Denmark's animosity, was much greater in the years 1739-1748 than in the preceding decade. In 1747, the Republic's war with France having necessitated extraordinary measures to get crews for the squadrons, a general obligation to give up one third of the crews to the Admiralties, or redeem them at the price of 40 florins per head, was once more laid upon merchant vessels in general; but the Greenland and Davis' Straits fisheries were expressly exempted from either charge, by a Resolution of the States-General, dated December 1st*. The favour was partly cancelled on February 19th of the next year, when the States-General resolved to allow the trade two men-of-war as convoyers without the retribution they had hitherto paid for them to the Admiralties, provided each whaling vessel should furnish five able seamen, or the whole fleet together should furnish five hundred such seamen to the Admiralties of the Maas and Amsterdam†. In other words, the whalers were to have convoying vessels without paying for them, but on condition that they should man them out of their own crews; for the men-of-war offered by the States were to carry forty guns and two hundred and fifty men each.

Besides these measures in their behalf, whaling ships were in 1750, upon the request of the Commission of Greenland

* *Gr. Pl. Boek*, vii. 515.
† *Ibid.* p. 1591.

Fishery, allowed exemption from excise duties on victuals, wine, spirits, &c., consumed on board.* The measure was indeed taken on a very liberal scale, for it was extended not only to the victuals actually consumed, but, as regards bread, to the whole quantity taken on board, even though some parts of it should be brought home again. Immunities of a similar nature were at the same time allowed to other branches of fishery; but there is reason to believe that whalers derived peculiar profit from theirs, as they were in the habit of dealing in divers commodities with the natives of the northern countries whither they were bound. It will be seen in another chapter that this propensity to do spurious business was one of the principal causes of the difficulties with Denmark; and it may be assumed that Dutch whalers upon occasion were not only petty tradesmen, but did by no means disdain smuggling on foreign coasts, towards which they were of course peculiarly benefitted by having some of the articles most heavily taxed in all countries at their disposal duty-free, by the States-General's express licence. Considerable light is thrown on this feature of the Greenland trade by a curious controversy kept up in the often-named periodical, 'Den Koopman,' in the course of the years 1772 and 1773.† A free-spoken letter-writer styling himself "Lubertus Piscator" is especially communicative on the subject. The results of whaling in itself, he says, now amount to average losses; and the trade is kept going by the profits of a fraudulent commerce in goods exported free of duty and smuggled ashore on the coasts of Norway and Scotland. These irregular profits are mostly pocketed by the manager (boekhouder) of the ship and a few of the

* *Res. Holl.* 1750–52, passim, *Gr. Pl. B.*, viii. 1253.
† Vol iv. p. 33, 90, 194, 199, &c.

chief partners, and dissimulated in such a manner as not to let the others have any share in them ; and most of the ships now engaged in whaling are kept afloat merely because a majority of votes in the partnership are in this manner interested against their being sold or broken up, although the returns of the whaling business proper are generally very unfavourable. Lubertus' indiscreet statements were indeed contradicted by other correspondents ; but the fact that much irregular business was done at the time by Dutch whalers is not positively denied by any of them. Some of these writers, who have all made a secret of their names, account for the continuation of the trade, in despite of unfavourable results, by the fact that the whaling vessels' purveyors were at the time generally part-owners, and recovered on the price of the stores what was lost on the business itself. And this state of things they approve, in virtue of a course of reasoning strongly and curiously illustrative of the economical notions of the period. The money lost on the voyage's balance, says an apologist of the trade in 1773, goes to the ship's victuallers, commander, and crew ; *it remains in the country*, and therefore is not lost to the nation ; and the value of every whale caught, however small their number, is to be accounted as a clear profit, though the sums made by the trade do not cover the expense !

If the above controversy sets one point beyond doubt, it is the fact that towards the end of the eighteenth century there was a rottenness in Dutch whaling. Its rapid decrease in the same period, shown by Appendix B, proves that even illegal proceedings could not cover losses as a rule ; and the demonstration is wound up by the fact that in 1775 the Commissioners of the Greenland and Davis Straits fisheries applied for a bounty, and were not behind-hand in the race for premiums which at this period characterises the whole of the sea-fishing concerns. The premium applied for was limited to 40 florins per head of the crews, besides exemption from export duty on train-oil, &c. Some objection was at first made to the plan. A Committee of the States of Holland, before whom the request was laid, considered premiums as a rule to be very useful in bringing a new trade to prosperity, but doubted their efficacy in upholding a business the decay of which was attributable to causes beyond the legislator's control, such as the development of whaling abroad, and the closing of some foreign markets. Still, the Committee were not averse to grant the trade some succour, and advised a bounty of 30 florins per head of the crew, for such vessels only as should return *clean*, i.e. empty. The matter was treated with the prolixity and slowness characteristic of the later years of the Republic's existence, and Holland did not take a decision till January 18th, 1777, when a premium of 30 florins was granted for all whaling vessels indiscriminately, and the immunity from export duty declined.* The premium was granted again in the next years.

The result of the application of the bounty system was as negative upon the whaling trade as on the herring fishery; and the table contained in Appendix B shows an actual decrease of the number of vessels sailed after bounties had been first allowed in 1777. The Whaling Commissioners accordingly in 1779 sued for an increase of the bounty to 80 florins per head of the crews; but the demand was declined. The war against England in 1781 next put

† *Res. Holl.* 1775, p. 607, 793, 990; 1776, p. 38; 1777, p. 73. The collection of printed documents emanated from and received by the States in these years, moreover contains a series of long memorials exchanged between them and the Greenland Committee.

a stop to all whaling expeditions for two seasons, in the course of which many vessels were sold out of the trade. A special permission was necessary for this, as the ancient laws against selling whaling ships to foreigners were still in vigour ; and this permission was granted by the States of Holland in 1782, provided that each person inclined to sell a vessel abroad should procure a licence from the Admiralty Board under which he resorted, and moreover that if the ship were sold to be used as a merchantman, the whaling implements should not be destroyed, but kept for better times. At the same time, the Admiralty Boards were empowered to grant permissions to hire out whaling sailors to foreigners, English excepted, under caution for their being sent back to the Republic after the war.* As a consequence, of the vessels formerly employed in the Straits fishery only nine were left in 1783, when whaling was recommenced ; and the business never recovered its losses. Premiums were granted till the end of the Republic, and were even determined for twelve years at their former amount of 30 florins per head, by one of the several Resolutions taken on April 17th, 1788, by the States-General for the fisheries' preservation from utter ruin.† Another, and a very peculiar form of encouragement was resorted to by a Resolution of the States of Holland dated October 3rd, 1788 ; viz., an "indemnisation" bounty of 50 florins for every quarter of train *wanting to a hundred* in a vessel's cargo. In order to prevent mock whaling trips, by which the said bounty might have been secured very easily indeed, certain conditions were added as to burden and equipment of ships, strength of crew and duration, and latitude where to fish. Even

* *Res. Holl.* 1782, p. 138, 174 ; *Res St. Generaal* 1782, p. 175, 232, 273, 289.
† *Groot Placaetboek,* ix. p. 1313.

this thorough application of the premium system was of no effect. As the institution of bounties had been followed by a decrease in the trade, so their continuation and extension proved unable to prevent its ruin; and at the close of the Republic's existence the Straits fishery, as will be seen from Appendix B, was nearly extinct, and the Greenland business reduced to utter insignificance.

CHAPTER III.

Cod Fishery.

THIS branch of the fisheries never was of paramount importance under the Republic. The name of "small fishery" (kleine visscherye) * which is commonly applied to it, as an antithesis to the denomination constantly given to the herring-fishery, sufficiently points out the fact. One part of the business, the cod-fishery off Iceland, was indeed an extensive concern requiring separate capital; and as the produce of this fishery was either salted or dried, it commanded an extensive foreign market. Cod-fishery in the North Sea, and on the Dogger bank especially, was a minor branch of the trade, and indeed more or less an appendage of the herring-fisheries, inasmuch as most of the vessels

* There has been some controversy about this denomination. Some state it to have been commonly used to designate the whaling trade; others the Iceland fishery, and the cod and fresh-fish business in the North Sea. As a fact, it has been applied to all three, but very seldom to the whale fishery, which by reason of its importance had no title to the name. In the States' official publications, "kleijne visscherije" is used for cod-fishery and for "the trade of the fresh" (*de neeringhe van den versche*). A Placard of 1665 expressly mentions "the Great and Small fishery, by which we mean the herring trade and the fishery on Doggersbank."

used in the latter after St. John's Day were in winter and spring sent to the Dogger bank for haddock and cod-fish. The method in which the trade was carried on by Dutchmen has always been the same as when, under the Bavarian Counts, political parties derived their names from it; viz. by lines to which were attached hooks baited with small fish of different kinds, or very early herrings. A Placard of the year 1612 expressly allowed cod-fishers to catch herring for bait before the 24th of June, provided they should not cure or salt such herrings, nor lay them in barrels, nor carry them ashore or sell them at sea.*

Keelless boats from the North Sea coast villages from early times downward combined cod-fishery on the Dogger bank with "the trade of the fresh," as shown by a Resolution of the States of Holland dated 1585, and mentioning "all fish caught by fishermen of the Side, *except cod and haddock*." Keeled vessels from the fishing towns on the Maas likewise fished for cod in the North Sea out of the herring season; and besides, the Iceland cod fishery, which could not be combined with herring fishery, centred in some of those towns, and Vlaardingen and Maassluis were prominent in the Iceland business long before they became " herring towns" of importance. The vessels sent to Iceland were called "hookers," from the fishing gear they carried; although by their build they were fit for the herring trade also, and were used in the latter in some years when the state of the several markets, or other circumstances made a voyage to Iceland unadvisable. Still a mixing up of both trades could not occur, as the seasons for both were the same; whence Iceland fishery was a separate business, and had an organization of its own. Its object was to cure the

* Art. 2 of the herring regulations, 1604-1632; *Gr. Pl. Bock*, i. p. 733.

fish either by salting it as "*Zoutevisch*" "*labberdaan*" (also called *abberdaan*) or drying it as *stock-fish*, in both of which conditions it was a considerable article of exportation. In the fresh state the two varieties of cod-fish most caught bear the Dutch names of *kabeljauw* (also called *bakkeljauw* or *baccalauw**) and "*Schelvisch*" (the latter appearing to correspond exactly to the English denomination of *haddock*).

There is no literature to my knowledge on this peculiar branch of Dutch sea-fishery, and very few legislative acts are on record relative to it ; whence its history must necessarily be very incomplete and succinct. North-sea cod-fishery had some importance as early as the establishment of the Republic, as appears from the fact that two men-of-war were sent " ter Dogge," i.e. to the Dogger bank, for the cod-fishers' convoy, in 1589 ; † and as the place, of

* The latter word was also used now and then for cod salted and dried. *Bacallao* is Spanish, *Baccalà* is Italian, and *Bacalhão* is Portuguese, for dried cod. The assonance between these words and the (now obsolete) Dutch term *baccalauw* is so striking that the question can only be whether the word was derived by the Dutch from the Roman languages, or the reverse. Holland in the 17th and 18th centuries exported great quantities of salt and dried cod to Spain, and never, so far as can be traced, imported any from that country ; whence it would seem natural that the name should have been exported together with the article. On the other hand, I am not aware of the Dutch etymological derivation for " baccalauw," and I have heard it said, upon authority which I can neither back nor question, that in Spanish and Portuguese the word has something to do, etymologically, with *stick* (Lat. *Baculum*). In the latter case, *Bacalhao* &c., might be literal translations of the Dutch term *Stokvisch*, and Holland, having first exported the article, might have re-imported its Romanized name. I beg to refer the question to professional linguists. Such dictionaries as I have at command do not show any close relation between the Spanish, Italian, and Portuguese words, for a cod-fish and a stick.

† *Res. Holl.* 1589, p. 14, 836, 840.

all the North Sea, was perhaps the one most exposed to every naval foe, orders for ships to convoy the "Doggers" are numerous throughout the Republic's history. There is, however, another circumstance to account for the extraordinary liberality with which they had convoy doled out to them, viz. the fact that fishery on the Dogger bank took place at a season when both herring and whale fishery stood still; whence it was possible for Holland, on Jan. 30th, 1597, to order the Admiralty Board of Rotterdam to send out *the whole* of their available vessels for the "Doggervaarders" convoy.

In spite of Government protection, cod-fishery seems to have been subject to severe losses by war, for a contract for their mutual insurance against damage by sea or foemen was passed in 1622 between the shipowners of the towns on the Maas concerned in the business, and ratified by the States of Holland in 1623, under their charter or "octroy." I have not found any positive information as to the contents of this document, which appears somehow to have been prejudicial to the steersmen's real or presumed private interest. The latter in the autumn of 1623 twice interfered with the publication of the Octroy (which took place, as usual, by cry, and by the posting of handbills), and got up a serious riot at Maassluis, whither soldiers had to be sent in order to maintain the peace. The matter was even of sufficient importance for a deputation from the Court of Holland to be sent to Maassluis with instructions to pacify the mutinous seamen, and the men of the law effected this object by putting a new interpretation upon the charter, in virtue of which "the pennies of the second word were to be left among the steersmen to the end of the fishing season, and then to be restored to the partners, if no damage had been incurred."* The true sense of these words can only be found out by detailed investigation; but even though not quite understood they make it evident that the terms between shipowners and skippers in the cod-fishery were then commonly regulated by some intricate contract, full of antiquated words of doubtful meaning, such as are still in use in the Dutch sea-fisheries, and are frequently the cause of protracted, and by the nature of the men concerned, violent disputes between employers and employed.

The Dunkirkers in the next years did not spare the cod fishery any more than the other branches. Cod fishers accordingly used to sail in squadron to the Dogger bank, under cover of two or more men-of-war supplied by Government, which convoy having been destroyed by seven Dunkirk privateers in April 1628, the whole fleet of the "small-fishery," reported to have, at the moment, been 180 vessels strong, retreated into port before the end of the season.† Three years afterwards, six men-of-war were allowed to "*de groote Abberdaan visscherije op de Maase*," at the request of their Committee of Shipowners and Steersmen.‡ These words of "great salt cod-fishery" were commonly used to designate the Iceland business, which accordingly must have had some organization, and a representative board, early in the seventeenth century. The mutual insurance contract just now mentioned may have been the beginning of a farther organization of the trade. An association called "*de Schelvis visscherije*" of Maassluis is mentioned as having in 1636 applied for

* "De Penningen van het tweede woord gelaten zouden worden onder de stuurlieden tot het einde der teelt, en dan te restitueren aan de Vennots, indien geen schade en viele." Cf. *Res. Holl.* 1622, p. 751; 1623 p. 94, 206, 214.

† *Res. Holl.* 1628, p. 444.

‡ *Ibid.* 1631, p. 171.

convoy by the organ of its commissioners,* and as Maassluis (then not yet a "herring town") was likewise the seat of the above-mentioned board, both names are perhaps indicative of one corporation. At any rate, the body representative of the several cod-fisheries was, like the Herring College, invested with more extensive powers in the course of time. In July 1678, during the protracted negotiations with France at Nijmegen, we find them engaged in negotiations with the States of Holland to obtain French passports; and when these were not obtained fast enough by diplomatic correspondence, the Committee offered to apply for the documents themselves.† On Sept. 5th, 1695, the treasurer and commissioners of the fishery at Maassluis were empowered by the States of Holland to levy, collect, or farm a tax of one penny per barrel of salt fish, including several kinds of cod-fish, plaice, and in general "everything that is salted between two bottoms," cured-herring of course excepted, which never was called "fish" in any publication of the period, and was moreover already subject to last-money under the herring laws. The contribution was to be due upon the fish being unshipped at Maassluis, and so bore the character of a local staple-duty. Annex to it, the Commissioners were entitled to levy the 40th penny on all fresh fish brought to market at Maassluis, whether alive or dead, and moreover to collect "ship-money" to the amount of fl. 12, upon each herring buss, and fl. 8 upon each hooker sailing either for herring or to Iceland. The privilege was granted anew for twelve years on Dec. 17th, 1706.‡ I should incline to conclude from these facts,

* *Res. Holl.* 1636, p. 394, 413.
† *Ibid.* July 8, 1678.
‡ *Gr. Plb.* v. p. 730.

that herring-fishery first began to develop at Maassluis towards the end of the seventeenth century, and that it was from the beginning under the superintendence of the same corporation who represented the cod-fishery. If the Commissioners here alluded to had been the delegates of one fishery only, the States would never have allowed them to levy a tax upon the other. A similar unity of interests and business probably existed in the other towns where both herring and cod-fishery were exercised.

These very scanty and incoherent indications are indeed quite insufficient to establish a notion as to the importance of Dutch cod-fishery in the seventeenth century. Besides the convoy usually granted them by the States, some testimony to the extension of the trade may be found in the fact that their salt or dried produce was constantly exported on a considerable scale. In 1657 a dispute arose about four Dutch vessels laden with "baccalauw" which had arrived at Cadiz, but were declined admission by the Spanish authorities on the plea that their papers where insufficient;* and it is apparent from the terms in which the matter was reported upon that Spain was a market of importance for Dutch salt cod-fish. So were many other Catholic countries, whose fast-day requirements were in part supplied by Dutch fish. The Catholic provinces now forming the Kingdom of Belgium were, in this respect, of particular importance, for their situation allowed Dutch haddock and cod, as well as plaice, sole, &c., to be imported there fresh, as a Friday delicacy; whence the protective measures applied to the Flemish fisheries by their Austrian Government, in the shape of elevated custom-house duties upon foreign fish, were particularly prejudicial to the Dutch Cod-fishery

* *Res. Holl.* 1657, p. 180.

and fresh fish business. Extensive correspondence was carried on between the Dutch Ambassadors at Brussels and their principals at the Hague, in the earlier years of the 18th century, on the subject of duties on salt-cod, and fresh fish of several descriptions; but all efforts to obtain the removal of these duties were in vain, and the decay of the Iceland cod-fishery in Holland appears to have taken its origin from protective duties in the Austrian Netherlands and France. Difficulties with Denmark, the nature of which I shall expose in another chapter,* were also particularly prejudicial to the Iceland cod-fishery in 1740 and the next years; and the first Dutch vessels confiscated by Denmark were not whalers, but cod-hookers from the Maas.

The actual effect of the differences with Denmark upon the Iceland cod-fishery cannot be traced, as no statistics of the trade are extant earlier than 1751, from which year they have been annually noted down in the 'Nederlandsche Jaarboeken," and collected into a table by the Committee on Sea-fisheries, 1854, from whose Report Appendix C to these pages has been derived. The striking ups and downs of the trade, as shown by this table, may frequently be accounted for by vessels being transferred from the herring fishery to the Iceland business, and *vice versâ*, as the state of the cured-herring and cod markets made such shiftings desirable. I should be at a loss, for instance, to find another reason why the number of vessels sailed to Iceland was 95 in 1756, and 111 in the next year, although the fishing returns of the former were miserable. A knowledge of fish-prices throughout the Republic's existence would be necessary to acquire a full understanding of this, as of other phenomena in the fisheries' history; and

* *See* Chapter v.

as statistics, if kept at all, were at the time incomplete and unwarranted, to obtain such a knowledge would alone be the work of years.

Besides "hookers" transferable from one business to another, there were under the Republic vessels fit for no other service than the capture of fresh fish, cod and haddock especially, and provided with wells to keep the fish alive. Such well-boats must have been in use from early times downward; for without them it would scarcely have been feasible to carry fish caught on the Dogger bank to the Friday-markets of the Catholic provinces unsalted. No mention, however, is made of well-boats till 1777, when, one Jongeneel of Rotterdam having built such a vessel to meet a foreign order, a petition to prohibit its exportation was preferred to the States of Holland by the Commissioners of the Cod-fishery of Vlaardingen and Maassluis. The States instantly appointed Rotterdam to take provisional steps to baulk the said Jongeneel's purpose; but as in point of fact there was no law against it, they at the same time applied to the States-General for a special prohibition to export well-boats (*vishoekers met bunnen*), which was accordingly enacted on January 5th, 1778, notwithstanding Jongeneel's remonstrances, who by reason of the depression then prevailing in the trade could hope for no chance of selling his vessel at home. The Placard of January 5th, 1778, contains prohibitions for the Republic's subjects not only to sell or hire vessels of the above description out to foreigners, or build them upon orders from abroad, but also to take service on foreign wharves towards the building of such vessels, or put wells into foreign vessels while staying in Dutch ports. All steersmen in the cod-fishery are, moreover, enjoined by this Act to take oath to observe the new law.* From these several enactments it may perhaps be assumed that the Dutch had then a reputation as well-boat builders abroad. It would not be safe, however, to give this law the credit of the considerable increase in the Dutch cod-fishery in 1779 (see Appendix C); for the latter fact is amply accounted for by the very favourable fishing returns of the two preceding years.

The "embargo" laid upon all Dutch shipping by the States in January 1781 brought cod-fishery to a full stop as well as its sister-trades; and several requests of the Commissioners of the Cod-fishery of Vlaardingen and Maassluis, to have their trade permitted in the North Sea and off Iceland, were declined in the course of that year and the next. The scarcity of fish resulting from this "embargo" took effect upon the cod-fish as well as upon the herring market. While, as shown in a former chapter, herring was now actually imported into the Republic, certain dealers in salt cod-fish applied for leave to import that article and re-pack and re-export it; which permission, however, was strongly opposed by the Commissioners of Maassluis. It would appear from these proceedings that some particular fashion of packing and arranging cod was then in use in Holland, and Dutch salt-fish and stock-fish were in some way distinguished from foreign produce of a similar nature. The request having been declined, the Commissioners in 1781 obtained from the States-General a permission to sail, by way of experiment.† It does not appear that the experiment was attended with any success; for several shipowners preferred to sell their vessels abroad.

* Res. Holl. 1777, pp. 1229, 1414, 1443 ; Res. St. Gen. Ibid. p. 866. Gr. Pl. Bock, ix. p. 1309.
† Res. St. Gen. 1781, pp. 1054, 1182.

As this, however, was contrary to the law of 1778, it was necessary to obtain the States-General's permission for it, who accordingly, upon the request of the Commissioners of Maassluis, empowered the Admiralty of the Maas to allow vessels to be sold out of the Dutch cod-fishery to foreigners, under the sole condition that they should be bought back at the end of the war. The condition probably was not very faithfully observed; for 63 hookers sailed in 1780, and only 49 in 1784. The next years were very unfavourable, and the trade had come to nought in 1787, when only two vessels are stated to have been employed in it. The bounty system was then applied to the Iceland as well as to the other fisheries. The Commissioners of Maassluis applied for a premium in June 1788, and were by Resolution of April 9th, 1789,* allowed fl. 500 per hooker, being the same sum promised to the herring busses the year before. But premiums failed in the cod-fishery, even more utterly than they had failed in other branches. Not one hooker sailed to Iceland in the next years; and the cod-fishery had virtually come to a close before the final overthrow of the Republic.

CHAPTER IV.

COAST FISHING.

In using this title, which is a common denomination of several distinct branches of the Dutch sea-fisheries, a previous elucidation is necessary to prevent misunderstandings. "Coast-fishery" is thus named because carried on, not *off* or *under* the Dutch coast exclusively, but *from* that coast; i.e. by flat-bottomed vessels owned there.

* *Groot Placactb.* C. vol. ix. p. 1314.

These vessels until recent years have been principally employed in two distinct trades, viz., catching herring to be smoked, and catching fish to be sold fresh, cod and haddock included. The former fishery was generally exercised off Yarmouth, in the so-called "Deepwater," and the latter all over the North Sea, on the Dogger bank especially. The name of "*neeringhe van den Versche*," or "trade of the fresh," is generally applied to the latter fishery only, although herring salted preparatory to smoking is frequently, though improperly, styled "*fresh herring.*" Both the trades now alluded to were under the Republic exercised only in flat and square smacks called *pinken* or *bomschuiten* (bum-boats) the model of which can have undergone no considerable variations, as they were and are bound from villages having no ports, and therefore must be built so as to bear going ashore and remaining on dry land at low tide, without prejudice to their soundness. The Zuider Zee fisheries, which have a history of their own, may also be comprised under the general term of coast fishery. This chapter will therefore treat of three subjects essentially different, viz., the fisheries for smoke-herring and fresh fish in the North Sea, and Zuiderzee fishery.

Bum-boats were, in the Republican period, owned at the North Sea coast villages of ter Heide, Scheveningen, Katwijk, Noordwijk, Zandvoort, Wijk op Zee, and Egmond. Vessels of the kind never went as far north as the coast of Scotland in those times, and consequently had no share in the earlier herring fishery. They went for herring only to "Deepwater," off Yarmouth, in autumn and in the latter weeks of summer; and although herring caught then and there was successfully cured in keeled vessels, *and bum-boat fisheries were at first not prohibited from curing it likewise*, they have long abstained from the practice, probably on account of the small size of their vessels. Herring caught in bum-boats was summarily salted, or strewn with salt, on board, and carried home in baskets to be smoked in the coast villages, and sold as "bucking." The salting process destined to preserve such herring until brought to the smokeries was, and is now, called *steuren;* whence smoke-herring is generally styled *steurharing.*

"Bucking," although an article of extensive home consumption, never fetched anything like the prices of cured herring ; but smoke-herring fishermen found a compensation for this inferiority in the nearly complete liberty of their business. They were at liberty to carry their fish abroad, and it appears from an entry in v. d. Lely's Recueil (p. 13) that they used, "from early times downward," to sell "fresh" herring at Yarmouth. As their produce never was held to be of a particularly fine quality, they were of course not subject to any of the laws on packing and branding. They were, indeed, subject to the St. John's rule ; for by the Placard of 1607, quoted in Chapter I.,* it was prohibited, in the most general terms, to wet any nets fit to catch herring before St. John's in midsummer, and the only exception to the rule was in favour of the cod-fishers, who were allowed at any time to catch unripe herring as bait for their hooks. Fishing steersmen from the coast were moreover obliged annually to take out a licence from the College of the Grand Fishery, which was only delivered upon their taking oath not to use foreign nets or buy herring from others at sea. As this obligation is first mentioned in the Herring Act of 1656,† it is probable that they sailed without a licence before, and were not brought under the College's rule till the said year. But

* *Gr. Plb.*, i. p. 733.
† *Ibid.* viii. p. 1242, art. 3.

the College's yoke was easy upon them so long as they abstained from curing herring, and therefore were not competitors of the Grand Fishery. In 1663, according to v. d. Lely, they were " suspected " of curing herring ; whence, in the said year, the college inserted a clause against such curing into the oath to be taken by steersmen from the coast previous to receiving their licence. The proceeding was clearly an encroachment, as the law did not prohibit the coast fishermen from curing their herring. But it has been shown in Chapter I. that the College did not usually shrink from extending the law to their competitors' prejudice. In this instance they actually conferred on themselves a very important monopoly, which was afterwards the object of much controversy and one of the main features of herring legislation ; but which, when first claimed, *was not based on any law.*

It appears that this monopoly was not always observed to the letter. In 1735 and 1736, coast fishermen from Katwijk were found to cure herring caught by them in the Deepwater, on the plea that a very warm season made it impossible for them to preserve their herring uncured till they should have reached the coast and brought the fish to the smokery. The proceeding, as they argued, was for the benefit of the smoked-herring industry ; for if they had not cured the earlier part of their catch they would have been obliged to smoke it some time after capture, whereas no herring above two days old was now carried to the smokehouse, and Dutch " deepwater " bucking thereby maintained its excellence over the Yarmouth bloater.* But the grand Fishery would not hear of admitting competitors into the cured-herring business upon a plea based on the smoked-herring interest ; and once more prohibited the coast

* *Ned. Jaarboeken*, 1751, p. 1043, sqq.

fishermen to cure, which prohibition their competency to grant or refuse licences to all herring fishermen enabled them to enforce.

The prohibition appears to have been generally observed till 1751, in which year the Stadtholder Prince William IV. paid a visit to the coast village of Katwijk, and the fishermen of the locality availed themselves of the occasion to petition His Highness for re-instalment in their ancient right to cure herring. The Grand Fishery's self-made curing monopoly being thus menaced, petitions in a contrary sense were immediately sent in from some of the towns concerned in the cured-herring business, and a controversy ensued, of which a full account is to be found in the periodical called 'Nederlandsche Jaarboeken.'* The College of the Grand Fishery, before whom the petition from Katwijk was laid, of course advised against it; and although the coast fishermen (or *parlevinkers* as they are called in a contemporaneous Act of the States of Holland)† presented another memorial to the Princess Governess‡ after the Stadtholder's demise, the question at issue was ultimately decided against them, and the College rule maintained.

The logic in this dispute was all on the side of the coast fishermen, and their opponents indeed contradicted their own arguments by using too many. First, said they of the Grand Fishery, the herring caught in bum-boats is of inferior quality and unfit to be cured. Secondly, fishing boats from the coast are equipped at less risk and expense than herring busses, and the former's owners are already

---

* *Ned. Jaarboeken*, 1751, p. 1043, 1181; 1752, p. 481.
† *Res. Holl.* 1751, p. 318.
‡ Princess Anne, as guardian of her son William V., then three years old.

privileged, inasmuch as they are allowed to sell herring at
sea and abroad; and it would be the Grand Fishery's ruin
to expose them to competition on such unequal terms as
these. Thirdly, the smoked-herring business will be upset
if coast fishermen take to curing, and English "bucking"
will gradually supersede the Dutch. To the first of these
arguments it was objected that there could scarcely be any
difference in quality between the herring caught by either
party, as busses and bum-boats, or "pinken" fished side by
side, in the same sea and season. Besides, if the herring
caught by the latter were unfit for curage, how could the
Grand Fishery fear their competition, or the extinction of
the smoked-herring business? The argument based upon
the Grand Fishery's greater risks and charges was met by
the query "whether it was more expedient for the country's
interest that much should be risked for little gain, or that
considerable profit should be made with little or no ex-
posure?" As for the liberty to sell herring abroad, any coast
fishermen would of course have had to give up that
privilege if he had taken to curing. As a last and conclusive argument, the petitioners from the coast showed that
the Grand Fishery, in prohibiting them from curing herring,
acted as judges in their own case. So they undoubtedly did;
but their judgment does not appear to have been further
appealed from at the time, and their monopoly of curing
remained in force long after the end of the Republic.

The coast fishery might indeed have proved serious
competitors to the Grand Fishery if they had been given a
chance. It is stated that in 1751 one hundred and twenty
boats sailed from Scheveningen alone* and the whole
number of busses in that year was not quite double the
figure. The smoked-herring business appears in the next

* *Europische Mercurius*, 1754, vol. i. p. 62.

years to have declined rapidly, chiefly on account of measures taken to prevent the importation of Dutch fish into the Austrian Netherlands, of which the fresh and smoked fish concerns were equally the victims. In 1777, the Grand Fishery having obtained a premium two years before, the owners of herring boats of Katwijk and Noordwijk in their turn petitioned the States of Holland for "such a bounty (*douceur*) as it shall please their Noble and Grand Mightinesses to grant" and they likewise sued for a prohibition to the busses to bring home uncured herring,* whence it may be inferred that they of the Grand Fishery, although anxious enough to shelter their own trade from competition by those of the coast, did not disdain occasionally to meddle with theirs. No resolution was taken as to the latter part of the petition, and the former was at the time declined. The application for bounties was renewed in November 1786,† and kept under consideration for more than a year. A premium of fl. 200 was awarded, on April 17th, 1788,‡ to the owners or managers of all such herring boats equipped in any of the villages on the North Sea coast as shall be used in the fishery, for "salt-herring or bucking" between Elevation day, or Sept. medio, and Dec. medio, "or thereabouts." The premium was granted for three years only, but the grant was renewed in 1791 and 1794. The fact of the coast fishermen being still

* *Steur-en Korf-haring.* Such herring was kept in baskets (korven) and strewed with salt (steuren) till brought home to be smoked, whence fish thus treated was called either *steurharing* or *korfharing*. The name of *zoutharing* (salt herring) is also occasionally applied to it, but this "salt herring" should be carefully distinguished from "cured herring." See *Res. Holl.* 1777, p. 928, and 1778, p. 880.

† *Res. Holl.* 1786, p. 4413.
‡ *Gr. Pl. Boek*, ix. p. 1314.

THE HISTORY OF DUTCH SEA FISHERIES. 151

at the time under obligation to take licences from the College of the Grand Fishery is evident from a clause of this Resolution, by which the said College is ordered to yearly state the number of boats sailed from the coast under their supervision.

The differences about the right to cure herring are, as has been shown, the main subject of the smoked-herring trade's history under the Republic. A very different point of working legislation has been contested between those concerned in the "fresh-fishery;" viz., the nature of the nets to be used by them.

It would appear to be still a point at issue between technical writers on sea-fishery, *whether the sea can be exhausted.* Whatever views may at present prevail upon this question among experts, the provincial legislators of Holland under the Dutch Republic held it possible to extinguish fish-life under their shores; and they accordingly at one time took steps to prevent its destruction by enacting penalties against the use of such nets as either sweep the bottom of the sea, and thereby are said to extirpate spawn and fry of certain fish residing on the ground, or destroy fry of fish by their undersized meshes.

Fresh-fishery of the North Sea coast, commonly called "the side" in former times, appears at an early period to have been of some importance, as a Resolution of the States of Holland dated December 7th, 1585,* proves that fresh fish from Scheveningen was at the time sold in the London market. Still the profits of the trade were small, and fishermen "of the fresh" are throughout the Republic's time styled "the poor, or miserable (*schamele*) fishers of the side." In 1595 they were allowed, on account of their

* *Res. Holl.* 1585, p. 808.

poverty, to fish on public prayer-days, "provided it should be done with good discretion."* Measures for their safety were frequently taken by the States of Holland, and they had generally one or two small ships of war for their special protection in time of war. Agreements to leave each other's coast fishery unmolested were concluded with Dunkirk, or their conclusion proposed, in 1606, 1644, 1674, 1703, and 1707 ; but as to the effect of these measures I have not found any evidence. The circumstance of Dutch coast fishery being mostly exercised at a short distance from shore, and by flat and shallow boats, liable to be stranded whenever a foeman hove in sight, may have induced the Dunkirkers to show forbearance to prey so apt to escape them, when the reciprocal safety of their coast fishery from Dutch privateers and men-of-war was to be gained by it. For the same reason "fresh-fishery" was sometimes permitted when the other sea-fisheries were prohibited on account of the wars.†

Measures to prevent the exhaustion of the coast waters are not on record before the year 1676, when at the request of the coast fishermen themselves, viz., those of ter Heide, Scheveningen, Katwijk, Noordwijk, Zantvoort, Wijk op Zee and Egmond, a Placard of the States of Holland, dated September 10th,‡ prohibited all such proceedings as were reputed obnoxious to the preservation of certain species of fish. "It has always been customary," says this Act, "that nobody should fish with narrower gear than plaice nets, being drift nets made upon a chip of the size of a full eight-and-twenty" (whatever that measure may have been). "Some time before this, however, certain gain-seek-

---
* *Res. Holl.* 1595, p. 531, 586.
† *Ibid.* 1666, p. 49, 621 ; 1667, p. 101, and others.
‡ *Ibid.* 1676, p. 385 ; *Gr. Pl. B.*, iii. p. 1366.

ing persons have begun to fish with nets composed of narrower meshes, and even with trawl-nets (*schrobnetten*)" ; and as by the former proceeding fry of fish are killed, while the latter destroys the spawn, and even the bait on which fish live, both are prohibited ·by the placard just quoted. An exception to this law was made on January 22nd, 1677,* in favour of those who should fish for shrimps within the sand-bars, with a light ground-net (*ligte sayingh of corde*). Bars of movable sand do indeed exist to this day close under the whole of the North Sea coast. "Sayingh" (now spelt *saayem*), is the name still used for the shrimp-net, which is indeed a kind of trawl. The sense of the word *corde* is explained in the first legislative act in which the implement is mentioned, viz., a placard dated April 19th, 1583,† by which it is forbidden to fish with this net in the river estuaries, and in which it is described as a net kept open by a beam and burdened with stones or lead, which is dragged along the bottom of the water behind a fishing vessel. "Corde," in short, is an equivalent for the now common word "schrobnet," and a general term for any trawling apparatus.

The permission to use the shrimp trawl was not the only mitigation grafted in 1677 upon the law of the preceding year. It was likewise permitted to use "sole-nets" (*tongewant*) the meshes of which measured "a two-and-thirty" being apparently a smaller dimension than the "eight-and-twenty" adopted as a minimum size in 1676.‡ But the use of all trawl-nets other than the

---

* *Gr. Pl. Bock*, iii. p. 1367.
† *Ibid.* i. p. 1274.
‡ It appears from these denominations that the dimensions of the meshes were indicated by the number of them which went to some standard measure. And it may therefore be supposed, although I

"sayingh," just mentioned was again prohibited in 1677, and a special clause was enacted against the sinking even of lawful "eight-and-twenty" nets by ballasting them with weights whereby they might be used as trawls.

The prohibition against trawling, although enacted at the fishermen's own request, was very ill observed. On March 29th, 1678, the States of Holland instructed their officers to strictly execute the law against all those who should fish with trawls (*corden of schrobnetten*); but nevertheless in the summer of that year the delegates from Haarlem to the States reported about grievous disturbances occasioned by trawlers at Wijk op Zee. Among the fishermen of this village one party stuck to trawling and therefore went by the name of "schrobbers," while another observed the law and were styled "scholders," by reason of their adhering to the lawful "scholnet," or plaice net. The trawlers acted upon a principle frequently followed by trespassers of every kind; they annoyed those who kept within the law by carving and destroying their gear, and occasionally laying violent hands upon their persons; and the local magistrates, stated to be "friends of the trawlers," made matters still worse by sequestering the "scholders'" nets under a pretence of their being sized contrary to the statute, and keeping them under arrest so long as to occasion their owners a serious prejudice, although the nets had to be ultimately released, being found in accordance with the law.* Fishermen of

---

have found no positive evidence to the fact, that the "eight-and-twenty" size here alluded to was the same which was in 1683 declared lawful for seines used in the Zuider Zee, viz. fourteen to half a yard. In the first quarter of the present century, the "eight-and-twenty" measure was three Netherland inches and nine-tenths (see the Laws of 1820 and 1825, in Part iii. of this essay).

* *Res. Holl.* 1678, p. 391.

other coast villages were not much better observers of the statute, and the placards of 1676 and 1677 had to be re-issued several times in 1679 and following years. On March 16th, 1680, a petition by the Side fishermen, to be allowed the use of "*cordens*" or trawls either of the twenty-eight or thirty-two size was declined by the States, and a strict application of the laws against such fishing once more recommended to all officers concerned.* On September 17th, 1687, the placard was once more renewed,† and the penalties extended to any in whose boats forbidden nets should have been found, even though they should not have sailed with them. But even this did not put a stop to the coast fishers' habit of trawling, and the prohibition had ultimately to be given up, chiefly because of the impossibility of enforcing it. In March 1689, the "*Corders*," of Wijk op Zee represented to the States that trawling went on in the other villages in spite of the law, as it was not possible to procure fresh fish by any other process during war time, when fishermen "of the Fresh," were obliged to keep within view of the coast. Whereupon the States ordered their officers on the coast to stop the execution of the laws against trawling,‡ and there is no evidence of their having been renewed under the Republic.

It is stated in some of the above-quoted laws against trawling, that at the time the fresh fishery "was already ruined for the greater part." Nothing precise is known as to its extent in still earlier times; but its decline certainly did not stop at the end of the seventeenth century. The Catholic provinces of the Austrian Netherlands were one of the principal markets for fresh fish from the Side, which

* *Gr. Plac. Bock*, iii. 1368.
† *Ibid.* iv. p. 1363.
‡ *Res. Holl.* 1689, p. 230; *Gr. Pl. B.* iv. 1365.

of course could never be carried far inland in those days of slow locomotion; and accordingly, when protective duties against foreign fish were resorted to in the Austrian provinces about 1725, the Dutch "*neeringe van den versche*" were the principal sufferers. Remonstrances against the Austrian tariffs were tried several times, but found unavailing; and although under the Republic statistical accounts of the fresh fishery do not appear to have been kept, the gradual closing of the Southern market may be safely assumed to have occasioned its lasting decline in the course of the eighteenth century. The "embargo" of 1781 of course contributed to hasten the downward movement; and when the sea was reopened in 1783, only ten bum-boats or "*pinken*" are stated to have sailed from Scheveningen for fresh fish. The trade's utter insignificance towards the end of the Republic may also be deduced from the fact that, of all the several branches of North Sea fishery, it is the only one which never was encouraged by a bounty. The phenomenon might indeed be accounted for by a very flourishing state of the Fresh trade in the year 1788, when premiums were lavishly dispensed to all other fisheries, and all of them were in a prostrate condition. But if the "*verschvaart*" had made such a favourable exception, there is not a doubt but the fact would have been mentioned on all hands; whereas the history of this trade is simply a blank at the period when sea-fisheries in general were distinguished by an ardent competition for bounties. Fresh fishery from the "side" might even be believed to have come to a complete stand-still at the close of the republican period, if some mention of it were not made a few years later, as will be shown in another part of this work.

The fisheries of the Zuider Zee have, as has been said

above, a history of their own, and one widely different from that of the several trades of which the North Sea is the area. As the Zuider Zee is an inlet, separated from the North Sea by a boundary of isles and shallows, no enemies used to disturb its fishermen, and the Republic's many wars never affected them. As regards the nature of their trade and of the gear and vessels used, they were entirely at variance with their brethren of the open sea. The most striking point of resemblance between the fisheries in the two waters is perhaps the jealousy respecting them between the inhabitants of the surrounding land. In the case of the North Sea, this jealousy raged between nations; in that of the Zuider Zee, between inhabitants of the Republic's several provinces. In both cases it led to repeated conflicts, accords, and treaties. While reading the Zuider Zee history, of which, as it can be of no very stringent interest to the foreign reader, I shall give but a very succinct account, it should be borne in mind that the shore of this inland sea belongs to several provinces, which under the Republic were distinct States, having sovereignty rights of their own, and in this case anxious to use them so as to ensure the greatest possible part of the Zuider Zee fishing returns for their own subjects. Something like the "Dominium Maris" question, on a reduced scale, is at the bottom of the history of Zuider Zee fishery under the Republic of the United Provinces, the gaps of whose union were peculiarly apparent in this very matter.

Salmon and sturgeon appear in old times to have been abundant along the Zuider Zee shore and about the mouths of the rivers descending into it;[*] where, however, they have

[*] Several towns on the Zuider Zee still carry salmon in their scutcheons. A present of salmon from one of them to Duke Albert of Bavaria is recorded as early as 1389.

been now for a long time extinct, or very nearly so. Flounder and turbot were always, as they are to this day, prominent among the produce of the Zuider Zee, and gave their name to the vessels most in use there (*botters*, from *bot*, *i.e.*, flounder). Herring fishery was also exercised in the said water from time immemorial ; but Zuider Zee herring never was branded, nor its fishery subjected to working rules, whereas the main object of legislation on Zuider Zee fisheries has for centuries been to prevent the destruction of salmon, sturgeon, and flounder, by regulations as to the width of the nets to be used. This object was pursued some time before the Republic was born. On January 8th, 1546, the Emperor Charles the Fifth, by a publication, fixed the minimum size of the meshes, at "five common seamen's thumbs." The towns of Holland, whose fishermen had from early times used to fish in the Zuider Zee with narrow nets, obtained the repeal of this edict on November 12th, 1547, when there was substituted for it a prohibition against dragging nets through the water, by which proceeding, according to the said law, fish are smothered ere they be full grown. It was likewise forbidden by this edict to land smothered unripe fish and sell them as food for cattle or pigs ; and all fish not quite full-grown were prescribed to be thrown overboard as soon as caught. Fishermen from Holland continued to assert their rights to unlimited fishery in spite of the law, whereas those of Gelderland and Overyssel insisted on its observation, and moreover claimed for themselves the exclusive right to fish within a certain distance from their shore ; and both subjects became a matter of protracted disputes between the several provinces.* A provisional edict of the year 1555, fixed the minimum width of the nets to be

* A paper on the subject has been contributed to Nyhoff's *Bydragen voor Vaderl. Geschiedenis en Oudheidkunde*, 1864, p. 309.

used at two common seamen's thumbs, and some limits were measured out in the next year, within which fishermen from Holland should not be allowed to approach the Gelderland and Overyssel shores. But they of Holland continued to overstep both boundaries of lawful fishing, and their fishing vessels of a peculiar description call "*waterschepen*,"* in which they used to carry arms and ammunition, and commit acts of violence and piracy upon the fishers of the other provinces, were the terror of the Zuider Zee. Nor did they amend their conduct when a sentence, or arrest, by the Grand Council of Malines, dated April 29th, 1559, definitively determined both the fishery limits of each province, and the minimum width of the nets to be used.

The Union of Utrecht by no means put an end to the protracted disputes and petty warfare between fishermen from the several provinces which acceded to it. Reciprocal complaints about fishing with unlawful nets, and within the established limits, were frequently laid before the States of those provinces. Gelderland and Overyssel having been occupied by the enemy in 1672, it was seriously considered in the States of Holland to exact from them, as a condition for their re-admission into the Union, a promise never to trouble Holland fishermen in the unrestricted fishery in the Zuider Zee in future.† The disputes ran so high in the next years, that Holland and Gelderland imprisoned several of each other's fishermen for unlawful fishing, and a conven-

---

* I have not been able to ascertain to what peculiarity these vessels, of which no mention is made in after years, owe their rather singular name of "water ships." None of the authors nor any of the laws upon the subject explain their nature. I suppose them to have been well-boats.

† *Secret Res. Holl.* February 65, March 24, 1674.

tion was at last agreed to between delegates from both provinces, on December 17th, 1682, in virtue of which the men detained were released on either side, and a set of rules for Zuider Zee fishery was established on March 21st, 1683, to be enforced as a law in both provinces.*

The principal contents of this regulation were as follows :—

No silken nets whatever to be used, and the nets of yarn not to be of a less depth than three feet measured between the floats at the top and the lead used to steady them ; the nets' meshes not to be narrower than twelve to the yard.†

All setting of nets (a practice very common especially along the Zuider Zee shores, by reason of their extreme shallowness), to be prohibited in the first three months of the year ; and all set nets to be placed seaward perpendicular to the shore line, and not parallel to the shore, and their ends marked by poles driven into the bottom, for sailing vessels to avoid damaging them ; the maximum length of these nets to be two hundred fathoms.

Fishers using either set nets of the above description, or fykes and weirs, to keep a convenient berth and not place their contrivances closer to each other than at intervals of one hundred fathoms at the least.

All fish caught unripe and unfit for consumption to be thrown overboard, whether dead or alive, and on no pretence carried ashore and sold, bartered or otherwise turned to account as food for pigs, ducks, or other animals.

The use of seines (*zegens*) to be prohibited in the months of April and May, and the meshes of such nets at all times to be of the size of fourteen to half a yard.

This regulation by treaty, issued as a law for Hollands fishermen by the States of Holland on April 10th, 1683, by

* *Gr. Plac. Bock* iv. p. 1358-9.
† " *dan van twaelf overgangen in een elle.*"

no means set the fishermen's minds at rest. On September 24th of the same year the prohibition to use silken nets was repealed as regarded set-nets fixed to poles, and used on the coasts of Holland only,* at the urgent request of the fishermen of Monnickendam and some neighbouring localities. Petitions to be allowed to fish with narrower nets than the sizes prescribed were examined by the States in 1685 ;† and Holland took upon herself to supersede till June 1st, 1688, the enforcement of the general prohibition against nets narrower than twelve meshes to the yard.‡ In 1698, conditions of a similar nature of those of 1683 were agreed between Holland and Overyssel ; and it is recorded that on January 21st, 1699, forty fishermen from Amsterdam, being ready to sail on the Zuider Zee in "water ships" were sworn by the Burgomasters of their city to observe the above regulations. In the next year, however, the State of Overyssel remonstrated with those of Holland about unlawful fishing by Hollands subjects,§ and in 1707, Holland in her turn complained of violence committed upon fishermen from Hoorn, by others from Vollenhoven in Overyssel. In 1728, Friesland, having likewise an interest in the Zuider Zee fishery, remonstrated with Holland about inhabitants of the latter province fishing for plaice before the fifteenth of April, against a law of Friesland which never was binding for Hollands subjects.‖ Though only now and then mentioned in the States' registers, such disputes as these may be presumed to have occurred as long as the Republic existed ;

* *Gr. Placc. Bock*, iv. 1361.
† *Res. Holl.* 1685, p. 88.
‡ *Ibid.* 1688, p. 265.
§ *Ibid.* 1700, p. 386.
‖ *Ibid.* 1728, p. 430.

for it was impossible to prevent them so long as every one of the provinces surrounding the Zuider Zee was entitled to legislate on fishery on its own hand, and the statutes of one were not binding for the others, except in so far as they had been agreed upon by treaty, as in the case between Holland and Gelderland.

The last legislative act on record relating to Zuider Zee fishery other than for herring, was not conventional, but issued by Holland at the request of her own subjects. The set-net fishermen of Marken (a small island close under the Hollands shore) in 1785 petitioned the States for protection against destruction of their weirs, traps, &c., by nets dragged through the water at a reckless speed, either between two vessels or behind one.* The matter was considered with the slowness and pedantic verbosity habitual in the later years of the Republic, and ended in a prohibition dated December 15th, 1786, "against the most pernicious drag-fishery between two vessels (or *botters*) coupled together," and against drag-fishery at night, even if only one vessel were used. It was also prohibited by this Act, to tow a grapnel behind fishing vessels; and from the latter clause, as well as from the deliberations relative to the law, it appears that drag-fishery was sometimes carried on with a view not only to catch fish, but also to destroy the set-gear of concurrents.†

Herring fishery appears to have been in the Zuider Zee as ancient a trade as that of plaice and sturgeon; but very

---

* These nets, by the description given of them, are evidently the very narrow anchovy nets (*wonderkuil*) against the use of which measures have recently been taken (see Part iii., ch. iv.). I have not however, found any distinct mention made of anchovy fishery in Zuider Zee under the Republic.

† *Res. Holl.* 1785, p. 5119; 1786, p. 2406; *Gr. Plb*, ix. 1312.

little is known about the former, except that its produce, being herring of a small size and often lean (*yele haring*) was never cured, but either sold fresh as "*pan-herring*," or smoked, the latter being the more habitual method. The only legislative act relative to the Zuider Zee herring fishery is a placard of Holland dated May 31st, 1752,* by which the Zuider Zee fishermen of the province were enjoined to bring all their herring to market in one of the fortified towns of Holland and West Friesland, and not to sell, or otherwise transfer any herring at sea. The object of this enactment (which appears to have been but a renovation of old laws fallen into disuse) was to uphold the smoking establishments of Holland, and prevent herring caught by inhabitants of that province from being landed in one of the ports of Gelderland and Overyssel. The law was mitigated by another dated May 9th, 1755,† by which it was declared lawful for two or three fishers to sail in company, and have their fish brought ashore by one of them ; and they were moreover during the week preceding Easter dispensed from the prohibition to sell herring at sea. The former clause is indicative of something like "sale-hunting" on a scale reduced in proportion to the small distances between the ports and the fishing area. Zuider Zee vessels indeed did not lose much time in sailing home to their ports of Edam, Monnickendam, &c. ; but their time was often peculiarly precious, as the Zuider Zee has at all times been subject to fitful invasions by herring shoals so dense as almost to fill up the sea. It is stated that in 1549 herrings were caught off Enkhuizen by simply scooping them out of the water

* *Gr. Plb.* viii., 1255.
† *Ibid* viii., 1259. An interpretation of this Act was issued in 1765, (*Gr. Pl. B.* ix., 1301).

in basketfuls, and that in 1665, some skippers of the same town landed eight hundred lasts, or eight millions of herrings in one month.*

CHAPTER V.

"DOMINIUM MARIS."

THE right to fish all over the open sea has always been to the Dutch Republic a matter of importance proportioned to that of her sea-fisheries. This right is now universally acknowledged to belong to all and sundry; but notions on international law were different some centuries ago, when the Sovereignty of the seas, or of some portion of them, was claimed by more nations than one. The Netherlands never set up any such claim, and by the number of their merchant and fishing shipping were always very closely interested in debating it, and maintaining the "Mare Liberum," theory, the very name of which reminds of its immortal Dutch exposer and defender, Hugo Grotius. As all pretensions to "Dominium Maris," were of a nature in the very first place to affect the sea-fisheries' most vital interest, this history, or that period of it which coincides with the international debate on the question, would not be complete without a brief account of the several phases of the quarrel, as carried on between the Netherlands and their two rivals in fishery, Great Britain and Denmark. The disputes with the former power are by far the more important, and have been made the subject of a profound historical investigation by Mr. J. Muller, Fzn., in his important work 'Mare Clausum.'† The compass of these pages of course affords

* See p. 20 of the Report by the Committee on Sea-fisheries, 1854.
† Edited by Fr. Muller, Amsterdam, 1872.

no space for any but a short survey of the question, and forbids entering upon its merits properly said, or treating its scientific side as a point of history and international law. The following is a very concise account of its actual bearings upon the Dutch sea-fisheries, i.e. of the effect taken upon them, at some periods, by such acts of foreign Governments as were based upon pretensions to a fishing monopoly in some portions of the sea.

It has been stated in Part I of this work, that as early as the year 1295, King Edward the First forbade his subjects to molest the Dutch, Zealanders and Frisons, while fishing off Yarmouth ; a fact peculiarly significant, as Edward the First was the first British monarch who styled himself sovereign of the sea. In 1439 a treaty concerning the rights of fishermen was agreed to between King Henry the Sixth and Isabel of Portugal as representing her husband, Philip Duke of Burgundy, then reigning Count of Holland. This treaty, stipulating that the fishermen of both parties should be free to "*paisiblement aler par tout sur Mer, pour Peschier et Gaignier leur vivre, sans Empeschement ou Destourber de l'une Partie ne de l'Aultre,*" originally covered only the natives of Brabant and Flanders on this side of the Channel. Having been renewed more than once, it was finally extended on the 24th of November, 1467, to the natives of "*toutz ler aultres Paiis et seigneuries,*" of the then reigning Duke of Burgundy, thereby including the Dutch and Zealand fishermen, and for the first time consecrating by international compact their right to fish all over the sea, "*sans qu'il leur soit Besoigne sur ceo requirer ne opteiner ascune Licence Congie ou Saufconducte.*" The treaty was again renewed at Lille, on July 12th, 1478, in the same terms as regards fisheries ; and was finally superseded by the "Grand Intercourse," or treaty concluded at London on the 24th of February 1496, which likewise stipulated, in Latin bad but explicit, the entire freedom of fisheries on either side. "*Conventum, concordatum et conclusum est,*" says the document, "*quod Piscatores utriusque Partis Partium praedictarum (cujuscunque conditionis existant) poterunt ubique Tre, Navigare per Mare, secure Piscari absque aliquo Impedimento Licentia seu salvo Conductu.*" This treaty continued in force for more than a century and a half.

The protection of the Sovereigns of Scotland was from very early times no less valuable than that of England to the Dutch fishermen, who as far back as the earliest stage of their history appear to have worked the more northerly parts of the North Sea and the Scottish coasts. A privilege granted to them by the King of Scotland is mentioned in the year 1341; and a treaty concluded at Binche on February 19th, 1540, between the Emperor Charles the Fifth (then Sovereign of the Low Countries) and James the Fifth of Scotland, stipulates that the fishermen of both nations shall be reciprocally protected against pirates and indemnified for damage received in time of peace at the hands of subjects of either state.

The second treaty of Binche, dated December 15th, 1550, explicitly stated "*circa Piscationem ac liberum usum Maris, ea quae per Tractatum anno* 1540 ... *inita conclusa ac conventa fuerint debite ac sincere observari debebunt.*" In virtue of this treaty, which was once more confirmed in 1594, and of the London treaty of 1496, the freedom and reciprocal protection of sea-fisheries was a settled point of international law between Great Britain and Holland, towards the close of the 16th century.

But at this period the Low Countries, hitherto an obscure province of a continental Empire, not only astonished the world by their declaration of independence of the Spanish dominion (1581), but entered upon a career of matchless prosperity, in spite at first of the most disastrous circumstances. Even while involved in the long and destructive war, which long before its end brought about the avowal and consecration of their independence by their late sovereign, their unfettered energies, spurred by self-given freedom, were strenuously directed towards economical progress, and their fisheries began to increase rapidly. A new State had sprung up in Europe, and was at once counted with and envied. Such rivalry as had from times immemorial existed between the British and Dutch fishermen, grew with the young Republic, and from the very beginning of its existence took the shape of an animosity between it and the British Empire, which centred in long-rankling disputes about the freedom or dominion of the North Sea.

Robert Hitchcock's extremely curious plan for the organization of British fisheries, which appeared in 1580,* is the first document in which this rivalry is tacitly avowed. The author proposes British herring-boats to be rigged on the pattern of "Flemishe Busses" and the fish caught by them to be cured in the Flemish manner (*Beukelsz's*). The competition of the Dutch herring fleet, then evaluated by Selden at four or five hundred sails, was considered by

* A Pollitique Platt for the honour of the Prince, the great Profit of the Publique State, relief of the poore, preservation of the riche, reformation of the Roges and Idle persones, and the wealthe of thousandes that knowes not how to live. Written for a New Yeres gifte to Englande and the inhabitantes thereof." It appears that there is now *but one* copy extant of this pamphlet, preserved in the British Museum. The author of these pages quotes it from Mr. Muller, who in his above-quoted work, '*Mare Clausum*,' quotes it from extracts transmitted by a friend.

Hitchcock to be the chief obstacle to his plan, but he did not consider it insurmountable, the fishing area being situated "within the Queene's Majesties Seas" and much closer to the British than the Dutch coast, thereby putting the Dutch at a considerable disadvantage on the markets of England and Scotland. Sir Thomas Overbury's 'Observations in his Travels' (written 1609, printed 1626) likewise contain a warning against the Dutch, and represent them as being England's natural rivals on the sea.

Still, under Queen Elizabeth's reign Dutch fishermen were not molested. Measures tending to alienate so desirable an ally against Spain were inconsistent with the politics of this far-sighted monarch. Things took a very different turn soon after James the First's advent to the throne. Besides considering himself personally affronted by Grotius' treatise on Mare Liberum, the contents of which agreed very ill with the King's passion for his prerogative, His Majesty felt sorely aggrieved, and by no means without reason, by the manner in which the Dutch exercised and overstepped their fishing rights; not only ousting the English from the trade by lawful competition in overwhelming numbers, but occasionally offering them such violence as has for centuries been usual with such of the rival fishermen as chanced to be the stronger in a collision.* Fishery and piracy were then, as indeed they have been since, concerns closely connected together on all hands. English subjects were loud in complaining, and the result was the king's "Proclamation touching Fishing" (May 16th, 1609) by which in consideration of the injury done to English by foreign fishermen, and in virtue of the Royal prerogative, foreigners were prohibited from fishing on

* For instances of this see *Müller*, p. 47.

British coasts and in British seas, unless licensed thereto by the king's officers, upon payment of the duties incumbent on such license. The great "Mare clausum" question was by this measure openly started.

It was at first discussed on amicable terms. The Dutch Ambassador, sent to London avowedly to thank the king for his good offices in the concluding of the twelve years' truce with Spain, had a debate upon the point against the king's counsel learned in the law, on the 16th of May, 1610 They based their remonstrance chiefly upon the liberties anciently granted to the Dutch, and upon their being the first in right to the herring fishery by reason of the best method of herring curage having been invented in the Netherlands, but were met by the assertion of the king's dominion over the seas, and would very probably have been unsuccessful had not the murder of Henry IV. of France suddenly turned the king's most earnest attention to the expedience of conciliatory proceedings towards all those in whom allies were to be found against Spain. Although fully maintaining his exclusive sovereignty in the British seas, the king consented to supersede the Proclamation, and the infliction menacing Dutch fishermen was for the time averted.

A conflict, however, could not long be averted between two seafaring nations, both anxious to promote their fisheries in the same seas. Spitzbergen, discovered in 1596 by the Dutch Admiral Jacob van Heemskerk, while in search of the North-West Passage, and by him appropriated in the name of his Sovereigns the States-General, next became the theatre of private naval war. English and Dutch fishermen set about working this new shaft at the same time; but as stated in chapter II., the first attempts of the latter were unfruitful, owing mainly to the plundering of two whalers from Amsterdam off Spitzbergen, in the summer of 1612, by a fleet of English whalers well equipped for warlike proceedings. The small Dutch fleet sailed home despoiled both of fish caught and oil made, and of the instruments to catch and make more. The "Mare clausum" controversy, just quieted in the British seas, sprung up in a fresh and very critical shape beyond the Arctic circle; for the whaling seas were included in the alleged "Dominium Maris" of Great Britain. And this time the king was not to be moved, though Winwood, late ambassador of England at the Hague, and just then called to the Secretaryship of State, interceded for the Dutch claims on behalf of the States, who on their part addressed to the king a memorandum, "Replicques fondées à l'encontre des propositions et pretentions des Anglais, d'avoir le commandement sur la Pescherie de l'île Spitsberge ou Terre Neufve," composed by the renowned Dutch cosmographer Plancius. There was nothing for it but to oppose violence to violence. A Dutch company was formed in 1614 (see chapter II.), and sent eighteen vessels north, under cover of three men-of-war. A truce was the consequence, and for the year 1614 the waters of Spitzbergen were divided between the parties who had come north ready to fight for them. The same armed peace again prevailed in 1615 and 1616, when the whaling fleets of both States came out under convoy, and seem to have fished in peace, keeping each other in respect. Diplomatic interference, in which the celebrated Grotius acted as a commissioner on the part of the States-General, and extensive memorializing on both sides, meanwhile led to no solution of the difference, as James I. inflexibly maintained his claim to Dominium Maris, and vouchsafed no answer to the Dutch Ambassador's remonstrances. Although peace was maintained between the two Courts, war between the British and Dutch whalers under the northern lights was, of course, inevitable under these circumstances. In 1617, the States having granted an insufficient convoy to their whaling fleet, the establishment built by them at Spitzbergen was destroyed by the English. Forcible retaliation was taken by the Dutch in the next year, when open warfare seems to have prevailed in the north all the summer, occasioning, on the 3rd of October, 1618, a sharp and menacing remonstrance to the States-General from the British Ambassador, Sir Dudley Carleton, whose "Lettres Memoires et Negociations" (edited in English and translated into French) are a source of much information upon the fishery differences between the two nations in the years 1616-20.

Nor, in the meantime, did peace reign in the North Sea. The works of Sir Walter Raleigh * and "Gentleman" † strongly contributed to keep the spirit of rivalry awake, by giving the British public highly exaggerated notions of the profits and prosperity derived by the Dutch from the herring fishery, and stimulating England to try and evict those competitors, whether by free competition or by legislatory checks. Welwood's books of juridical controversy ‡ at the same time directed the public attention afresh towards England's alleged monopoly of fishing in the British waters. King James I. did not long remain deaf to exhortations so congenial to his own notions. In August, 1616, without any previous renewal of the publication of 1609,

---

* *Observations touching Trade and Commerce with the Hollanders* (published about 1610).

† *England's Way to Win Wealth* (published 1614).

‡ *Abridgment of all Sea Lawes* (published 1613); *De dominio Maris* (published 1616).

the king's officers by his orders demanded of Dutch fishermen a tax or retribution of one angelot, or a barrel of herring and twelve cod-fish for every vessel fishing in the British seas. The tax was paid by most skippers until two of the convoying men-of-war's captains interceded and reported matters home. Bitter remonstrances from the States to the king ensued, but the tax was appointed to be levied again in 1617. This time, however, the officer entrusted with the duty met with a flat refusal, in the name of all the Dutch fishermen, at the hands of the captain of one of the convoying ships. Having so far executed his orders, the British officer was about to leave the Dutch herring fleet, when Captain John Albertsz, of the convoying vessel from Enkhuizen, one of those who had parleyed with the English officer in the preceding year, alleged orders to arrest him, and carried him to Holland. Two Dutch captains were instantly taken by the English, and kept as hostages. The States and Stadtholder hastened to utterly disavow Captain Albertsz' rash act, turn him out of office, and release the captured English officer. Still King James's wrath required further satisfaction, and the Dutch hostages were not returned until one of the guilty Dutch commanders, Tlieff (Albertsz being retained by sickness), had been sent to England and had been rebuked by the king in person with such asperity as might be expected in such a cause.

Scarcely had the quarrel been thus adjusted upon the offender's back, when complaints of ill-treatment by the Dutch were heard from some Scotch fishermen. A fresh interpellation from the British Ambassador at the Hague gave rise to an examination of sundry fishing skippers, which of course led to no result. The States, however, emitted a sharp edict against ill-treatment of Scotch fishermen,*

* *Gr. Pl. Boek*, i. p. 707.

charging all Dutch seamen, whether serving in herring busses or convoying men-of-war, to refrain from violence towards the subjects of His Britannic Majesty, and keep "true friendship, neighbourship and good correspondence" with them, on pain of being "punished in the body as pirates and men of violence."

Matters, then, were scarcely on an amicable footing in the North Sea, when, in the year 1619, a Dutch Embassy went to London to treat, among other matters, of the Greenland and Spitzbergen fishery question. The herring fishery was not mentioned in their instructions, a circumstance sufficient in itself to ensure them a cold reception; and as regards the Arctic affairs they were met with an assertion of the king's unlimited sovereignty over Spitzbergen, which left small hope of coming to a definitive agreement. The king indeed in a verbal audience consented to let the Dutch fish off Spitzbergen for three years, but the restitution of goods and chattels unlawfully taken by both parties remained an unsettled question, and in point of rights " Mare clausum " as regards Spitzbergen was maintained as firmly as ever.

Another Dutch Embassy came to London in Janaury, 1621, with directions to negotiate on various matters of importance then pending; and although unprovided with precise instructions regarding the fishery question, they had that question broached to them by the British Government. The States at the time were anxious to keep this delicate point out of discussion and leave it *in statu quo ;* but the king required an end to it, and the ambassadors were obliged to promise the speedy opening of negotiations on the subject, with a view to a definitive settlement of the claims of both nations. The fact that the individual claims of several Scotch herring-fishers for damage sustained on the hands of the Dutch were in the meantime secretly settled by order of the States, stands as a proof of their anxiety at the time to conciliate England as far as it might be done without serious injury to Dutch interests.

The fresh Dutch Embassy, which sailed for England on December 8th, 1621, carried instructions which, as regards the matter of fisheries, amounted to an order to tergiversate as much as feasible. The king treated them to such language as might be expected from an aged and querulous invalid feeling wronged and aggrieved in one of his favourite pretensions; and in consequence of the tergiversating policy adopted, the Greenland and the herring fishery questions as well as the British claims for damages were as unsettled as ever when the ambassadors left England in February, 1623.

The States, who at the time had good reasons of general policy to avoid any rupture with England, towards the opening of the herring season issued orders for Dutch herring boats to refrain from approaching too near the British coast,* as, indeed, it had been tacitly understood for years that they were to keep out of sight of that coast. The damages question, however, remained unsettled, and the Dutch fished off Greenland and Spitzbergen, as well as in the North Sea, by the king's tacit acquiescence and without any agreement as to their rights to either. The demise of James I. and the Anglo-Dutch Alliance of 1625 made it possible to continue matters in this state without any serious collision, although the ancient rivalry between the nations continued, and petty claims and disputes occurred even in this period, in the causes of which there is reason to believe the misconduct of Dutch fishermen had a fair share. The publication or

* *Res. St. Gen.* June 12th, 1623.

"placard" against violence to the Scotch was renewed twice in this period of quiet, in satisfaction to British complaints.

Charles I.'s politics involved the strengthening of England's navy and the most strenuous measures to uplift her fisheries. The establishment of an Act on herring fishery, on the pattern of the Dutch laws upon the subject, and the chartering of a company for the herring fishery in 1632, are decisive instances of this tendency. But as yet the competition of Dutch herring fishermen, whose trade at the time had obtained immense development, was a serious obstacle to its progress in England, and the company founded there had but a short duration, and nothing like success.

It was not in Charles I.'s character to suffer this state of things for a long time. Selden's work on "Mare clausum," intended as a refutation of Grotius' "Mare liberum," was published in December, 1635, by the king's express order. The work instantly received general attention, the more so because, being dedicated to the king and approved by Council, it bore a semi-official character. Holland, where Selden's work was very soon reprinted, very soon also was visited with its effects. On April 5th, 1636, the king notified to the Dutch Ambassador his intention to subject all fishing in the alleged British seas to his royal license and recognizance in the shape of a special tax; and notwithstanding the States' immediate protest, a proclamation renewing the one issued by James I., and drawn in high-sounding terms, was issued on May 30th, 1636.* The king, indeed, in an audience granted to the Dutch Ambassador

* This proclamation is printed as an appendix to Mr. Muller's work before-quoted, and translated in Aitzema's *Matters of State and War*, ii. p. 306.

on the 27th of July, represented the measure as being of a peaceful nature and intended to benefit the Dutch fishermen by the protection of England against their enemies, the Dunkirk privateers. But at the same time twelve British ships of war sailed from the Downs to the Dutch herring fleet's fishing grounds; and though most of the fleet had already left, the rest were made to take the license and pay the recognition demanded of them, which indeed amounted to but two shillings per last for the year, and was paid by the fishermen without hesitation. The British Admiral, the Earl of Northumberland, nevertheless took the commander of a Dutch convoying vessel prisoner, and the Dutch Ambassador Joachimi, sent in haste to England in order to obtain redress, was met with a more than ever decided assertion of the king's right to exact last-money from any who should fish in the alleged British seas. The Dutch fishermen's readiness to pay the amount demanded of them had, as Joachimi observed to the States, greatly compromised matters.

Dutch fishermen complained loudly to the States of the proceedings in which some of them had acquiesced readily enough; and in August, 1636, a fleet of fifty-seven Dutch ships of war sailed under admiral van Dorp, with instructions to give the herring busses efficient protection, "against the Spaniards and *all others inclined to molest them.*" Van Dorp was late at his rendezvous, where he found a British squadron had already arrived, and levied the tax from most of the Dutch fishing vessels; and having no orders how to act in such a case, his presence was useless, and his position awkward. The admirals of both nations, having met in presence of the Dutch herring fleet, reciprocally asked each other why they were there? and each answered, "to protect the fishermen." Both squadrons soon afterwards left the spot for other business, and the net result of the season's proceedings was the carrying off of some twenty thousand florins as license-money by the British admiral, and the establishment in England of a general, though unfounded, notion that the Dutch States had tacitly acquiesced in the tax for the future, and acknowledged the sovereignty of England in the North Sea. The notion was so far from being exact that the Dutch admiral van Dorp was punished for his insufficient protection of the fleet by having his demission pressed upon him, in the following year, in such terms as moved him to instantly retire from office.

Although far from acquiescing, the States were still anxious to evade a definitive settlement of the sea-sovereignty question. When, in October, 1636, they negotiated an alliance with England against Spain, the king's promise to leave the Dutch fishermen unmolested as long as the proposed alliance should last, was asked for as a set-off against certain concessions on the Dutch side, without anything being said on the principle of "Mare liberum" or "clausum." Pending the very intricate and delicate negotiations on the Anglo-French alliance, in which the whole of European politics were at issue, Charles had reason to pacify the Dutch Republic, and accordingly left her fishermen in quiet during the herring season of the year 1637; and the States on their side managed to keep the question out of view, though they never once departed from their alleged right of free-fishing. A learned treatise in refutation of Selden's "Mare clausum" was about this time composed by the States order, by one Dirk Graswinckel; but it was thought advisable not to publish it, and Grotius himself, then in Swedish service after his disgrace and escape from his mother country, had good reason not to meddle even with the merely scientific side of the matter any more, because, as he wrote to his brother in 1636, "*Ego, cum Suecia multum teneat orae maritimae, quid aliud praestare possum quam silentium?*" The policy of "not waking sleeping dogs" was in those days prevalent on all hands, and a summer's unmolested fishing was the result for the Dutch herring busses.

The naval battle of the Downs (October 21st, 1639), in which the Dutch fleet under Tromp routed that of Spain within the so-called "King's chambers," and in spite of Charles the I.'s inclining towards Spain, was of wide consequence even for the fishery interest. The engagement constituted a most flagrant breach of Charles's alleged sovereignty of the sea; but at the same time it showed to what a pitch the Republic's naval power had in the meantime ascended. The British pretences to sea-kingdom were virtually at an end after the affront of the Downs, which never was resented openly. The king having on October 10th, 1639, pressed the States to accede to the Franco-British alliance, under promise that their freedom to fish in the straits should ensue from such accession, their answer was: "they did not intend to stipulate that right from any one," being, indeed, in tranquil possession of it. Striking instances of outrageous treatment from Dutch fishermen to British subjects occurred at this period.* Feeling themselves masters of the sea, they indulged in acts of piracy, which Charles, then sorely

---

* Such acts were committed even before the battle of the Downs. On the 26th of May, 1638, the States-General examined the matter of a captain from Enkhuizen who appears to have gone ashore on a piratical expedition, and plundered and sacked the house of one Robert Sherret, a merchant of Ireland.

intent on home affairs, was not at leisure to resent. The events of 1640 utterly broke the king's power to make himself respected abroad, and the impending fall of the House of Stuart put an end, for a long period, to open contestation between the two nations as regards the right to fishery in the North Sea. Under Cromwell, other and still more important questions than that of the free sea fishery were at issue between the two then greatest naval powers of Europe; and their next collisions were the beginning of that series of naval wars, the effects of which upon the Dutch sea fisheries have already been described in former chapters. Nor does the "Dominium Maris" question, as between Great Britain and the Dutch Republic, appear to have told upon the actual state of the fishery in later years, though it continued for some time to influence the diplomatical relations between the two countries, especially in 1661, when British influence considerably retarded the conclusion of a treaty between France and the Republic, by which the former power engaged to protect the latter's fishermen.

Besides England, Denmark has at several periods pretended to "Dominium Maris," in the shape of a fishing monopoly within a certain range from the shores of Greenland, Iceland, and Spitzbergen. The Danish claims never had anything like the importance of the British; for, besides being preferred by a power much less formidable, they bore exclusively upon two minor branches of sea fishery, viz. the whale and the cod-fish business. Still, as Denmark more than once actually interfered with Dutch fishery in virtue of these claims, they are entitled to a brief mention in these pages.

The first instance I have found of controversies on

fisheries with Denmark dates from the year 1615, just after the first successes of the Arctic Company. On February 18th of the said year the King of Denmark wrote to the States-General about the Dutch whaling expeditions, and claimed for himself the exclusive right to allow his subjects to whale off Greenland, to the exclusion of all foreigners unless provided with a Danish licence. The reason given was, that "the waters in question are off the northerly shores of our Empire." Some contribution from Dutch whalers had already been pretended to by a Danish ship of war in the season of 1615, but had then been refused by the former on the plea that they knew of no title to the exaction. The British claims to the whaling monopoly off Spitzbergen probably moved Denmark to a similar measure relative to Greenland. But the States-General, in their answer to the Royal Dane, politely but peremptorily declined the latter claim as well as the former; and Denmark preparing for violent interference with the Dutch whalers, the States accommodated the latter with artillery and ammunition, besides granting them such convoy as kept the Danes in respect.*

Next, in 1635, the Danish Sovereign preferred similar pretensions to a fishing monopoly off Iceland. A letter from the King remonstrating against the Dutch fishing off the shores of that island was laid by the States-General before those of Holland, who took the advice of the Arctic Company upon it. The latter were just then engaged in difficulties about the renovation of their charter, and owing, perhaps, to this circumstance, although the King of Denmark renewed his protestations, and even employed a Dutch merchant residing at Copenhagen to remind the States of them, he got no answer for two years. A

* *Res. St. Gen.*, April 13th, 28th; May 11th, 12th, and June 2nd, 1616.

memorial was addressed to Denmark in 1637 to refute their claims to a whaling monopoly off Iceland, and as these claims are not mentioned again in the States' Resolutions of the next years, they appear to have been suffered to drop, as had the Greenland difficulties in 1616. Still, pretensions of the said nature were not given up by Denmark. In 1639 Dutch whalers were menaced and annoyed by Danish men-of-war, in virtue of a law issued against all who should fish off Spitzbergen without a Danish passport; and once more a "well-reasoned memorial" from the States appears to have settled matters. It would indeed have been indifferent policy for Denmark to push them too far against a power whose navy had just then beaten Spain and kept England at bay in the famous battle of the Downs. I have found no further mention of fishery difficulties with Denmark till a century later, when the Danish claims for the first time gave rise to actual violence, the first motive for which, however, was taken not from a fishing but from a trading monopoly.

It has been recorded in another chapter that Dutch whalers used in the eighteenth century to apply themselves, besides the exercise of their industry properly said, to traffic with the natives of the Arctic countries. This trade first occasioned a collision between Denmark and Holland in the year 1739, in a bay near Disco Island, Greenland. A Dutch whaler anchored there, and doing business with the natives, was arrested and captured by a Danish man-of-war, and four more Dutch vessels, equally trading with the inhabitants, soon after endured a regular bombardment by three of the King of Denmark's ships, whose commander, having captured the vessels and crews, launched the latter off to sea in open boats, and brought the ships to Denmark as prizes. The Dutch sailors only escaped death from starvation by their happily falling in with some of their countrymen's vessels after a few days' navigation, who carried them home and reported what had happened. The Commissioners of the Greenland fishery of course lost no time in petitioning the States for redress; and the proprietors of the captured Dutch vessels meanwhile resorted to retaliation by arresting a Danish vessel then lying at Amsterdam. This at once called forth a protest from the Danish Ambassador Griis (or Grys), who, while demanding the release of the arrested ship, stated the alleged cause of the proceedings against the Dutch in Greenland to be a monopoly of trade granted to a Danish subject on certain parts of that coast, including the bay near Disco where the above-mentioned facts had occurred. The Republic was then no longer as formidable a naval power as a century before, and the States saw fit on this occasion to use the utmost forbearance. They showed to the Danish diplomatist that the arrest laid on one of his country's merchant vessels was a matter of civil litigation, and therefore could not occasion an intervention by the political authorities; but at the same time they prevailed upon the magistrates of Amsterdam and the parties concerned to release the Danish vessel, a measure dictated by *comitas gentium*, which, as the States did not fail to represent to the Danish Ambassador, they expected to be responded to by the release of the four captured Dutch vessels. Denmark, far from consenting to such an amicable termination of the difference, gave it considerable extension by falling upon the Dutch cod-fishing fleet, then assembled round Iceland to the number of about one hundred vessels. After some chasing and annoying of this fleet, Danish men-of-war ultimately captured four of the hookers; but while being brought to Denmark one of them succeeded in effecting her escape, and carried to Holland, as prisoners, a Danish midshipman and three common seamen who had been put on board to bring the prize into port. The quarrel, which had at first revolved upon an alleged monopoly of trade ashore, thus became a fishery question; and from the diplomatic correspondence which was at once opened on the matter it appeared that Denmark based her action on a pretended *exclusive right of Danish subjects to all fishery and navigation within four miles of the coasts of all Danish possessions in the Arctic seas.* Whether or not it may have been true, as was stated in a petition to the States by "the common shipowners of the cod fishery about Iceland," that while chasing and capturing Dutch fishermen the Danes had left those of France and England unmolested, here was "Dominium Maris" come to life again, and the matter therefore called for the Republic's utmost vigilance and energy.

A series of remonstrances were accordingly presented to the Danish Government by the Dutch Ambassador at Copenhagen in the course of the years 1740 and 1741. As regards the means of actual compulsion, Holland indeed spoiled her case at the very outset, by reiterating the extreme forbearance used towards the Danish vessel arrested at Amsterdam in 1739. Upon the Danish Ambassador's request the States in 1740 ordered the Admiralty of Amsterdam to set the captive Danish sailors at liberty, whereas the captured Dutch ships had been declared by the Danish magistrates to be lawful prizes, and eventually sold in public auction at Copenhagen. The point of law meanwhile gave rise to extensive memorializing on both sides. It was alleged by Denmark that all foreign vessels were prohibited from approaching within four miles of the

Iceland coast, by a law issued in 1733, in confirmation of a privilege granted in 1682 to a Danish trading company; and that the Dutch cod fishers made unlawful trading, contrary to this act, their principal business, to the ruin of the Danish traffic on the Iceland shores. To this, the Dutch Ambassador opposed the non-acquaintance of his Government with the law and privilege in question, and the fact that Dutch vessels had, up to the year 1739, constantly been allowed to fish and trade unmolested on the coasts of both Greenland and Iceland. The right to both was averred to belong to the Dutch in virtue of certain ancient treaties, one of which, dated 1447, established the rights of the Dutch to free navigation " usque ad Boreæ oras." In this, as in former disputes of the same nature with England, the historical side of the question was strenuously discussed, without leading to acquiescence on either side. The Dutch pretensions were advocated with considerable energy by Mauricius, then Dutch Ambassador at Hamburg, who though not called upon by his diplomatical duties personally to act in the matter, made the rights of both parties the subject of very profound and ample historical investigation, the results of which, in the shape of a series of memorials, he sent to the States-General, who drew from them the materials for the notes and remonstrances they ordered their minister at Copenhagen, Coymans, to present to the Danish Government.* Far from bringing about an agree-

* Mauricius' several Memorials on the subject, together forming a goodly folio volume, have been printed, and a copy of them is extant in the Royal Netherlands Library. The volume gives astonishing evidence to the mass of labour bestowed by this learned diplomatist upon a matter alien to his own professional duties at Hamburg, from which town the whole of the documents are dated. For the course of facts and negotiations see *Res. Holland,* 1739, 1740, 1741 ; *Res. St. Gen.* of the same years ; the secret *Resolutions of Holland,* 1740, 1742, and

ment this diplomatic debate only led to the question at issue assuming more and more serious proportions; and finally, when remonstrances on both sides had gone on for more than a year, a distinct pretension to " la domination de la Mer du Nord" as the source and origin of the right to exclude foreign vessels from the coasts of islands in the said sea, was set on foot by the Danish Government in August 1741. The States-General immediately ordered their ambassador to deny this pretension in the most energetic terms, " because other potentates might follow the example of Denmark, to the inestimable prejudice of these countries' trade and traffic in general." Denmark at the same time sent a squadron north to enforce her claims, and the Dutch Whaling Commissioners obtained convoy from the States. A warlike conflict between the two naval Powers seemed imminent, but was ultimately averted by the intercession, in favour of the Republic, of the British and French Ministers at Copenhagen. " Mare liberum " was the base of their joint remonstrance, in which it is worthy of note that a British diplomatist should have been employed, in opposition to another naval Power's pretension to " Maris dominium." The matter was subsequently adjusted by an understanding that Dutch vessels should not trade within the precincts of the Danish provinces in the Arctic seas; and a placard against such trade was issued by the States-General on April 15th, 1762.* The limit of four miles from the shores of these provinces appears to have been afterwards interpreted by Denmark, not as a prohibition

---

the periodical called *Europische Mercurius*, 1741, vol. i. p. 313. Wagenaar (*Vad. Hist.* xix. p. 279) gives but a very incomplete account of the matter, and plainly was not acquainted with its true bearings, having never read the Mauricius papers.

* *Res. Holl.* 1762, p. 508.

to fish within that region, but as a precaution against foreign fishing vessels going ashore for trading purposes, and the commanders of Danish men-of-war in the Northern Seas constantly had orders not to molest such fishermen as should occasionally be found within the said limit, provided they should not show any disposition to trade.*

PART III.

SEA FISHERIES SINCE THE END OF THE DUTCH REPUBLIC.

CHAPTER I.

1795-1813.

THE Revolution of 1794-5 transformed the Republic of the United Netherlands into a Batavian republic, at first based upon the principle of the former United Netherlands, and some time afterwards remodelled upon the pattern of the French Republic. A gradual reform of ancient rotten institutions attended these events; but the rules and rulers of sea fisheries survived the wreck of the rest.

The "College of the Grand Fishery" was indeed abolished in 1795; but a similar body was at the same time appointed, under the more modern and French sounding title of "Committee for the Affairs of the Grand Fishery," by a decree of the provisional legislative body dated May 12th. The members of the new Board appear to have been freshmen in their business; for the committee was unable to make the necessary provisions before the

* *Res. Holl.* 1761, p. 974; 1762, pp. 314, 650; 1774, p. 494.

busses' sailing day (June 24th), and some herring shipowners were, at their request, appointed by the representatives of Holland to arrange matters, under the title of a " Provisional Committee for the Direction of the Grand Fishery."

Besides taking the necessary steps towards the timely sailing of the fleet, this provisional Board tried to make out the financial status of the ancient college's administration. They found this an arduous task ; for the college's accounts were scarcely in a creditable condition. Their secretary was dead ; their chief clerk declined to give up the more important papers to the new committee ; and the latter, in such accounts as were delivered up to them, found many instances of maladministration. Considerable sums had been spent in banquets, the inevitable appendix of every meeting of a Dutch Government Board in former times. Herrings for the customary presents to certain authorities had been bought from some privileged shipowners at the very highest prices ; the towns of the south quarter represented in the college had rendered no accounts, and their " buss convoyer," or " hospital ship," to equip which was one of the college's principal duties, had been taken by the French two years before, and not replaced. Commissioners from the " Committees of Public Welfare, Marine and Finance," had to intervene in order to make the refractory college clerk give up such part of his books as he had chosen to secrete. In a word, it was shown that the college's administration had latterly been anything but an exception to the general rottenness and mass of abuses prevalent in the old Republic's later years.*

Sea fisheries were scarcely then in a better condition than the books of their administrators. The war with France in 1794 had forced part of the herring fleet to

* *Vervolg op Wagenaar*, vol. xxxiv. p. 138 *sqq.*

return into port as early as the first days of July; and in September the French had taken the whole of the cod fishing fleet.* To apply for pecuniary aid was therefore one of the first acts of the new committee; and the several immunities previously granted to the herring fishery were accordingly continued by the government of the new Republic. As for subsidies, the committee in 1795 refrained from applying for them, in consideration of the exhausted state of the country's exchequer; but at the same time directed the attention of Government towards the expediency of ulteriorly granting the Grand Fishery the same aid which they had enjoyed under the defunct Republic.† But there was little occasion for subsidy in the next years, as the protracted war with England, which at one time nearly swept the Dutch colours away from the face of the seas, stopped all or most fishing expeditions. The main feature of this history in the years between the overthrow of the Republic of the United Netherlands and the restoration of 1813 is, that there was some legislation, but very little fishery. Sailors and vessels belonging to the latter were often pressed into the country's service; and a publication against resisting such requisitions had to be issued by the Executive Board on July 4th, 1798. A re-organisation of the committee for the Grand Fishery took place on November 20th of the same year, but as yet only the title of Provisional Committee was given them, and there is no evidence of the extent of their business transactions having warranted another name. Their only act in the last two years of the century is indicative of the very depressed condition, if not the utter stand-still, of the

* *Nieuwe Jaarboeken*, aº 1794, p. 1218; *Gevers, de magno sive halecum piscatu*, p. 61 *sqq.*
† *Gevers, de magno sive halecum piscatu*, p. 63.

North Sea herring fishery. Some export trade in herring was then kept up by the unlawful processes of re-packing imported foreign herring and cured "pan-herring," caught in the Zuider Zee; a sure proof that the Grand, or North Sea Fishery could not supply the market. But, although obliged by the troublous times to refrain from their trade, the Grand Fishery would not allow others, who acted under more favourable circumstances, to interfere with it. Several herring dealers in July 1799 applied to Government for a prohibition against the re-packing of foreign herring, and a strict application of the herring laws of the former Republic, which had never been repealed, and were expressly maintained in force by publication of November 20th, 1798; and the Committee of the Grand Fishery of course seconded the application. In consequence, on May 30th, 1800, a publication was issued to the effect that all herring imported from abroad should be re-exported in the same barrels, without undergoing any manipulation whatever; and that no "pan-herring" caught in the Zuider Zee should be cured or laid in barrels as pickle-herring. The considerations upon which this edict is based are a remarkable instance of the spirit of monopoly surviving the trade, and excluding competition even when competitors had the market all to themselves. Zuider Zee herring, says the publication, cannot be packed so as to acquire the taste of the Grand Fishery's produce; the former is never cured on board, but always ashore, and while being carried home uncured is crushed into a jelly,* by the motion of the vessel; and it is generally caught in spring, when it can be sold at very low prices, so as to seriously depress those of early cured-herring from the North Sea, and injure the reputation of Batavian brand-herring abroad. The same

* "*Als in hare pap wordt gaar gekookt.*"

contradictory statements in which the Grand Fishery were found out while insisting upon their curing monopoly against the North Sea coast fishermen in 1751[*] were now repeated by them against those of the Zuider Zee. Letting alone the improbability of herring getting "crushed into a jelly," during a transport home which upon the Zuider Zee must have generally been of but a few hours' duration, how could herring so crushed be cured with a result so satisfactory as by its competition to endanger the Grand Fishery? As a fact, Zuider Zee cured-herring was certainly of worse quality than Dutch, or, as it was styled at the time, Batavian brand cured on board in the North Sea; but the former was taken by the markets abroad, where it certainly was more profitable to sell Zuider Zee herring than to sell none at all.

The Grand Fishery's stand-still at the time is proved, if not by any positive testimonies, by the fact that even the coast fishery had come to a dead stop. If Dutch bum-boats could not fish under the Dutch coast in 1799 because of the English cruisers, Dutch busses certainly could not venture into their fishing areas off Shetland and Yarmouth. And as regards the former, the forced stoppage of their trade in the season of 1799 is established by several petitions preferred by the municipality of Katwijk, suing for a subsidy to maintain their poor, "because in the present circumstances no fishery whatever can take place in the North Sea." They applied for a weekly bounty of fl.40 for each bum-boat and fl.8 for each of the smaller or shrimping boats, instead of which the first Chamber decreed to allow the village a subsidy of fl.2000 down, towards the maintenance of their poor. But the second Chamber declined to ratify the edict; and the "poor fishers

[*] See part ii. chap. iv.

of the Side," of whose often very miserable condition we have had evidence in a former part of this work, had to go without any relief from Government. It might have been found advisable under such circumstances to let Zuider Zee fishermen at least have the full benefit of the exceptionally sheltered position of their fishing water. But, as shown above, the spirit of monopoly bore them down and kept them within the old legislative trammels, even when they were virtually the only branch of sea fishery still in action.

In the midst of this general stand-still of the business the legislative bodies gave birth to a very prolix and detailed fishery law, viz., the Publication of July 28th, 1801 ; the preparation of which, although it was mainly a repetition of existing regulations, had lasted since the summer of 1800. This law has been in vigour for a very few years only, and during the fisheries' greatest decay. It is nevertheless important in the history of Dutch fishery legislation for more reasons than one. In the first place, it is a thorough proof that the Revolution had brought no change whatever into the fishers' and fish dealers' notions. Secondly, the law is, so to say, a crystallisation of the various statutes and rules which emanated on the subject under the republic of the United Netherlands, and reflects the whole of the herring legislation from its beginning downwards; while in its turn it has been the model for Acts of later date. Thirdly, the law of July 28th, 1801, contains many clauses apparently taken from bye-laws made by the ancient College of the Grand Fishery, of which I have not found the text in any official publication of earlier date.

The greater part of this herring law of 1801 is a faithful, and in many clauses a literal reproduction of the placards on the Grand Fishery of 1582 and following years, the contents of which have been exposed at some length in Part II. of the present essay. The "Committee for the Grand Fishery" was definitely organized by this law, and their competency was much the same as that of the college of old. They were to deliver licences (*acten van consent*) to the masters of all herring busses and sale-hunters, and of such cod-fishing vessels as should carry herring nets; to swear in the masters, and two of the crews of all the said vessels to observance of the law; to provide "hospital ships" (the nature of which will be shown hereafter); to issue instructions to the captains of the same, levy last-money, and advise Government on all matters of fishery legislation. The working rules relative to the opening and close of the herring season (June 24th —Dec. ult.):—to the curing, sorting, packing and further handling of herring on board; the prohibition to carry herring to a foreign port, or transfer it at sea to any but licensed sale-hunters, or to any one after July 15th; the interdiction from selling salt and fishing implements to foreigners, or from taking service on foreign fishing vessels; the police regulations for fishermen at sea, and the rules relative to the hiring and payment of sailors, and the terms between them and the busses' masters and owners; to the salt to be used, the packing of herring, and branding of barrels ashore—these several rules were all re-edited to nearly the same effect, and partly in the very same terms, as in the several placards in vigour under the Republic of the United Provinces. Laws of many dates, and scattered over many volumes of the Grand Placard Book, were now assembled into one statute, in virtue of the principle of codification brought into use as one of the far-spreading consequences of the French Revolution.

Of the clauses now sanctioned for the first time by the law of the realm, aad most probably taken from former

College bye-laws, the following are the most interesting :—

No herring-buss to put to sea without a complete 'fleet" of forty nets at the least (Art. 2).

No buss to sail home during sale-hunting time (i.e. between June 24th and July 15th), or come into port before July 19th, unless with a complete cargo, i.e. with the whole of her barrels packed full of herring treated according to law (Art. 15). This is the first legal sanction of the *monopoly of sale-hunting*, of which more shall be said in a following chapter. The institution may have existed before, as a College bye-law, but not before 1753, as it is not mentioned in v. d. Lely's 'Recueil.'

Herring-nets to be subject to control, as well as herring barrels. A complete set of regulations relative to the nets to be used in the cured-herring fishery was enacted in 1801 (Arts. 67–73).*

The sizes of both nets and meshes, and the quality of the hemp to be used in them, were prescribed in detail. Previous to delivery to the owner, every herring-net was to be submitted to inspection by a male or female "counter" (*teller of telster*), i.e. a sworn official entitled to verify and certify to the size and number of the meshes and the dimensions of the net; and the very hemp intended to be spun into yarn for herring-nets was to be previously

---

* The style of these articles is in some parts so antiquated and different from the usual wording of laws in the first years of the present century, as to make it particularly probable that they were modelled upon some bye-law of the former College's making, and of a much older date. An "order" relative to herring-net making, dated 1579 and arrested by "the *four* towns" then incorporated in the College, is mentioned on p. 15 of v. d. Lely's *Recueil*, without further reference to its contents.

inspected by a "keurmeester" or assayer. Other materials than Dutch hemp were prohibited from being used in herring-nets. No nets were to be used unless marked by the "counter" with a leaden seal bearing the name and arms of the town, and the official's own initials.

The most important innovations contained in the law of 1801 are, however, the clauses relative to the rights of the several branches of North Sea Fishery; about which rights, as has been shown in Part II., differences had formerly arisen. The several monopolies, the limits of which had in the course of the eighteenth century been for the greater part established by College bye-laws, were now, for the first time, sundered and defined by ordinary legislation.

The Grand Fishery having the monopoly of curing, was restricted to that business, and forbidden to use the process called *steuren*,* i.e. to salt herring in baskets ungutted, for the purpose of ulterior curage by smoke. The busses' steersmen were allowed to preserve herring in this fashion in two cases only; viz., when all the barrels on board should have been filled with cured herring, in consequence of an exceptionally felicitous catch, and when it should be impossible, by reason of foul weather and high sea, to use the proper method of curing (*kaken*), which required considerable attention from the whole of the ship's hands simultaneously. If any herring had been salted in the former manner by reason of either of the said circumstances, a peculiar oath to the fact was to be taken by the vessel's steersmen and two of her crew, immediately upon entering port (Art. 19).

The monopoly of the "*steurharing*" business being

* See part ii. chap. iv.

thus assured to the fresh fishery, the latter were likewise subjected to a complete set of rules. They were, in the first place, strictly forbidden to cure (*kaken*) any herring either on board or ashore, under any pretence or for any purpose whatever (Art. 93). For the better enforcement of this prohibition, which as will be remembered existed under the former Republic as a bye-law of the Herring College's making,* steersmen of the fresh-herring fishery were prohibited from sailing before September 14th, or from casting their nets before September 20th of each year (Art. 91). They were, as formerly, obliged before sailing to take out a peculiar licence under the seal of the Grand Fishery Committee, and take oath to observe the laws and regulations relative to their trade (Arts. 88, 89). They were subject to last-money to the amount of fl. 3 per twelve thousand herrings, the same amount being due for every last, of fourteen barrels, of cured-herring brought into port by the herring busses (Arts. 17, 99). To ensure the recovery of this tax, which, as formerly, was levied by the committee's officers for the benefit of their treasury, the steersmen of all fresh-herring smacks were bound to have their cargoes of "steurharing" examined and counted by municipal officials, who made the necessary declarations to the committee's last-money collectors. The steersmen of the Grand Fishery were subject to no such obligations, for they had to deliver up their barrels of cured herring (or *pickle-herring*) to the assayer, whose examination was sufficient control over their declaration for last-money to be paid.

In the third place, the North Sea cod-fishermen's attributions as regards herring-fishery were established in detail by the law of 1801 (Arts. 21, 22). They were, as

* See part ii. chap. iv.

formerly, permitted to catch herring for bait at all seasons; but if sailing before the 15th of July were not allowed to have more than eight herring-nets on board, and ten if sailing at a later date. In the former case, they were prohibited from curing or preserving any herring whatever unless for immediate use as bait for cod-fish; and all sale, barter, or transfer of salted herring was strictly interdicted to them. If sailed after the 15th of July, they were allowed to cure the remnant of their herring left after providing the necessary bait; but such herring was not to be sold unless in open barrels, and qualified as "mixed" (*ongezonderden*) herring, subject to previous inspection by the assayer, who was to destroy the herring thus brought into port if found unfit for consumption. The object of these rules was to secure the Grand Fishery the unrestricted monopoly of curing till the 15th of July, i.e. the day on which the last "sale-hunter" was to leave the herring fleet and sail home; and even after the said date to prevent the cod-fishery from offering the cured-herring business any serious concurrence.

Such are the principal contents of the Herring Law of 1801. It was, as has been shown, a codification of the rules in vigour under the Republic of the United Netherlands, whether established by the legislator of the realm or by the Herring College's ill-defined but seldom-questioned authority.

Besides the law itself, which is composed of no less than 109 clauses, and a series of forms of oath annexed to it in imitation of the Placard of 1656,* the publication of July 28th, 1801, contains two more documents requiring peculiar mention, viz., an instruction for the members of the "Grand Fishery Committee of the Batavian Republic,"

* See part ii. chap. i.

THE HISTORY OF DUTCH SEA FISHERIES. 197

and a form of commission for the commanders of their buss-convoyers, or hospital ships.

The former instruction, issued in lieu of the provisional organisation of the year 1798, contains the following principal clauses:

The committee is to superintend the whole business of the Grand Fishery (and indeed, as appears from the terms of the law just mentioned, much of that of the fresh-herring trade) under the supreme supervision of Government (then the "Uitvoerend Bewind" or executive board of the Batavian Republic). The committee is to be composed of nine members, *all of whom are to be privately concerned in the herring-fishery*, and appointed, subject to approbation by Government, by the managing owners (*boekhouders*) of herring busses in the towns and villages most concerned, viz., four by Vlaardingen,* two by Maassluis, two by Enkhuizen, and one by de Rijp. If the Grand Fishery be ulteriorly exercised or extended in other towns, such towns shall be entitled to appoint one further member of the committee if fifteen busses be equipped there; and if the number of such busses exceed forty, they shall be entitled to apply to Government for their further representation in the committee. The latter body's place of meeting, formerly Delft, is now fixed at the Hague. They are entitled to appoint their several officers and last-money collectors, and to regulate the latter's salaries and cautionmoneys under Government approbation. They shall annually elect their chairman, and hold their first and

* This town was not a prominent "herring town" in the earlier times of the old Republic, and was repeatedly declined admission to the College of the Grand Fishery. Vlaardingen's greatness in the trade seems to date from the latter half of the 18th century; it has been foremost in it ever since.

second meetings on the first Mondays in March and May, having previously conferred with the shipowners in the several towns and on the sea-coast, and taken their instructions as to the subjects to be considered for the several interests of the cured and fresh-herring fisheries. They shall annually render an account of their financial administration to a delegate from Government, in presence of such shipowners as shall choose to attend their meeting designated for the purpose; and their account is to be ultimately submitted to the Commissioners of the National Accounts (or supreme Government Board of Control) for liquidation. The said administration involved, as receipts, the last-money mentioned in the above law, and Government subsidies; as expenditure, the equipment, manning, and victualling of hospital-ships, the salaries of committee officers, and other general expenses. The committee's members were entitled to nothing beyond travelling expenses under a certain tariff. They were under oath to Government strictly and honestly to fulfil their several duties.

The form of commissions for commander of hospital-ships annexed to the law of 1801 throws much light upon the convoying institutions of the time. The hospital-ship, also called "buss convoyer," appears to be the ultimate result of a gradual transformation of the "direction-ships," anciently sent by the college after the herring fleet to protect them against enemies, and to enforce the rules of fishery police upon them.*

The "hospital-ships" of 1801, if they were still armed

---

* "Hospital ships" were sent out with the herring fleet under the old republic, *in time of peace*, when convoy properly said was unnecessary; v. d. Lely's *Recueil* mentions the cost of two "hospital-ships" in 1714 and following years, without stating their precise nature at the time.

convoying vessels like the "direction ships" of old, were mainly intended for peaceful purposes. Their captains' instructions indeed contained an injunction "to use good seamanship *and soldiership*," but the rest of their vessels' attributes, as apparent from the same document, are such as no man-of-war could carry out without very serious prejudice to the latter function. They were to be floating lazarets, marine stores, and wharves for the busses' convenience, whom they were bound to assist with surgeons and carpenters, spare rigging, and all such materials as they should require. They were to relieve the busses of their sick, and provide them with able seamen instead, and in general see that no buss should be obliged to sail home prematurely by reason of avary or lack of hands. In some cases the captain was instructed to act in concert with the commander "of the other hospital-ship;" whence it is evident that no more than two used as a rule to be sent after the fleet; and both of them were constantly to sail round the herring fleet, and carry signals to enable busses in distress to find them out.

A short while after the establishment of the law of 1801, and the definitive organisation of the Committee of the Grand Fishery, the preliminaries of London were signed; and in the next spring the short-lived Peace of Amiens opened the sea for peaceful pursuits. Sea-fishery was instantly recommenced, and of course its beginnings were attended with such financial difficulties as shipowners had in former years been accustomed to overcome by the aid of bounties. Accordingly, to sue for premiums to herring-busses was one of the first acts of the now established committee; and besides, they applied for the subsidy which the provisional committee had not enjoyed during the stagnation of herring-fishery. A subsidy of fl.3000 was granted them on January 15th, 1802, and on May 21st the sum was increased to fl.12,800, by the addition of the ordinary subsidies, which had been kept back in the preceding years. Besides the subsidies, which as formerly were intended to cover general College expenditure, a premium of fl.700 for each buss to sail in that year was allowed by the Legislative Body on April 27th, somewhat to the committee's disappointment, as the sums applied for by them were fl.800 for 1802, and fl.500 for the next ten years. The other branches of sea-fishery likewise applied for premiums to recommence their business. The Commissioners of the Greenland fishery * had the highest pretensions of all, and sued for fl.3000 as a premium for each whaler carrying forty men and seven boats, besides fl.5000 as an indemnification for each of twenty-nine whalers which had been sent north in 1798, and all taken by the English. As, however, the Treasury could afford no such largess, they had to be content with fl.2000 for each whaling ship equipped and sailed in 1802, besides the "indemnization" † formerly held out by the Placard of October 3rd, 1788,‡ to the amount of fl.50 for each quarter of train oil wanting to a hundred in each cargo. The commissioners of the small, or Iceland cod-fishery at Vlaardingen and Maassluis § were likewise accommodated with bounties to the amount of fl.700 for each vessel, and the fresh-herring fishery of the Side had fl.200 held out to them as a premium for each bumboat.‖ One hundred and sixty-eight busses sailed in this memorable year of peace, 1802; and it may be readily

* See part ii. chap. ii.
† "*Premie van dedommagement.*"
‡ See part ii. chap. ii.
§ See part ii. chap. iii.
‖ *Notulen van het Staatsbewind*, Dec. 1801—June, 1802, *passim*.

assumed that, as a consequence of the re-establishment of the premium system for all the several branches, the revival of sea-fisheries was general, and shared by the other branches besides the Grand Fishery. At any rate, such a revival of the fisheries and the trades dependent on them was counted upon as certain after the peace of Amiens, as is proved by a publication dated April 22nd, renewing the prohibition issued by the States-General in 1778,* against exporting well-boats for cod-fishery.

As an instance of the spirit of enterprise infused into those concerned in sea-fisheries in the year 1802, the institution of an African whaling society may be cited. A report had spread that whales were very plentiful about the Cape of Good Hope, so that, although they were of a small size and yielded train of an inferior quality, a renewal of the ancient Greenland Company's first successes might be hoped for. Accordingly a corporation styling itself "South Sea Whaling Company" was started in 1802, and subscriptions to it soon reached the considerable figure of fl.790,000. They obtained a Government charter of monopoly to last twenty years. Government (then the Executive Board called "Staatsbewind") indeed judged all monopolies "hateful and contrary to that equality" of all citizens, which formed one of the fundamental principles of the Batavian Republic; but they undertook to reconcile monopoly and "equality" by an ingenious wording of the charter. As a precaution against their superseding the ancient Greenland whalery, the new company were obliged by their charter to take a one-eighth share in every vessel sailing to Greenland, if the owners of such a vessel should demand it, and to a maximum of one-fourth of the company's paid up capital.†

* See part ii. chap. iii.
† *Vervolg op Wagenaar*, vol. xlv. pp. 54, 327.

The rupture of the peace of Amiens in the next year stopped these hopeful beginnings. The blow was the heavier, as considerable preparations for sea-fishery had been made in the first months of the year, under the continued stimulus of premiums, which were granted again in 1803, to the amount of fl.700 and fl.500, for the next eleven years, for busses and hookers employed in the cured-herring and cod-fisheries. To prevent the utter loss of the capital invested in vessels and equipment by the time war had recommenced, the Committee for the Grand Fishery asked Government to apply for passports from England; but far from acceding to the petition, the "Staatsbewind" on June 6th ordered the Committee to prevent the sailing of busses. Several shipowners next applied for permission to sail under the colours of neutral Powers, but were likewise forbidden to carry out their purpose. Coast fishermen were subjected to particularly rigorous measures. Napoleon's grand project of a descent on the British shores was then so far ripened as to make him anxious for the preservation of a store of flat-bottomed vessels in the hands of his ally and subordinate the Batavian Republic; whence England was, with excellent reasons, peculiarly anxious to capture and destroy Dutch fishing craft from the coast. Many smacks were taken in the beginning of the war; and so great was the terror spread by these events, that an order against the sailing of bum-boats from the side was soon followed by another, purporting that all such boats should be secured out of the enemy's sight *behind* the downs. It is, and probably was always customary to haul the "*pinken*" or bum-boats up the beach, close under the outer declivity of the sand-downs, either for repair or during the short interval between the herring and hook-fishery seasons, so high as to be beyond the highest tide. But I am not aware of another instance of their having been hauled completely across the first range of downs, and the operation must certainly have been a very difficult one. Government, however, set much store by the order being strictly executed. It was feared that, if the smacks were left ashore so as to be visible from the sea, they might be destroyed by British artillery, or burnt in some successful landing razzia; and such an event would not only have been a severe infliction upon shipowners, but also have brought down upon the Batavian Government the displeasure of their powerful ally in the south, who wanted the boats to be preserved for his ulterior military views The coast fishermen of Scheveningen, Katwijk and Noordwijk opposed the measure, and baulked its execution for some time, but it was ultimately carried out all over the coast, and as regards Scheveningen was enforced by the intervention of the municipal authorities of the Hague. As an instance of the extreme reluctancy of shipowners to subject their bum-boats to the operation prescribed, some fishermen of Noordwijk tried to evade the order on the plea that their boats were no longer subject to the Batavian law, having been sold to Prussian subjects.*

And now there was virtually an end of Dutch sea-fishery for some years. Herring shipowners in the course of the year 1803 tried, but in vain, to obtain a premium as an indemnification for having equipped their vessels to no purpose,† and some of them ultimately sought to cover part of their outlays by fishing for cod on the Dogger bank, and occasionally trying a cast for herring, towards which end

* *Vervolg op Wagenaar*, p. 249, sqq. *Notulen van het Staatsbewind*, June-Dec. 1803, Jan. 1804, passim.
† *Notulen Staatsbewind* 1803, passim.

they obtained from the Legislative Body a dispensation of the law of 1801 as regards the restrictions put upon herring-fishery by cod-fishing vessels.* The premiums decreed in 1802 were in the next years paid for the very few ships which ventured to sail; but the dread of British cruisers was generally stronger than the hope of a bounty. Matters became still worse under King Louis' reign, when Holland was virtually a province of France, and the Emperor, as omnipotent there as in the lands under his own direct government, kept the fishing fleet constantly in readiness as instruments for the one great plan he never could put into execution, viz., the descent on the British shores. A "Dutch Herring Company" was formed at London in 1809, for the purpose of cultivating the Dutch method of curage; and employed some captive Dutch herring-fishers, without, however, obtaining a durable success. The period when Holland was actually annexed to France (1810-1813) is remarkable in the history of Dutch sea-fisheries, not, of course, because of anything like prosperity for them, but because during this short period *the Dutch fishery-laws were cancelled.* As a consequence of this, coast fishermen, who alone could sail now and then with hope of escaping the British cruisers, used their new-gotten freedom to cure fresh-herring caught off the Dutch coast; and so good was the produce of their curage that dealers from Vlaardingen and Maassluis, whose busses could not sail to their accustomed rendezvous off the British shores, did not disdain to buy cured herring from the coast and sell it under their brands. The only instance of French sea-fishery legislation is an Imperial Decree of April 25th, 1812† by which the herring, cod, and fresh-fisheries were permitted, but under such rules as to

---

* *Notulen Staatsbewind*, May 22nd, 25th, 1803; April 22nd, 1805.
† *Bulletin de Lois de l'Empire Francais*, 4me série, vol. xvi. p. 373.

the duration of their absence from home, their obligation never to enter any port but their own, and always to rally there at an appointed signal, and the inspection of their vessels and men, as kept them constantly under the hand of the military and naval authorities, to be gathered at a moment's notice. It was the Emperor's object, not to secure for his subjects such freedom of sea-fishery as was not precluded by his disastrous wars, but merely to use their ships as instruments for the ever-proposed expedition against England. The fishery boards of the country were swept away, and the Decree of 1812 substituted for them a College of "*prud'hommes pêcheurs*" in each fishery port, whose main duty was to supervise the regulations relative to the well-known French "*inscription maritime.*" The chiefs of the Imperial Navy were by this law made the supreme ordainers of all fishermen's conduct, and the vessels employed in sea-fishery were considered in no other light than that of ferry-boats, to be kept handy eventually to land a French army across the Channel. And yet the whole of this military organization was set up under a pretence of consummate benevolence and liberality towards the fishing interests; for the 12th article of the above quoted Imperial Decree expressly stated that it was made, "*voulant dégager ceux de nos sujets qui s'adonnent à la pêche de toutes les entraves qui peuvent gêner leur industrie, et les éclairer des leçons de l'expérience !*"

CHAPTER II.

PROTECTION AT A CULMINATING POINT.

ON November 30th, 1813, the Prince of Orange crossed from England to take the hereditary government of the ex-Batavian Republic. On December 1st, he was proclaimed Sovereign Prince of the Netherlands at Amsterdam; and one of his very first acts of economical legislation was to cancel all fishery laws of French origin and re-instate the herring law of 1801.[*]

The old system of fishery regulation and protection was further rebuilt in the next years. Premiums were held out to encourage a fresh beginning of the several fisheries, to the amount of fl.500 for every cure-herring buss equipped, for every vessel employed on cod-fishery in the North Sea during the winter months, and for every voyage made by a vessel in the Iceland cod-fishery; of fl.200 for a fresh herring bum-boat, and fl.4000 for each of the first twelve whalers to sail in the next years, besides, as regards the latter, the "indemnification bounty" of fl.50 for each quarter of train wanting to a hundred, under the same conditions as to equipment, strength of crew, and duration of voyage, which had been enacted in 1788 and 1802.[†] In virtue of the latter premium, a whaler was entitled, if returning "clean," i.e. without any cargo, to no less a sum than fl.9000 as a bounty. The permission to send a few sale-hunters direct from the fleet to Germany, was also granted once more in

---

[*] Decree of January 10th, 1814 (*Staatsbl.* No. 6).

[†] *Staatsblad* 1815, Nos. 2, 27; 1816, No. 6; 1817, No. 3; 1818 Nos. 13, 42, 43. *Bijvoegsel op het Staatsblad*, 1818, p. 892.

1815;* and although this grant had been constantly made in the last years of the ancient Republic, the fiction of its exceptional character was upheld even now, and the permission was given for one year only, and renewed afterwards. The old exemption from excise duty on salt was likewise restored, for the benefit of all herring and cod fishery, by the law on salt excise duty of September 15th, 1816;† and a Decree of May 30th, 1817 ‡ besides establishing peculiar facilities for the enjoyment of this immunity, in the shape of credit for excise duty not subject to the common bonded warehouse rules, held out a special premium of fl.3 per last of salt cod-fish brought into port, and a general bounty on exportation of salt cod or herring. Another decree, dated July 31st, 1817,§ established facilities of a similar nature for unrefined salt used free of excise duty by the North Sea coast fresh herring (or steurharing) fishery. In a word, no efforts were spared to promote a speedy rising of the national fisheries; and as the sea was now free, and national labour anxious to take avail of the withdrawal of the fetters imposed by foreign domination, the herring-fishery, and its corollary the North Sea cod-fishery, soon reached something approaching their status of the latter part of the former century.

Whaling was likewise attempted afresh, under the stimulus of the very important premium offered; but the attempts were timidly made, generally in old and wretched vessels, and the trade never regained anything like a rank worth mentioning among the Dutch sea-fisheries in the present century. A whaling company (limited) was chartered at

* Staatsblad, 1815, No. 34.
† Ibid. 1816, No. 36.
‡ Bijvoegsel tot het Staatsblad, 1817, p. 220.
§ Ibid. p. 236.

Harlingen in 1824,* the King being one of the principal participators. A similar company was formed at Rotterdam about the same time. Notwithstanding the very considerable amount of premiums awarded, I have not found any evidence of these whaling attempts having been successful; indeed the "Nederlandsche Hermes" of December 1826 distinctly states the contrary, and whaling was the only branch of Dutch sea-fishery which did not perceptibly survive the ruin of the ancient Republic.

Not content with restoring every detail of the ancient system of fishing regulation and protection, the Government of the Kingdom of the Netherlands soon began to out-Herod Herod, and add fresh fishery restrictions and monopolies to those made in former times. A minimum charter for herring busses allowed to cure and entitled to the premium of fl.500 was established, by a Decree of June 16th, 1815; † twenty-four lasts and thirteen men being prescribed as the minimum size and crew for such vessels. The same Decree contained a clause by which the Grand Fishery College's virtual power was very much extended, and it became indeed a matter of some difficulty to assign its exact limits. All laws whatever emanated on fisheries in former years, and aiming at the maintenance of the credit of Dutch herring were declared to continue in vigour, unless expressly repealed; and the publication of May 30th, 1800, against curing Zuider Zee "*panherring*," and importing foreign herring unless for re-exportation in the same

---

* *Bijvoegsel op het Staatsblad*, p. 612.

† *Staatsblad* No. 39. Although virtually a modification of the law of 1801, the enactment was disguised in the shape of a simple regulation prohibiting the College of the Grand Fishery from issuing licences for vessels not responding to it.

barrels, was expressly renewed. By this enactment the whole of the ancient herring legislation of the United Provinces was virtually re-established, although the essence of it had already been, so to say, crystallized in the law of 1801. It was not easy to apply the tangled mass of the old Republic's fishery laws to the modern kingdom, or indeed to make out what part of the countless Resolutions of the States-General and the States of Holland, on the subject, was still lawfully in vigour, and what part repealed. There was now, in short, *too much* general legislation on sea-fisheries; and a simplification was found necessary. To promote this end, without detriment to the principles of the existing laws, the King, on February 20th, 1818, laid a Bill before the States-General, the leading idea of which was to leave all detailed working rules to the provincial authorities, under Government approbation, and have only general precepts laid down in the law of the realm. This law, promulgated on March 12th, 1818, (Staatsblad No 15) was the last general statute regulating sea-fisheries in the Netherlands. It contained the leading principles of the system on which fishery protection was built, and its several clauses have been an object of much debate down to the final overthrow of the system in 1857. For these reasons I have found it expedient to add a translation of the full text of the law of 1818, as Appendix D. to these pages.

The law, as will be found upon perusal of the said Appendix, repeated the outlines of the system in vigour ever since the beginning of the ancient Republic, and described in Part II. Chapter I., of the present essay. It moreover contained one important novelty, viz., the utter prohibition from importing any foreign herring whatever, whether for transit or for home consumption. Both under the Republic and by the law of 1801, it had been permitted to import foreign herring for re-exportation in the same barrels, un-opened and unbranded; and the general Customs tariff of 1816 admitted such herring for home consumption, although subject to a heavy duty. Fish dealers in 1818 were, for the first time, utterly deprived of a branch of their business for the better preservation of the Grand Fishery's monopoly.

The law was not established without serious opposition. The importing prohibition just mentioned was, in the first place, the subject of a warm remonstrance in the Second Chamber, on the part of no less a personage than Count Hogendorp,* who found sufficient motive in Art. 6 to vote against the Bill, although favourably inclined towards it in general.† But the main brunt of antagonism was borne by the sixteenth clause of the law, by which the Grand Fishery's monopoly of curing herring after Beukelsz' ancient method was once more consecrated, to the exclusion of the fishermen of both the North Sea and Zuider Zee shores. This monopoly, which we have seen established in the eighteenth century by the potent Commissioners of the Grand Fishery, and maintained by the laws of 1800 and 1801, had already been expressly re-enforced by a special law dated November 25th, 1814 (Staatsblad No. 108). Of all the several items of protection to which the Grand Fishery had learned to cling for two centuries and more, they held this curing privilege the most precious. Fresh-herring fishermen, on the other hand, still considered their

* One of the illustrious men who led the revolt against the French authorities, some time before the arrival of the allied forces. This great and wise statesman has, throughout his career as such, advocated the principle of Free Trade.

† Hogendorp, *Bijdragen* t.d. *Huish. van Staat*, ii. p. 249. The entire debate upon the Bill is to be found in Mr. Noordzick's collection of *States-General Records*, 1817-18, p. 288.

exclusion as the main cause of their trade's insignificance, and took occasion from the general revision of the fishery statutes ordained in 1818 to strenuously claim the right to cure their herring. Their petition,* besides the arguments used by their fathers in 1751,† had now some still more stringent reasons as a base. Under the French Government in 1812 and 1813, fishermen from the Side were allowed to cure ; and as they of the Grand Fishery could not venture into their ordinary fishing waters, herring caught and cured by the despised bum-boats closer to the continental shore was carried to Maassluis and Vlaardingen, and those towns were then anxious enough to export it under the Grand Fishery brand.

The petition from the coast villages (viz., Scheveningen, Katwijk, Noordwijk, Egmond aan Zee and Zantvoort, the rest having meanwhile given up fishing), was this time echoed higher up than its predecessor in 1751 had been. Four sections out of the five into which the Second Chamber, or Lower House of the legislative body, was then divided for the preliminary examination of Bills brought in, desired more ample elucidation respecting the curing monopoly.‡ Government answered them with assertions either unfounded or not to the point. Firstly, it was said, the early herring which really constitutes the renown of the Dutch brands abroad is caught off the Shetlands, whither no keelless boat can sail ; a statement in flat contradiction to the representations of the coast fishermen, who in their petition alleged the early herring caught off Shetland to be,

* Published as Appendix XIX. to the Report of the Committee on Sea-Fisheries, 1854.
† See part ii.
‡ See the Report of the Central Section, in *Bijvoegsel tot het Staatsblad*, 1818, p. 1006.

as a fact, unfit for exportation. Next, said the Minister in defence of the Bill, it is a requisite for first-rate cured-herring that the fish be cured quite fresh, whence buss-fishermen are enjoined to throw overboard in the morning all such herring of yesterday's capture as they have been unable to cure in the night ; and bum-boats, being much less strongly manned, could not carry out this point of the law with sufficient precision. To this argument it might have been objected that if bum-boats carried fewer hands, they also shot fewer nets, and had less fish to cure in one night. Subsequent events have fully proved that herring can be cured in bum-boats with entire success. Thirdly, Government argued that it had been enacted in 1801, that no vessel should sail home in the early part of the season unless with a full cargo ; and the smaller vessels, having sooner completed theirs, could have the immense privilege of the early market all to themselves if allowed to cure. The true reason for maintaining the monopoly, to wit, the preponderance of the Grand Fishery interest, peeped through this last argument ; and in preferring it, Government omitted to take into account the institution of sale-hunting, by which the first cured-herring was annually brought into port much earlier than a bum-boat could ever hope to make the shore with a complete cargo. Another pretended danger of allowing bum-boat fishers to cure, viz., that of their divulging the professional secret of curage in the ports of Great Britain, and Yarmouth especially, which they used to visit, was indeed altogether visionary. Keeled busses as well as bum-boats were in the habit of holding communication with the British shore ; and the danger of the former's crews promulgating abroad the mysteries of Dutch curage was much the greater. Bum-boats from the coast were all manned exclusively by Dutchmen ; whereas the greater part of the busses' crews was, at the time now spoken of, composed of foreigners, Germans especially, whom nothing prevented from teaching their countrymen, or other foreigners, the process on which they were employed during the summer. If Dutch curage was not generally practised abroad, it was because other methods were used in foreign countries with such success as made English, Germans, Swedes, Danes and Norsemen the victorious competitors of the Dutch in the great herring markets, as early as the beginning of the present century.

The point at issue being so far elucidated on both sides in the Parliament papers, the oral discussion could not of course bring any fresh arguments into the field. Still it did not lack interest. The speech of Mr. Kemper, who employed himself most strenuously in defence of both the curing monopoly and the importing prohibition, is a fair specimen of the peculiar logic customary to protectionism. The first-named measure, according to Mr. Kemper, was in reality not a monopoly at all. Bum-boat owners were left perfectly at liberty to exchange their vessels for keeled busses, and take their share in the profits of curage. And so they certainly were, as far as the words of the law were concerned. But no keeled vessel could sail from, or anchor in safety at a convenient distance off one of the villages on the Dutch sea coast; so in order to adopt the orator's advice, shipowners from the coast would have had to transfer their establishments to the riverside towns, and abandon the capital primarily sunk in their business, besides the many other expenses and disadvantages always attendant upon shifting the seat of an industry from one place to another. As coast-fishermen pithily said in their petition, their liberty to equip busses was equivalent to a merchant's liberty to sell certain wares, under an obligation to pack those wares in bales too big to be got through his warehouse doors.

Yet another point of the Bill was forcibly illustrated in the course of the debate, viz., the King's faculty to allow dispensations from the prohibition to cure issued against coast fishermen. This clause was never meant for anything but a decoy to win the opposition over. The parliamentary system was at the time in its infancy in the Netherlands. There was no ministerial responsibility ; and to oppose a Bill emanating from the King himself was something awful, on which many members of the House did not care to venture so long as they could somehow keep their consciences at rest in acquiescing. To provide a sedative to this effect was therefore a means to shut up importunate mouths. One member distinctly stated his intention to vote for the law in the hope that the King would use his faculty to establish exceptions ; whereas, as he justly observed, the Bill's rejection would be the continuance of the laws of 1800 and 1801, by which the monopoly was sanctioned without any perspective of relaxation. It is probable that many members tacitly embraced the same course ; and it certainly was a clever piece of parliamentary tactics to make such members vote the continuation of a monopoly obnoxious to their views, by asking them to empower Government to overthrow its own handiwork and system. But such an overthrow was no part of the King's intentions. The Minister's speech in defence of the Bill has unfortunately been lost ; but it is more than probable that Mr. Kemper fully expressed the Government's views upon the subject, by stating that he did not look forward to any breach in the monopoly, and would rather have abandoned the reservation clause. This was straightforward speaking ; and the law having been voted by a majority of fifty-one to sixteen, coast fishermen had not many illusions left. Of the several provincial regulations on herring-fishery subsequently issued under the Royal approbation, not one permitted coast-fishermen to cure until long after King William the First had ceased to reign ; and the privilege was thus maintained, which prevented them from making above fl.10 or fl.12 for a quantity of herring, to which their concurrents imparted by curage a value of fl.50 and sometimes more.

The details of the system, as regulated under the law of March 12th, 1818, fully responded to the legislators' rigorously conservative spirit in fishery matters. No change was at first made in those details. For four years and a half, in virtue of a Royal decree dated June 9th, 1818 (Staatsblad, No. 27), the working rules laid down in the law of 1801 were continued in vigour, while a new set was under consideration with the Provincial authorities, now appointed legislators, under the royal approval, for all such working details as were rather vaguely defined by the law of 1818 as "internal police" of the herring-fishery. "Provincial authorities," of course, meant those of the province of Holland, now, as in former centuries, the only one where herring-fishery was exercised on a considerable scale. On December 31st, 1822, the royal approbation was given to a set of rules drawn up by the Provincial States of Holland, relative to herring-fishery in their province.*

Two Regulations were made in 1822 ; one on the Grand and one on the Fresh-herring Fishery. They were mainly a repetition, in a more prolix wording, of such details of the law of 1801 as had not been transferred to the law of March 12th, 1818. Very little was added to the virtual contents of the statute ; and that little tended to make the rules even more stringent than before. A minimum size for herring busses had been determined in 1815 ; the provincial regulation added that such busses should carry

* *Bijvoegsel op het Staatsblad*, 1822, pp. 1018 *sqq.*, 1358 *sqq.*

square sails (*razeilen*). The law of 1801 had ordered every buss to carry forty nets ; the regulation of 1822 added the size of those nets for each voyage. The former statute prohibited cure-herring fishermen from salting herring in baskets ungutted (*steuren*), unless in urgent cases, when it should be impossible to cure the fish ; the latter made away with the exception, and prescribed all herring caught in a buss to be either cured (*kaken*) immediately or ·thrown overboard. Besides these, and a few more tightenings of the old fetters, the Regulations of 1822 offer one important new feature, viz., the institution of two distinct boards for the cure-herring, and fresh-herring fisheries. The former was to sit at the Hague and exercise exactly the dominion formerly held over the cured-herring business by the Committee for the Grand Fishery. The latter board was to meet at Katwijk, as the most centrally situated among the North Sea coast villages, and hold sway over the smoke-herring concern. As a novelty, the whole of the coast fisheries, including those for pan-herring and fresh fish in both the North Sea and Zuider Zee, and even shrimping, were brought under the supervision of the College assembling at Katwijk, who were enjoined to keep their eye upon these several branches of the trade, and from time to time to draw up the necessary regulations regarding them for the Provincial States' approval. Last-money was to be levied by both colleges under similar provisions as made in 1801 for the committee's sole benefit ; and the forms of oath, instructions for steersmen, and hospital-ship captains, &c., &c., ordained in 1801, were renewed in pretty much the same words.

Another novelty of some importance in the Grand Fishery Regulation of 1822 is, that it first gives a legal definition of the several qualities of Dutch cured-herring, viz., *full, maatjes, ijlen*, and *kuitziek* (*homziek*). The former and latter terms had indeed been used from very early times downward, the former meaning herring full of spawn or milt, and the latter fish about to shoot the same, and consequently unfit to be preserved for a long time " *Ylen*" is a common word for lean, or empty, and was applied to herring, in its literal sense, down from old times. The word *maatjes* first occurs, without any positive statement as to its meaning, in the 14th clause of the Herring Placard of 1656. The Regulation of 1822 defines this very important description of cured-herring as containing neither milt nor spawn, but much fat, and "maatjes" herring is stated to be a great delicacy, but not very durable. The " maatjes " and " ylen " qualities were formerly certified on board by the skipper, by means of "girdings" or circles drawn round the barrels. Positive *brands* for them, to be given of course ashore by the brander, are first prescribed in the Regulation of 1822, besides the old brands stating the season of catch and described in Part II., Chap. I.

Besides the aforesaid regulations, a Royal Decree of April 4th, 1824 (Staatsblad, No. 28), extended the clause of 1818, forbidding Dutchmen to fish " between the rocks of Scotland, Hitland, and Norway." They were now prohibited from fishing, or even without urgent reasons from approaching, within two hours (twenty making a degree) of the British shores. The main object of this statute appears to have been to stop Dutchmen smuggling on the British coast ; but as cure-herring fishery off " Hitland," Fairhill, and Yarmouth, and all fresh-herring fishery, were expressly dispensed from the rule, it is not easy to see what can have been its real force at the outset. It was carried into full effect, and the exceptions were withdrawn, by a new regulation on cure-herring fishery enacted by the Provincial States of Holland in 1826, and approved by Royal Decree of June 5th, 1827,* which regulation did not otherwise materially alter the existing rules.

The edifice of legislation on herring fishery was now more complete than ever. Its base, construction, and general outlines still responded to the Placards of 1582; and the only material alterations wrought since then were such *novellae* as had been, in the course of two centuries and a half, invented by the ingenuity of many generations of fishermen, the better to secure their several monopolies against home and foreign competition. As regards the former, the rules now as formerly proved efficient enough. As for the latter, no laws or monopolies had in former days shielded Dutch fishermen from the effects of war, or of elevated tariffs and active concurrency abroad; nor could they now, under profound and continual peace and industrial activity, make the Grand Fishery regain anything of its splendour of a hundred and fifty years ago.

But the spirit of monopoly had not yet done its utmost. The narrow-minded greed of parties interested had still more stringent measures of Protection in store. Before speaking of these it will be necessary to relate how the herring fishery fared between 1814 and the time of which I am now speaking.

About one hundred busses sailed in 1814; and as herring prices were very high in the next two years, and premiums, as has been shown, were lavishly given, enormous gains were made. The returns of one season sometimes amounted to fl. 10,000 per vessel, besides the bounty.† An organization of the sale-hunting business was agreed upon during this period of 'success, in

* *Staatscourant*, 1827, No. 278 (Bijvoegsel).
† See a Memorial on a Herring Association, written in 1828. (*Notulen Holland*, 1829, p. 211.)

virtue of which cure-herring shipowners annually clubbed to equip sale-hunters, and each buss, while at sea, sold her early herring to these for a price fixed beforehand. The much higher prices made in the home market for this "hunted herring" (*Jaag-haring*) were then divided among the participators in the "Hunting Association" (*Jagery-vereeniging*), according to the number of barrels sold to the hunters by each buss ; and a managing Committee of shipowners regulated the sale and expedition of the early herring so as to prevent an overstocking of the market and a downfall of prices early in the season.* Under the very favourable circumstances mentioned just now the number of the vessels of course increased fast, and reached 160 in 1817. A series of exceptionally bad years, during which the catch was very scanty, and most busses "sailed money overboard," notwithstanding tolerable prices, reduced the number of busses to 145 in 1821. In the said year a shipowning company established at Emden transferred its fleet of twenty-five busses to Enkhuizen and carried the total of the Dutch fleet up to 170. Fishing returns in 1821 were once more plentiful ; but prices went down to an extremely low level, mainly on account of the competition of Scotch herring in the foreign markets ; and several firms were in jeopardy. At this juncture, a herring dealer from Amsterdam, in the spring of 1822, proposed a measure which, being adopted by the principal shipowners of the towns on the Maas, led to some amelioration of prices. They agreed not to sell herring under fl.17 a barrel before October 15th, whereas fl.10 had been paid in the preceding year. This was a considerable extension of

* After steam navigation had come in, the Dutch Government annually supplied a steamer to the Hunting Association to act as the first "sale-hunter."

the principle on which the Hunting Association used to act; for the former did not meddle with prices after the close of hunting time, generally July 15th, and left competition in the market entirely free at all times beyond the first three weeks of the season. The measure was repeated in 1823, and by it prices on the Dutch market were indeed kept at fl.17 or upwards, but three hundred lasts* of herring remained unsold in the winter of 1823, and had to be thrown on the market for fl.8 in the next spring, before the opening of the season 1824. A "Herring Company of Amsterdam" ("Amsterdamsche Haringreedery") was created and chartered in the said year, in the hope of exploiting the fixity of prices caused in the two preceding years by the general association of shipowners. But such an association was not again formed, as its results had upon the whole proved unsatisfactory, and some doubts had arisen as to the faithful observation of the contract by many of the participators. Meanwhile prices went down again; and in 1825, although the bounty of fl.500 was carried to fl.750, most shipowners sustained severe losses, which in that and the next three years were shared by the Amsterdam Company, based on an unfulfilled expectation. The cause of these losses might have been manifest to any unprejudiced observer. Scotch, German, and Norse herring was now prevalent in most of the European markets. Herring had become an article of common nourishment in some countries, by reason of its cheapness, the result of vastly increased international competition. In order to sell a fair quantity of herring it was now necessary to catch it at little expense and sell it

---

* The "last" of herring at this time and afterwards was a quantity of 14 barrels; the barrel contained on an average 800 herrings. In former centuries the "last" averaged from 12 to 14 barrels.

cheap; and the Dutch herring laws, instead of pointing out the way to cheap production, were based on the bicentennial principle that Dutch cured herring was to be, not an article of daily food, but a delicious, and of course expensive, luxury. The legislation had been built up in a time when the Dutch were, if not the only, at least by very far the greatest herring-fishers of the world, and enabled by the absence of serious competition to put their own prices upon their own brands. Thus the notions of Herring and Monopoly had for centuries been closely interwoven in the Dutchman's mind; and he was not able to disentangle those notions, even when foreigners began to go far ahead of Holland in competition upon the herring markets. Other countries at the same time retaliated on Holland for her former ascendency and present exclusive policy, by closing their markets against Dutch herring by heavy customs duties. This state of things had not been realised in the course of the eighteenth century; whence the continued downfall of the Dutch herring fisheries, in spite of premiums and regulations without number. It was not realised in the first part of the present century; whence the impossibility of keeping up competition abroad. Nor could home consumption, being curtailed by prices artificially high, sustain the business even under a prohibition of foreign herring. Herring Protection, more than two centuries old, had been bringing down its own punishment for one century or more; and yet nobody saw the evident effects of the great social law against which they had been striving in vain.

As a very conclusive instance of this blindness, the "*Amsterdamsche Haringreedery*" before mentioned in 1828 presented a petition to the King, which, though not fully carried out, led to a very masterpiece of monopolising policy. They asked that, by the abolition of clause 46 of the Herring Regulations for the province of Holland, it should be made lawful for every buss to transfer herring to every other, during the whole of the season ; and that the whole of the fishery should then be formed into one Association, whose committee should at all times determine a minimum price for the last of herrings, and regulate the sale so as to keep up that price. The accession of all shipowners to this association, and their submission to its rules, they required to be enforced by depriving all outsiders of the premium of 500 florins, and dividing the sums which would have been due to them as premiums between the members of the Association, whose premiums might thereby exceed the former amount.

The arguments preferred for this plan by those who moved it were the following. As things were under the Provincial Regulation of 1827, herring might only be transferred to the licensed sale-hunters between June 24th, or the opening of the season, and July 15th ; and the large supply of herring during this "hunting-time" (*jaagtyd*) was apt, in spite of the monopoly of "hunted herring" in the home markets secured by the prohibition against busses sailing home unless with a full cargo, to drive prices down to a level insufficient for that precious delicacy, the noble early Dutch cured herring. After the close of "hunting time," i.e. when it was no longer permitted to transfer herring from one ship to another, a scarcity of herring frequently set in, for it was manifestly contrary to the shipowners' interest to have their ships home, and stop fishing for a couple of weeks, unless the necessity of bringing in a complete cargo compelled them to do so. Thus, in consequence of the "hunting" monopoly and its restricted time of operation, many lasts of prime herring remained afloat and lost their freshness, while foreign orders upon the Dutch market could not be executed for lack of adequate supplies. Prices unnaturally low were thus succeeded by prices unnaturally high, or rather by a grievous understocking of the market. As a fact, this arrangement was certainly a monument of stolidity in economical legislation. But the remedy proposed by the men of Amsterdam was little better. They wanted, indeed, to have herring-hunting free throughout the season, but only in order to have all the herring brought in confided to the care of one central committee, who should limit the sale so as never to severely depress the market. They wanted, in a word, to monopolise into one single hand the whole of a trade already monopolised for the benefit of those few who could afford keeled and square-rigged vessels. While the law limited the cure-herring fishery to comparatively few ships, they wanted to limit the marketable production of those ships to such quantities as should suit the convenience of a body of narrow-minded shipowners and dealers, anxious, not to sell much fish, but only to make a high figure for such fish as they could manage to sell. The main end of the plan was, *not to extend, but to restrict the business.*

There has been a vast amount of written and oral discussion of this plan. The permanent Committee of the Provincial States,* before whom the matter was laid, called a meeting of parties concerned at Lisse, and had heaps of memorials presented to them, both before and after that meeting. The College of the Grand Fishery for Holland was then, as in former times, divided into two Chambers or "Departments," one for Amsterdam and the towns in North Holland, and one for the towns on the Maas; and

* *Gedeputeerde Staten.*

of these Departments the former sided for the plan proposed by the "*Amsterdamsche Haringreederij*," and the latter opposed it in the most strenuous terms. Of all the clamouring parties in the debate, this latter official Board was the only one which showed discernment, by starting from the premise that "not high prices, but abundant capture, were the means to restore the Grand Fishery." But even they were anything but faithful to their principle, and indeed disavowed it wofully in some of their subsequent reasonings. One of their objections to the plan of Amsterdam was, that if the "hunting" monopoly were removed, and all and sundry left free to carry home herring at any time, prices, now in some measure kept up till July 15th by the Hunting Association (*Jagery-Vereeniging*), would be frightfully depressed from the very beginning of each season.

Volumes of memorials were, as said before, written for and against the Amsterdam plan.* The numeric majority was against it; for the whole of the shipowners' companies and herring firms on the Maas of course took the side of the southern department of the College. Still the argument of Amsterdam prevailed in part. Having to suggest a decision to the King, the Provincial States determined upon a plan for conciliating the views of both parties, which was perhaps the worst solution they could possibly have contrived. By their advice, the King in 1829† maintained the 46th clause of the Regulation, but authorised the Provincial States to postpone the closing of the "hunting"

---

* The whole of the documents are preserved in the record-books (*Notulen*) of the Provincial States of Holland, 1828, p. 102, *seqq.*, and 1829, p. 180, *seqq.* They form about a hundred pages of folio print.

† Decree of May 5th, 1829 (*Bijvoegsel op het Staatsblad*, vol. xvi. p. 14).

season till a later date than July 15th. On the other hand, the new monopoly sued for by Amsterdam was granted by this Decree, and premiums were withheld (although without accretion to others) from all such herring shipowners as should decline to accede to a universal Association, since famous under the name of "*Vereeniging der Zoutharing-reederijen.*" The constitutive rules for this Association were shortly afterwards drawn up by a committee of dealers and shipowners, and approved by the Provincial States.* Four local Boards, residing at Vlaardingen, Maassluis, Amsterdam and Enkhuizen, were appointed by the herring shipowners, each buss conferring a vote on her owner. These boards were to buy up *all* branded herring brought in by the partners, and sell it out again; the prices for both purchase and sale being fixed, from day to day, by a central Board residing at Vlaardingen, "to the furtherance of the shipowners' interest, by preventing *unnecessary* depression of prices, and on the other hand, moderating them so as to leave no herring *unnecessarily* unsold." The Board, though a wholesale and monopolist dealer, was not to export directly, but sell to second-hand inland dealers only; and all herring left unsold on April 1st of any year was to be sold in auction at any price, and the returns recovered before May 1st. As herring kept till April 1st of the year succeeding its capture is comparatively worthless, this fresh monopoly was equivalent to throwing away part of the herring caught, in order to enhance the price of the rest. The measure was just the reverse of what ought to have been done. The only chance of upholding the herring business, even under the laws which bound it down, lay in altogether removing the preposterous "hunting" monopoly and restriction, and leaving the supply of the

* *Bijvoegsel op het Staatsblad*, vol. xvi, p. 16.

article to regulate itself; whereas Government now proceeded to cap the measure by having the sale monopolised and restricted likewise. The regulation and protection system, as applied to herring fishery, was now screwed up to its very acme. A cure-herring fisherman was not much beyond a machine as regards the management of his business. He was accurately prescribed how, in what vessels, with what nets, when, and where to fish; how to prepare his fish; how, when, and in what vessels to convey it home; and he was obliged to let others decide for him whether, when, and at what prices it was to be sold. He had not the slightest liberty of action; a knowledge of his business, of prices, markets, &c., was unnecessary for him; and he would have been fined large sums had he tried to improve his business by any technical innovation. Anybody could, so to say, be a herring shipowner, if he had a knowledge of the several regulations of which the above chapters contain a brief, and far from detailed, account. It is a marvel that a trade should have lingered so long, in which all vitality and spirit of enterprise was so utterly extinguished by regulations; the more so as the avowed object of some of these regulations was, not to extend, but to restrict the business. Of this baleful policy of directly and *openly* keeping back part of the supply of an article in order to enhance its market price, the history of the Netherlands in former centuries can show more instances than one; but I doubt whether in the present century there is an example of such a thing applied to *food*.

As regards the principle, the Dutch fish monopolies were decidedly worse than the British Corn Laws; and the reason why the latter affected the general welfare much more seriously is merely that they were applied to an article without which no one could do. Nor was the revival of

Government regulation under the reign of King William the First limited to the herring fisheries. Coast fishery for plaice, flounder, sole, &c., shared the general reinforcement of old rules, and close attention to their observation. Laws against trawling, for the protection of fish-life under the Dutch coast had, as related in a former part of this work, been enacted in 1676 and relinquished in 1689, as unnecessary vexations. A statute of this nature was once more set up by Royal decree dated January 12th, 1820.* Trawling was not prohibited altogether by this edict; but it was forbidden to trawl within view of the coast in November, December, and January, and at any time to use trawls or any other nets narrower than the "eight-and-twenty" size of old, i.e. a width of three (Netherlands) inches and nine-tenths, or about one inch (English) and a-half, for each mesh. Another decree of November 15th, 1825, † prescribed that the reglet, or spatule (*spaan*) determining the meshes' width of nets for the coast fishery should be made of copper, and subject to assay. The use of trawls for fishing herring along the coast was altogether prohibited by this Edict of 1825; but, at the same time, the general prohibition of all trawling was limited to the period between November 15th and February 15th. The latter date was afterwards shifted to February 1st by Decree of August 29th, 1837 (Staatsblad No. 56). It is worthy of note that the Decree of 1825 was only enacted for the province of Holland, whose States held it to be necessary; whereas the provinces of Antwerp, Zealand, and Occidental Flanders,‡ whose inhabitants, like those of Holland, exer-

* *Staatsblad*, No. 2.
† *Staatsblad*, No. 75.
‡ It should be remembered that, from 1815 till 1830, the provinces now forming the kingdom of Belgium were part of the kingdom of the Netherlands.

cised coast fishery on the North Sea shores, declined to have them enforced within their precincts. The States of these three provinces were so anxious to maintain their fishers' liberty in the choice of their gear that they bought it by the loss of a considerable advantage. A premium of fl.250 was held out, by the Decree of 1825, to every boat from the province of Holland (bumboats included) which should fish in the North Sea with hooks and lines,* without interruption, between November 15th and February 15th of any subsequent year. As this premium was not limited to any definite number of years, it afforded considerable encouragement to the coast-fishery of Holland; and yet the southern provinces chose to forego this benefit in order to maintain their right to use the trawl.

The premium awarded in 1825 to hook-and-line-fishery during winter was by no means a superfluous bounty. Hook-and-line fishery was, upon the whole, a good substitute for winter trawling. Plaice, turbot, &c., besides cod and haddock, were caught on the hooks; whence, though trawling was the more convenient, and it would appear the cheaper of the two methods, the other offered better chances of a fair return. But this was not the only consideration. Trawling was till then the coast-fishers' chief, if not their only, source of livelihood in winter, after the close of the smoke-herring business; and, being forbidden to use the trawl, they were, in common equity, entitled to some equivalent to keep them from starving. I have shown in former chapters that severe penury used to prevail in the coast villages during winter; and the premium for hook-and-line fishery during prohibited trawling time was, at the outset, a preventive measure against over-burdening of the Poor Boards. It soon wrought a considerable increase of

* " *Beug- of hockwant.*"

the hook-fishery by bumboats in winter, and even in autumn and summer, and subsequently occasioned a curious incident in the race for premiums characteristic of Dutch sea-fisheries between 1775 and 1850. Fresh-herring or "steurharing" fishermen, who had only fl.200 a year as a premium, began to desert their business for the more favoured hook-fishery; and the owners of herring smokeries in the coast villages complained of a scarcity of herring supplies to their establishments. The premium for "steurharing" fishery was therefore augmented to fl.300 per boat, by Decree of July 11th 1835, No. 72; whereupon a shifting in the opposite direction took place, and hook-fishers from the coast turned fresh-herring fishers to such an extent that the municipality of the Hague complained of their market being under-stocked with fresh haddock and plaice. A sliding scale of premiums was now adopted; and it was enacted by Decree of November 6th, 1840 (Staatsblad No. 71), that such of the two rival fisheries as should have the greater number of boats engaged in it in any year should in the next be entitled to the premium of fl.250, and the other to the full bounty of fl.300.

Besides the prohibition from trawling in the winter months, another measure for the preservation of fish-life along the coasts was taken in 1842. It will be remembered that the use, within the sand-bars, of the shrimp trawl, known in the Placards of the seventeenth century by the name of "sayngh" had been permitted at all times by those enactments, while they prohibited trawling at greater depth and distance. The several laws and Decrees of 1820 and following years had likewise left the use of the "saayem" (as the implement was now styled) unrestricted. But it was now discovered that, although the spawn of plaice, &c., was supposed to be deposited on the bottom at some distance from the coast, immense shoals of fry of such fish, quite unfit for consumption, sometimes approached so near the shore as to be caught in the shrimpers' nets, when they were either thrown away or used as pigs' food or manure. It was deemed advisable, as a supplement to the law on trawling, to prevent such waste of the fisherman's future stock; and towards this end it was enacted that, whenever a shrimper should find more than one-eighth of the contents of his "saayem" to consist of fry, or unripe fish, he should report the fact to the member of the Coast Fishery College or to the municipal officer nearest at hand; when all use of the shrimp-trawl should instantly be prohibited in the locality for eight days.* An estimate of the utility of this measure cannot be formed, for the prohibition was not applied above a few times, and the statute was repealed in 1857. But there is little or no probability of it having, till then, been faithfully observed. It was of course impossible to efficiently control the shrimpers' nets; and they were interested, if finding a quantity of fry of fish in those nets, in concealing the fact in order to avoid a compulsory holiday of a week or more.

CHAPTER III.

THE END OF PROTECTION.

THE present narrative has now come to a turning-point, viz. the period when the ancient system of sea-fishery legislation was abandoned, as inadequate to the *régime* of modern production and exchange. Before entering upon the details of the system's overthrow, it may be useful to resume its plan and outlines in a very few words.

* Royal Decree, January 7th, 1842 (*Staatsblad* No. 2)

There were no less than three monopolies in the Grand Fishery, or business of fishing for herring to be gutted and salted on board as soon as caught (*kaken*) ; to wit :

Firstly, the *fishing and curing monopoly*, restricting the business to those who owned keeled and square-rigged vessels ; forbidding them to fish unless between June 24th and January 1st, or carry fish elsewhere than into Dutch ports ; and subjecting fish, barrels, and fishing implements to obligatory and strict assay.

Secondly, the *carrying monopoly*, restricting the liberty to buy cure-herring at sea and carry it home to the earlier part of the season, and virtually monopolising the supply of herring, during that part of the season, in the hands of the body called " *Vereeniging van de Haringjagery*," by an enactment prohibiting fishing busses from sailing home during " hunting time," unless with a full cargo.

Thirdly, the *selling monopoly*, empowering a wholesale-dealing corporation called " *Vereeniging van Zoutharing-reederyen*," during the whole of the season to determine the quantity of cure-herring to be thrown on the market, and the price to be put upon it. In order to enforce adhesion to the rules established by this corporation, premiums were only granted to such buss-owners as were partners in it.

To make up for the first-named monopoly, the owners of vessels excluded from it were invested with a monopoly of the curing process called "*steuren*," i.e. salting herring ungutted, preparatory to curage by smoke. But they were prohibited from fishing for herring and preparing it in this way until the beginning of autumn, when the other branch, or " Grand Fishery," was no longer exercised on a large scale.

All herring fishery, including the cured, the smoked, and the fresh, or " pan-herring " business, was protected by a prohibition from importing any herring caught by foreigners, or by Customs duties amounting to such a prohibition.

All sea-fisheries, including, besides those just named, those of whale, cod, flounder, plaice, &c., were encouraged by bounties more or less considerable.

It will be noticed that this system, whatever its faults, was in its kind a well-ordained and finished organization. Its main parts completed each other so that no single stone of the building could be removed without endangering the whole. The curing monopoly of the Grand Fishery, and the smoking monopoly of the coast fishery, made the prohibition from importing herring an absolute necessity, it being impossible to let foreigners import articles which some or most natives were forbidden to produce. Again, the importing prohibition necessitated obligatory assay of brand-herring ; for it would have been impossible to prevent foreign cured-herring from being imported if Dutch fishermen had bought it at sea, which they would have done, in spite of the legal prohibition, if obligatory assays at home had not made detection highly probable. Next, Dutch fisheries being thus prevented, by a complete set of legislative trammels, from following their natural course of development and effectually facing the overwhelming competition of English, Germans, and Norsemen, they could not of course go without direct government assistance, and would have altogether ceased to exist if their losses had not been covered by premiums.

Finally, as the whole of the system was pointed towards the main object of *maintaining Dutch cured-herring as a fine and expensive delicacy*, and as this object was still aimed at when the delicacy ceased to be in great demand abroad, there could of course be but one chance of selling Dutch herring at high figures, and that chance lay in restricting the supplies. Thus, no considerable *item* could be missed out of the system; and if the public's eye should once be thoroughly opened to the evils of one part, it must of a necessity open to the wrongs of the whole.

We have now to consider the effects of the system of which a sketch is given above, in the short period between its reaching the highest degree of perfection, and its final break-down. For a summary view of those effects, I beg to refer the reader to the statistical tables contained in Appendices E, F, G, H, and I. The leading fact at once apparent from the first three of these, is: *that the Grand Fishery, to whose interests the other branches of herring-fishery were sacrificed, languished and decreased under extreme protection and regulation; whereas the smoke-herring fishery, being free in its own sphere of action, increased rapidly, although the law precluded its produce from being prepared to advantage.*

Next, it will be seen from Table G, that from 1845 downward, *the greater part of the herring caught by Dutchmen, was prevented from being cured, or prepared to advantage, in order to keep up the prices of the lesser part.*

Exports of herring of course followed a course analogous to that of production. Cured-herring exports remained stationary, being prevented from increasing, firstly, by the artificial dearth of the article and the lower prices of foreign herring, and secondly by the elevated customs tariffs against Dutch fish in most foreign countries, the inevitable consequence of the prohibitive measures against foreign herring in Holland. Smoked-herring, or "*bucking,*" being a cheap article, and fit for a poor man's food, was better able to withstand these duties, and its exports actually increased, though not in proportion to its production.* As regards the operations of the Salt-herring Shipowners' Association, or "*Vereeniging van Zoutharing-reederijen*" before alluded to, this corporation did in two ways contribute to keep Dutch brand-herring at high prices. Firstly, it limited the supply in the markets as soon as a tendency to fall became manifest. Secondly, it greatly enhanced the cost of production of the article as delivered to dealers. The association's expenses of management, warehousing, &c., were excessively high, so as often to swallow up the whole of the premium, and make it the shipowner's interest to forego the bounty and keep free of the association. Most shipowners indeed kept within the latter, but mainly, it would appear, because the association in course of time acted not only as their sole client but their banker, and embarked in credit operations entirely alien to its primitive sphere of action.†

Of the other branches of sea-fishery little need be said during the period now under consideration. Whaling was extinct, or very nearly so, and when mentioned at all in the writings of the period, is spoken of as a trade lost to the country. The somewhat reckless enterprise of the African Whaling Company had been wrecked long ago, during the English war. Of the several whaling companies started within a few years from the renewal of premiums in 1815, the greater part liquidated shortly afterwards. One corporation, of which King William I., a strenuous promoter of all national industries, was a shareholder, continued to work two old whaling vessels until a much

---

* *Vide* Appendix xxii. and xxiii. to the Report of the Committee on Sea-Fisheries, 1854. I have refrained from reproducing these, and other interesting statistical documents, in order not unnecessarily to extend the volume of this work.

† Report of the Committee on Sea-Fisheries, 1854, p. 199.

later period; but the results were very unsatisfactory, and the vessels took out of the country's pocket in premiums some four-fifths of the total value they brought into it in blubber and whalebone. Such was the effect of the "indemnification" bounty before mentioned, which was paid to whalers, not for the fish they caught, but for those they failed to catch.*

Iceland cod-fishery also continued in a state of extreme insignificance,† having never recovered the effects of the prohibitive duties on salt cod and haddock levied in foreign countries, in the latter part of the eighteenth century.‡ Hook-fishery in the North Sea continued to be of importance, as a complement of the several herring-fisheries.

This branch of sea-fisheries, as to which I have not succeeded in finding sufficient information at earlier periods, at the time now spoken of bore something of an universal character. It was exercised in herring-busses or "hookers," in sloops, and in bum-boats. Herring-fishers of all descriptions made hooking their business at times when nature provided no herring, or law forbade to catch it. Most or all herring-busses used to go for cod and plaice in spring, and continue the business till the end of May or the first days of June, when the time came to prepare for the first herring voyage. The lines used in this early hook-fishery were made out of a peculiar kind of hemp named *kol;* whence this branch of hook-fishery was commonly called *kolvaart,* and a hooking voyage arranged so as to be back in time to equip the vessel for the cure-herring season took the name of *kolreis.* Besides, some

---

* See Minister Thorbecke's speech on premiums in the Second Chamber, on December 21st, 1850.

† See Appendix H.

‡ See part ii. chap. iii.

herring-ships fished for cod in winter, using a gear of somewhat different description called *beug;* whence the business was called *beugvaart.* Hook-fishery was thus a resource for all herring-fishers to keep their capital constantly in activity; and the concern was the more profitable, as several kinds of fish (cod, haddock, plaice, &c.) were caught on the hooks, and an abundance of one sometimes made up for a scarcity of another. I have not found any separate and complete accounts of hook-fishery by busses during the period now spoken of.* But whatever its actual importance, it certainly served to keep busses afloat at times when market restrictions could not squeeze a profit out of the herring returns, nor premiums cover herring losses; and it will be observed that this precious resource in all seasons and for all fishermen was solely due to the fact that, beyond a few restrictions as to herring caught by cod-fishers, which have been spoken of above, *there was no legislation on hook-fishery.* And even these restrictions served to show the futility of the herring laws. Hook-fishers were allowed to cure herring caught by them after the 15th of July; but in order to prevent any dangerous competition for the Grand Fishery, they were enjoined to pack their herring as " mixed " (*ongezonderd*), sell it *in open barrels,* and have it branded with a peculiar mark.†
In spite of these several disadvantages, and, so to speak, marks of infamy, it is fully proved that herring of this

---

* The importance of winter hook-fishery on the Dogger bank (*beugvaart*) is shown by Appendix I.

† The mark consisted in the word "*kerf.*" North sea hook-fishers were called *kervers* (or, in former centuries, *corvers*), from the customary carving of haddock and flat-fish; whence herring cured by them, although it was not apparently submitted to any other carving than consistent with the common method of curage, used to be called *kerfharing.*

THE HISTORY OF DUTCH SEA FISHERIES. 237

description brought to market by coast-fishermen from Katwijk did, about 1850, *fetch the same prices* as regular brand-herring sold at the same time.* It could not be better proved that the vaunted superiority of herring caught by busses over herring caught by bum-boats, and the latter's unfitness for any curage unless by smoke, were either fictions or rules fraught with many exceptions; a fact as to which the experience of later years has not left the shadow of a doubt.

Of fresh-fishery I have not found any peculiar account during the period now spoken of. It was, indeed, no longer a separate business, being exercised by bum-boats of the North Sea coast, concurrently with hook and smoke-herring fishery, and especially at seasons when the latter was not permitted; and all the year round, by a multitude of small craft of various descriptions, in river-mouths of Holland and Zealand, and in the Zuider Zee. The trawl was the fresh-fisher's favourite implement in the North Sea during the months when its use was not prohibited. The capture of *anchovy*, of which I have found scarcely any positive mention made in earlier times, became an industry of some importance in the first half of the present century, when the Zuider Zee was especially its area, and it was commonly carried on with a net of conic shape, and of course very narrow, dragged between two ships; probably the same practice which we have seen prohibited in the latter part of the 18th century. Anchovy-fishery has always been subject to strong vicissitudes, and often gave rise to reckless speculation on future fishing returns. Thus, the annual quantity of anchovies brought to market at Monnickendam between 1847 and 1853 averaged about

* Report of the Committee on Sea-Fisheries, 1854, p. 90.

forty million; but it was sixty-eight million in 1851, and little more than one million in the next year.

I have now briefly to narrate why and how the system of sea-fishery regulation and protection was relinquished.

The main cause of this most important reform was the fact that rational notions on political economy began to prevail in the Netherlands in the second quarter of the present century, especially after the secession of the Belgian provinces in 1830. It was between 1830 and 1850 that Free Trade was decidedly adopted as the base of the kingdom's commercial policy; and to its adherents nothing could be more objectionable than sea-fishery protection in its actual form. The evils of monopoly, and the folly of paying bounties out of the public funds to encourage an industry while keeping it down by rules, began now to be fully realised, and public opinion, led by able writers in periodicals, gradually turned away from the system. It did indeed continue after most other items of protection had been abandoned; and the main reason of this is, that the public at large were still kept in a state of excitement by wonderful accounts of the herring fishery's ancient greatness, and taught to believe that this greatness had been attained by similar protective measures as were now in force; whereas I have shown *that the principal, and most stringent of those measures were invented long after the fisheries' decay had begun.* But this was not known at the time now spoken of. Whenever the subject was broached, writers and speakers in the fishery interest used to declaim out of Semeyns' and Raleigh's tales of wonder, and to take it for granted that those splendours, in which they still believed implicitly, were owing to our ancestors having done as we did now. The curious cry of "Try not to be wiser than thy fathers" was never raised with a more boisterous obstinacy than it was in matters of sea-fishery, as soon as modern ideas began to prevail in the question.

Considerable light was thrown on the subject in 1842, when Belgium increased its import duties on foreign fish, to the prejudice of Dutch sea-fisheries; and fishing shipowners loudly clamoured for more efficient protection. The public mind was then strongly turned towards the question of fishery protection; and it became apparent that *it was impossible to allow the several fisheries more protection than they enjoyed;* while at the same time that naked fact, that *the branches most strongly protected declined in spite of protection*, was urged on the public's notice. The measures proposed by the writers in the fishery interest were to augment premiums, which expedient the Treasury interest forbade to adopt, and to retaliate on Belgium by elevating the duties, not on their fish, which was prohibited as it was, but on sundry other articles imported from the former southern provinces. The duties in Belgium were reduced some years afterwards. But, in the meantime, the brisk interchange of pamphlets and leading articles occasioned in 1842 by the Belgian protective measure, had the result of bringing the subject of sea-fishery legislation in its full extent before the Dutch public's eye.

A breach in the system, however, was not made till 1846; and it was not then a wound in a vital part. It was reported by the Grand Fishery Committee in Holland, that in 1845 herring entirely ripe had been caught by Scotch fishermen some time before the consecrated opening of the Dutch cure-herring fishery, so that the produce of the latter was late in the market, much to the shipowners' and dealers' detriment. A Bill was brought in, and passed without opposition, by which Government was empowered to anticipate the opening date of the Grand Fishery by a period not exceeding a fortnight, i.e. fix it at any day between June 10th and 24th. The power was granted for two years, but renewed for three more in 1848; and the anticipation term was extended to twenty-three days in 1851 and 1854. Under these laws, the date on which the first casting of herring-nets should be permitted was fixed by Government on June 10th in the years 1846–50, and on June 1st in the years 1851–55.* The measure was not attended by any decided success. The first experiments of early fishing were indeed successful; but in nearly all the following years the results were unsatisfactory, and most shipowners returned to the observation of the ancient St. John's Day rule, finding the returns of early fishing did not cover the additional expenses necessitated by it, or compensate the disadvantage of having to quit the spring hook-fishery, or *kolvaart*, at an early date, whereas that business was generally most profitable in the latter part of May. The advisability of early fishing for cure-herring was a point of pretty constant debate in the course of the above-named years; shipowners generally advising to observe St. John's Day rule, in spite of the concurrence by early Scotch herring, and dealers urging early voyages because of that concurrence. Now dealers, although represented both in the College for the Grand Fishery and in the Salt-herring Shipowners' Association, were in a minority in both Boards; and consequently the College, after a few years' trial, advised against

---

* Laws of May 9th, 1846 (*Stbl.* No. 35); May 18th, 1848 (*Stbl.* No. 21); May 2nd, 1851 (*Stbl.* No. 23); and April 10th, 1854 (*Stbl.* No. 21). Decrees executive of these several laws, of May 12th, 1846 (*Stbl.* No. 41); May 19th, 1848 (*Stbl.* No. 24); May 8th, 1851 (*Stbl.* No. 51); May 3rd, 1852 (*Stbl.* No. 21); April 28th, 1853 (*Stbl.* No. 24), and April 22nd, 1854 (*Stbl.* No. 70).

continuation of the early fishing system, recommended by them in 1846. The main cause of opposition to early fishing was the Herring-hunting Association's contrary interest. This corporation, or rather annual covenant between shipowners, generally found it inconvenient to equip one or more "hunters" for the sole benefit of the few shipowners who chose to try an early cast of the nets; and all shipowners were obliged to be partners in the association and act upon its rules, in order to have some of their fish brought into market early and sold at the high prices prevalent during the first days of the season. As a fact, the liberty to fish before St. John's Day, though in itself desirable because good herring was sometimes caught at an earlier date, could only be of real use if the sale-hunting monopoly were abolished, and any buss allowed to transfer fish to any other, or sail home at any date with or without a full cargo. Thence the discussion of the laws for early fishing served to throw some light on the evils of the hunting monopoly, and are therefore of importance in the history of the regulation system, although the lawful opening date of the fisheries was not in itself one of its constitutive elements properly said, and could be altered without necessarily affecting the rest. Wherefore the measure of 1846 was not, properly speaking, the beginning of the system's destruction.

Premiums were the vital point in which the system was attacked. It has already been shown that, as sea-fisheries were regulated, bounties to them were necessary and equitable; and that, on the other hand, the fallacies of the bounty system were by this time found out in Holland, not only by political economists, but by the greater part of the enlightened and disinterested public. Fishery bounties threw a peculiarly strong light on the inherent defects of the system: for the trade declined in spite of them, and had, indeed, been in constant decline since bounties had first been given. Accordingly, when in the course of the years 1830-50 Parliament began seriously to oppose protection, the annual budget debates usually brought on a discussion on fishery premiums. The latter were especially the object of pretty general censure in the course of the debates on the budget for 1850, when their gradual abolition was demanded in unequivocal terms. Sea-fishery bounties at this period occasioned an average annual expenditure of about two hundred thousand florins, or some £17,000 sterling, a large sum for so small a State, especially as it was now felt to be poured into a Danaid's vat ; and Government, besides being opposed to premiums as a principle, was of course anxious to reduce or if possible to stop this drain upon the Exchequer. The Department for home affairs, under which matters relative to national industry at the time resorted, was then headed by no less a statesman than the great Mr. Thorbecke ; and he saw clearly that bounties must be stopped, and fishery laws must ultimately follow. A reversed order of repeal might have been preferable, but a good deal of inquiry had yet to be gone through before determining how far the fishery law reform was to go. The subject was dark and delicate, and it was not easy to procure information upon it unless from fishermen, who one and all clung to the wisdom of their fathers and to the country's money, and did their best to oppose or retard reform. Meanwhile, to save money by simplifying institutions (*bezuiniging door vereenvoudiging*) was at the time the popular cry in home politics, and the treasury interest was imperative against the continuation of premiums. Their abolition (by degrees of course) was therefore resolved upon ; and all sea-fishery bounties were reduced by one-tenth by royal decree of February 27th, 1851 (Staatscourant No. 52), under express statement that the step was taken preparatory to the entire abolition of premiums. The stone was now set rolling; and it was generally understood that the whole of sea-fishery legislation was at issue.

The measure of course elicited strong opposition. The whole of the fishing interest, from this moment downward, clamoured against a step which, as they represented it, deprived their tottering trade of its sole support; but failed to see and to appreciate the equivalent of liberty for bounties, which was being prepared for them. Parliament had approved the measure before it was taken. The budget estimate of sea-fishery bounties for 1851 had been lowered by about one-tenth, in accordance with the intentions of Government, and upon previous recommendations by a majority in the Second Chamber. During the debates on the budget, in a memorable night sitting on December 21st, 1850,* a Conservative member, Mr. Wintgens, who in the next years gave much of his attention to fishery matters, moved an amendment to carry the estimate up again to fl.172,000, or the sum granted in the preceding year. The honourable gentleman declared himself, as protectionists without number have done since, an adherent of free trade in principle, and, as such, averse to bounties as a rule; but he claimed circumspection in the rule's application, and this circumspection, in his opinion, was inconsistent even with a 10 per cent. reduction of premiums. A protracted debate ensued, in which the whole of the arguments for premiums, such as they were, were brought out. The importance of the Grand Fishery, even in its then reduced state, and the folly of letting it go to ruin, were exposed at a length the more remarkable, as the debate opened at one and lasted till past three in the morning, an occurrence extremely rare

* *Handelingen* v. d. *Staten-Generaal*, 1850-1, p. 461, *sqq.*

in Dutch parliamentary habits. But no one succeeded in proving, or indeed attempted on logical and historical grounds to prove the point at issue, viz. *that bounties could save the fisheries*; and the fact that British herring-fishery had increased rapidly since the discontinuance of bounties in 1830, was the only truly relevant and conclusive argument preferred in the course of the debate. The result of the night's proceedings was the rejection of Mr. Wintgens' amendment by forty-five votes against sixteen; in other words, a sentence of death passed on premiums, and implicitly on the fishery legislation system in general.

A very important point was now gained; and a reform leading to the ultimate establishment of free fishery was but a matter of time. Government made no secret of its preoccupation to examine into the subject of fishery law repeal, and on several occasions declared in Parliament that the matter was under its constant consideration. It was now to be considered how far, and how fast, the reform was to go. A considerable majority in the Second Chamber of the States-General (or House of Representatives) from 1851 downward lost no occasion to demand immediate and complete repeal of all fishery laws and regulations; but as yet the many evident and latent difficulties of the subject forbade such a course. Existing laws were extremely complicated, sundry interests were involved in the matter; and although in a rational state of things those interests might have been in perfect harmony, monopoly laws had since centuries brought them into collision. Some points, such as the propriety of laws for the protection of fish-life, were overhung with positive uncertainty; all were darkened by contending one-sided representations from the various parties concerned, each of whom, as usual in cases of this nature, nervously clung to its own *prima facie* interest ; and yet Government could scarcely hear any but parties concerned, as no one else was supposed to be a judge of a matter so dependent on personal experience. Cure-herring fishers, for instance, insisted on their monopoly, which smoke-herring fishers wanted to be overthrown ; the case was exactly the reverse as regarded the smoke-herring or "steurharing" monopoly ; and whom could the Minister consult, unless either cure or smoke-herring shipowners? Three Fishery Boards were then in existence : one for the Grand Fishery, one for the fresh-herring and coast fisheries, and one for the Iceland cod-fishery ; and on the several monopolies, the cod-fishers' permission to cure, and the distribution or abolition of premiums, no two of these, when consulted by the Home Department, were of one mind. The whole of the questions involved in the fishery laws were therefore peculiarly hard to elucidate ; and the inquiry preparatory to further measures took some years to lead to a result. And yet Government was at first resolved to rely solely on such information as could be collected by the customary canals of office. Mr. Wintgens, the member of Parliament quoted above, in October 1852 proposed an Inquiry into the whole of the subject by parliamentary committee, an institution then just introduced into Dutch constitutional law. There was much opposition to the plan ; the more so, as a suspicion prevailed that its mover's intention was to have bounties re-established, or at least to counteract their gradual suppression. Mr. Wintgens strongly denied the charge ; but he nevertheless withdrew his proposition at the Minister's request, who declared that a Government inquiry was then proceeding and about to be terminated.

Political events entirely alien to the fishery questions

occasioned Mr. Thorbecke's Cabinet to withdraw from office in the spring of 1853, before the inquiry had led to satisfactory results. Before this, however, the great statesman had taken further steps in the path npon which we have seen him enter. By decree of January 10th, 1852, the reduction of bounties had been carried, for that year, to 25 per cent.; and it was carried to 50 by decree of January 5th, 1853. The prohibition from trawling in winter contained in the decrees of 1825 and 1837, and mentioned in the preceding chapter, was also withdrawn under Mr. Thorbecke's administration ; the initial term of prohibited trawling being shifted from November 15th to December 15th, in November 1852, and the prohibition removed altogether in January 1853.* The latter measure consisted in the entire repeal of the decree of November 15th, 1825, including the control over the nets used in coast fishery, and the premiums for hook-and-line-fishery, during the time when trawling was prohibited. Coast fishery was now free, both in the choice of its implements and the regulation of its fishing time ; and the only measure for the protection of fish life still in vigour was the decree of 1842, on the use of the shrimp net or *saayem*.

Minister van Reenen, Mr. Thorbecke's successor in the Home Department, found the sea-fishery question in this state on coming into office. Being unacquainted with the precise bearings and antecedents of the matter, he was not prepared at once to act in it, and for the moment stopped the process of repeal, by leaving premiums for 1854 at the rate of the preceding year, or half the original amount.† The Minister stated his intention to this effect when laying

---

* Decrees of November 24th, 1852 (*Stbl.* No. 202), and January 29th, 1853 (*Stbl.* No. 8).

† Royal Decree, January 9th, 1854 (*Stbl.* No. 9).

the budget for 1854 before the States-General; and the result was a sharp debate on December 3rd, 1853, in the course of which an amendment to continue the reduction of bounties was moved, and rejected by a majority of only one vote.* The Minister's principal reason for leaving matters *in statu quo* for the nonce was, that he saw a rashness in a farther reduction of premiums unless attended by repeal of the fishery regulation laws, which thorough measure was not as yet warranted by the information obtained by Government inquiry. The debate once more showed the extreme anxiety of a strong majority in the Second Chamber to go through with the matter, and have done with the fishery laws; and this moved Government, at the outset of the year 1854 to appoint a Royal Committee to inquire into the question "whether all sea-fishery laws and regulations could be repealed altogether, or whether it was desirable to maintain, or reenact any part of them."†

Parties immediately concerned in sea-fishery, as may be readily supposed, had not in the meantime been silent in the debate. Both the actual reduction of premiums and the proposed repeal of protective laws, were the object of violent criticism and passionate appeal by the organs of the fishery interest. Kemper's advice in favour of the law of 1818, although given in circumstances long gone by, and overthrown by forty years' experience, did daily service in this discussion. The importance of the fisheries as an ancient branch of genuine national industry, as having been once the "principal gold-mine of the country,"

* *Handelingen van de Tweede Kamer*, 1853-4, p. 288 *sqq.*
† Royal Decree of February 9th, 1854, No. 57. The Committee's Report was published 1854, and has been quoted more than once in the course of this work.

as a recruiting-school for the navy, &c. &c., was passionately urged; and the two main points to be established, viz., the possibility of upholding the business by maintaining bounties and laws, and the certainty of destroying it by repealing both, were taken for granted without examination. The nation was used to such demonstration. Outcries of a similar nature had been raised in succession against each of the several reforms by which, since the Belgian revolution of 1830, Free Trade had gradually been established as a standard principle in Dutch economical policy. There had been a majority, both in and out of Parliament, to back those several measures; and the evils prophesied as sure to attend them had not been felt. Free Trade at the time was implicitly believed in, and was successful. Wherefore on the public at large, and on Parliament especially, the fishery opposition made little or no impression.

Nor was Fishery Law Reform entirely stopped during the first part of Mr. van Reenen's administration. The States of the several Provinces, actuated by the several fishery colleges, and subject to Government approbation, were, as has been shown, legislators in most of the detailed fishery rules; and in this quality they took a share, even before the legislative power of the realm, in the removal of fishery regulations. The rules concerning fresh, or smoke-herring fishery first underwent considerable alteration at the fishers' own request, as preferred by the college for the fresh-herring and coast fishery. The decree relative to the subject, dated December 31st, 1822, had been repealed in 1848, and replaced by two consonant statutes for the Provinces of North and South Holland, into which the former province of Holland had been divided in 1840; but as regards their principal contents, these two enactments were not at variance with the Statute of 1822.* In 1854 at the request of the States of both provinces, the Regulations were altered on two important heads, by the abolition of last money, till then levied from all freshherring fishers by the College, and the shifting of the freshherring fishery's opening date from September 20th to August 20th of each year.† The latter alteration especially indicated a slackening of the monopolising spirit, as on August 20th cure-herring fishery was still in full activity on the Scotch or English coasts, whereas the former opening date of the fresh-herring business had been contrived with a view to keep bumboats out of the herring seas altogether during the height of the cure-herring season. A month afterwards the States of South Holland, (in whose province nearly the whole of the Grand Fishery was then centred) took another and much more decisive step towards the abolition of the curing monopoly, by permitting bumboats to cure all herring caught in the course of any voyage commenced after October 10th. The measure had been strongly urged by the Fresh-herring and Coast Fishery College in the course of the preceding year, and was then retarded, not by any unwillingness on the part of provincial authorities, but by the naked fact of the request having been preferred too late for sanction by the Provincial States ordinary summer meeting.‡ This very important breach in the Grand Fishery's curing monopoly was sanctioned by Royal Decree of September 5th, 1854 (Staatsblad, No. 132), in virtue of the Royal qualification, established by clause 16 of the law of

* Royal Decrees of August 22nd, 1848 (*Staatsblad*, Nos. 36, 37)

† Decrees of August 7th, 1854 (*Staatsblad*, Nos. 109, 110).

‡ See Mr. Gevers van Endegeest's speech on premiums in the Second Chamber, on December 3rd, 1853.

1818,* to grant dispensations from the said monopoly. It will be remembered that the said royal qualification had contributed to make the law of 1818 acceptable to such members of Parliament as then objected to monopolies as a principle. *It was now used for the first time*, at a moment when the repeal of the law itself was looked for on all hands, and in immediate perspective.

On September 29th, 1854, or exactly a fortnight after the momentous date on which the curing monopoly was thus broken into, the Royal Committee appointed in February of the same year laid their Report before the Home Department. If any doubt remained in an unprejudiced mind as to the propriety of doing away with the whole of the sea-fishery laws, this very remarkable document was sufficient to dispel it. It was the result of an inquiry at once thorough, impartial, and dispassionate; and it laid before the public, in a clear and terse resumption, the whole outlines of the sea-fishery system, its faults, and its effects. The Committee's members, four in number, had been selected out of the Permanent Committees of the Provincial States (Gedeputeerde Staten) of South and North Holland ; they had, therefore, had ample occasion in the fulfilment of their daily official duties to acquire well-founded views on sea-fishery questions. Their secretary, now Professor Buys, has since achieved an eminent career in science and political literature. The report was henceforward the elementary handbook for any one desirous to form an opinion in sea-fishery matters. The public at large, as has been said, was then strongly disposed against Protection ; but it is more than probable that most were unacquainted with the exact bearings of the case for and

* Appendix D.

THE HISTORY OF DUTCH SEA FISHERIES. 251

against Protection as applied to fisheries, until they had read the Committee's Report.

It is needless here to dwell on the contents of the document, as most of the matter contained in it has been more amply developed in the preceding pages than in the Report itself. A special mention, however, ought to be made of Appendix I to the Report, containing an account of witnesses examined. Nearly all these witnesses were concerned in fishery or trade in fish; and their evidence, taking all in all, was a mass of contradiction. Parties concerned in the Grand Fishery in 1854 stoutly maintained that obligatory assay of cured-herring was the only way of warranting its quality, and fairly did warrant it; whereas two great dealers in fish stated in as many words that assay, as then practised, gave no warrant whatever, and one of them added that, if made facultative, it might be quite as efficient as when obligatory. Cured-herring fishers and their representatives denied that herring caught by bumboats could yield a tolerable article when cured; fresh-herring bumboat owners, as well as herring dealers, were entirely confident as to the contrary, and if they did not strongly insist on the removal of the Grand Fishery's monopoly, it was chiefly because their own was expected to be withdrawn together with the other. One dealer averred that the "Vereeniging van Zoutharing-reederyen" was ruining herring commerce by enforcing artificial prices and restraining supplies. Another (who was also a shipowner) stated that, as things were, the association acted for the best of both fishers and dealers by regulating the market; but added that entire liberty was the only chance for the herring fishery, whereas delegates from the College of the Grand Fishery strongly insisted on having existing laws maintained, and one buss-owner from Enkhuizen went the length of stating, in the face of the most conclusive statistical evidence, that no decline of the cured-herring fishery had occurred under those laws for twenty years.

Summing up the results of its inquiry, the Committee came to a set of conclusions, which may be rendered as follows:—

The aim of the fishery laws is to have herring sold in small quantities at high prices. The interest of both fishers and consumers requires herring to be abundant and cheap. Therefore the laws ought to be abolished.

And to this end, the Committee laid the draft of a Bill before Government, the chief purport of which was as follows:—

Everybody to be free to fish when, how, and where he finds convenient. Foreign sea-fish to be imported duty free.

Assays of herring to be made facultative. Government to have assayers and branders at the disposal of all who shall require their herring to be branded. Assayers to be appointed by a College for the Netherlands sea-fisheries, *which shall have no other administrative functions whatever*, but be a Consultative Board to Government on sea-fishery matters, *a majority in which shall be composed of men not personally concerned in the trade.*

As exceptions to the general rule of free fishery, the Committee advised to re-enact the prohibition from trawling in winter along the coasts, and to maintain the law against the use of the shrimp-trawl whenever fry of fish should have been found in it. The reason for these exceptions was, that most of the fishers examined by the Committee believed in the exhaustibility of the coast waters by the unrestricted use of ground-nets.

The case had now been heard to satiety. All parties had pleaded their side of it; both the public and the legislative power were fully enabled to pronounce; and a termination of debate was an urgent necessity, as the state of uncertainty about ulterior measures, combined with the suppression of premiums while restrictions remained, for some years reduced the herring fishery at a fast pace indeed. More than a year, however, was still suffered to elapse before a final decision was asked from the legislative power; and the only steps taken in 1855 were a further reduction of both premiums and monopolies, within the range of Government competency. By Decree of January 9th (Staatscourant, No. 10), the reduction of premiums, which had been stopped at 50 per cent. in 1854, was carried to 75 per cent.; and no provision for premiums was made in the budget for the next year, so that none were paid from 1856 downward. Next, the Grand Fishery's curing monopoly having been impaired in 1854, by allowing coast-fishermen to cure herring after October 15th, the coast-fishers' monopoly was reciprocally broken into in 1855, by allowing buss-shippers to salt herring for smoking (*steuren*) after August 20th, or the coast fishery's opening day.* Competition was thus opened, within certain limits, in both branches of fishery; and buss and bumboat owners. from the season of 1855 downward, were each others' competitors on tolerably fair terms, except so far as the latter continued to be precluded from curing in summer.

This remnant of the curing monopoly, besides those of carrying and selling, the prohibition against importing foreign fish, and the rest of the edifice of sea-fishery protection, were now to be cancelled. A law was necessary for this; for the said institutions were either contained in or directly based upon the law of 1818.

* Royal Decree of August 2nd, 1855 (*Bijvoegsel op het Staatsblad*, p. 347).

On December 4th and 7th, 1855, Minister van Reenen brought in two Bills for the final abolition of the system the development and effects of which have been the principal subject of the preceding pages.

One of these Bills, treating of sea-fisheries, was a reproduction of the draft made out by the Committee more than a year before. The other, treating of Customs duties on fish, reduced these duties to an amount equivalent to 10 per cent. on salt and cured-herring and miscellaneous salt fish (*rommeling*) of foreign catch, and abolished them for all other descriptions of fish, whether fresh, salt, dried, or smoked, including shell-fish. The duty on salt-herring was fixed at fl. 1·50, or two shillings and sixpence, on the barrel of 150 pounds. The duty on herring was simply meant as a transitory measure not to expose the fishery at once to the full effect of unrestrained foreign competition. It should be noticed that the absolute prohibition to import any foreign herring contained in the law of 1818 had in the meantime been slightly mitigated. As the Customs tariff stood in 1855, cured-herring was still prohibited, but salt-herring not cured was permitted to be imported in the months between November and May, subject to a duty of fl. 3 on the 100 pounds, and "bucking," or smoked-herring, was admitted at all times under a duty of fl. 0·90 on the thousand.

These two Bills were kept under consideration for a year and a half, owing to a series of mutations in office actuated by political motives alien to the subject of this work. As far as the prevalent opinions in Parliament were concerned both Bills might have been passed in a few weeks. Free Trade, as said, strongly prevailed in Parliament; and as every system is carried to extremities in the first period of its triumph, so "doctrinarism" in Free Trade, and the uncompromising principle of "laissez faire, laissez passer," was predominant with the Liberal side in politics. Thence the history of the Fishery Bills may properly be contained in a very few words. Government went a fair length Free Trade way, and Parliament urged them still farther.

Opposition to the leading idea of the Bills was now confined to the circle of fishery interest, and to those few publicists who, in the days of which we are speaking, openly advocated Protection. In Parliament scarcely a show was made of opposition to Fishery Law Repeal. The Sections' Report on both the Bills commenced by the auspicious statement that the principle laid down by Government had met with nearly universal approbation. Everything which looked like an exception to that principle was objected to. Not a few members wanted the fishery law to consist solely of a clause repealing all existing laws and decrees on the subject—in other words, they wanted the facultative assay, the advising College, and the measures against destruction of fish-life, to be removed out of the Bill, and all Customs duties on fish to be abolished at once. Assay of herring, they said, yielded no proper warrant as to quality, and retarded those expeditions of early herring by which very high prices were made during the first days of each season. The trawling and shrimping restrictions were regarded as unnecessary ; and it was shown upon the occasion that, as to the period when, and the place and depth where, spawn of plaice, sole, flounder, &c., are found in the sea, the opinions of pisciculturists and fishermen were then anything but consistent. Some said that spawn of these fish lay on the bottom, and was therefore destroyed by the trawl-net ; others averred that it swam in the water, and did not suffer from a trawling apparatus. According to some, the period when spawn and fry required undisturbed development lay between November and February; others stated that plaice full of spawn had been caught in May. A conclusive argument against restrictions was drawn from the fact that they did not exist in the Zuider Zee, where plaice, flounder, and turbot survived the effect of the most absolute fishing liberty. It might have been added that the trawl had been used in the North Sea without a restriction for centuries; that its use had only been interrupted or curtailed between 1676–89, and 1825–53; and that exhaustion of the coast waters, or scarcity of fish positively attributable to over-fishing, had never occurred, and the year 1856 was particularly beneficent for trawlers and coast-fishers in general. Besides, foreigners were not subject to the prohibitive laws, and were free to trawl off the Dutch coasts in all seasons; and, as a writer on the subject not inadequately remarked, "if the sea could indeed be emptied or *fished dead* (*doodgevischt*), it was but fair that Dutchmen should have their share of the burial feast." The rule for a temporary prohibition of the use of the shrimp net, whenever fry of fish should have been found in such a net, was opposed on similar grounds. It sacrificed one branch of fishery to another; and many held that fish born under the Dutch coast will migrate to other waters ere it be full-grown, whence to protect such fish in early life would be to put bread into the mouths of Belgians, French and Germans, who would have the benefit of the lives so preserved, although they did not use reciprocity in the matter. Even a College, or Board of Fisheries, was objected to, although its proposed attributes were merely to supervise assays, and advise Government in fishery matters. The paralysing sway so long held over fishermen by Boards, Colleges, and Associations of a very different nature evidently scared some of the more uncompromising Free

Traders, and made them shun the notion of having a Board at all.

These men of thorough measures did not, however, ultimately carry the day. The Fishery Bill was debated on March 7th, 1857; and facultative assay of herring, as well as an advising College, obtained a majority. On the other hand, a learned and lengthy speech by a member versed in natural history settled the fate of restrictions on trawling and shrimping, and they were removed by amendment. The law, as ultimately adopted,* simply established the entire liberty of all sea fishery in the largest sense of the word, and repealed all prohibitions of the importation of sea-fish. Next it established facultative assays of herring caught in Dutch vessels, and instituted a College to appoint assayers and generally promote the sea-fisheries' interests by advising Government in matters relative to them. The Bill on Customs duties on fish underwent some vicissitudes. It was amended so as *at once* to abolish all such duties; and the amendment was carried in the Lower House by a majority of one vote. The Upper House, or First Chamber of the States-General, then rejected the Bill by a slight majority. Government brought it in once more, in its primitive wording, in September 1857, when a fresh conflict was avoided by an amendment reducing duties on salt-herring and "rommeling" to half the amounts proposed. Their entire abolition took place two years afterwards.†

Provincial regulations were repealed soon after the new law was passed, as contrary to its purport; and a new law as a base for future administrative rules on the immunity of

* Dated June 13th, 1857 (*Staatsblad*, No. 86). An error in the text was removed by law of August 13th, 1857 (*Staatsblad*, No. 102).

† Laws of Dec. 11th, 1857 (*Staatsblad*, No. 122) and Dec. 23rd, 1859 (*Staatsblad*, No. 136).

salt excise was established simultaneously with the new Customs tariff on fish.* Some control against fraud is of course inevitable whenever an article subject to excise duty is exempted from it when consumed for one special purpose ; and the object of the new regulation was to make that control as easy as possible for fishermen, as a compensation for eventual damage by foreign competition attendant upon the reduced tariff.

A regulation upon assays of herring was made in time before the opening of the herring season of 1858.† The new rules were as simple as was consistent with maintaining the accustomed appearance of Dutch brand-herring. The old distinctions of "full-maatjes," "ijlen," any of these either sound or "*wrak*," were maintained, with a brand for each. To these was added a new brand for "overnight," or herring cured the day after its capture, which process was now permitted, whereas former regulations forbade such herring to be cured. A new distinction was likewise made between herring caught in deep sea, under the North Sea coast, and in the Zuider Zee ; the latter two qualities being now allowed to be cured as well as the one first named. Every barrel of assayed herring was thus to carry two brands, one stating its description, and the other where it was caught. The figure of the brand, formerly representing a lion, was altered into the royal crown ; and it will be shown in the next chapter what evil consequences attended that alteration. Assayers were to brand all herring presented to them, unless the barrel were defective, or not stamped with the owner's mark and filled from top to bottom with herring of one single description. Care was thus taken that there should be a Dutch brand as of

* Law of Dec. 11th, 1857 (*Staatsblad*, No. 123).
† Decree of January 11th, 1858 (*Staatsblad*, No. 2).

old, to which foreign dealers were used; but any one who chose was free to sell or export unbranded herring.

Sea-fishery Reform was now complete, and the trade allowed entire liberty in every respect. I shall briefly relate, in a last chapter, what effects were wrought by the measure.

CHAPTER IV.

REVIVAL.

IT is, I believe, a fact now known on every considerable fish market that Dutch sea-fisheries have been increasing fast for the last fifteen years. There is no need of words to state the fact; it may be seen at a glance from the fishery statistics of the last twenty-five years, the leading figures of which I have compiled from the annual Reports of the College, or Board of Sea-fisheries, instituted in 1857, and beg to lay before the reader in Appendices K, L, and M. It now remains to be shown how the increase, and indeed the entire revival of the business, was a direct consequence of fishing liberty substituted for fishery regulation. The task is an easy one; for, from 1857 downward, the above-named Reports contain every particular relative to the history of Dutch sea-fisheries.

The revival alluded to is nowhere so apparent as in the herring fisheries; for a general survey of which, from 1857 downward, I refer the reader to Appendix K. It will be seen from this table:—

1st.—That bumboat fishers in the coast villages used their new-gotten right to cure herring on an insignificant scale for some ten years after they had obtained it.

2ndly.—That the prices fetched by their cured-herring were, on an average, not much inferior to those of "buss-herring" cured in keeled vessels.

3*rdly.*—That they began to cure herring on a much larger scale in 1866 and subsequent years.

4*thly.*—That the whole production of cured-herring, and the number of ships employed in that production, took a leap upwards about the same time, and they have since then been constantly increasing.

5*thly.*—That a gradual lowering of cured-herring prices (see the *lowest* prices in columns 12 and 14) coincides with the increase of production.

Thus the irrefutable verdict of statistics now corroborates what *one* corporation realised in 1829, and what the Committee on Fisheries in 1854 set down as the fundamental idea of reform, viz. *that abundant capture, and not high prices, were the means of restoring the Dutch herring fisheries;* whereas the ancient system was based on the opposite theory.

Abundant capture (setting aside, of course, the vicissitudes of herring seasons) could only be, and was, obtained by means of improvement in the fishing processes. The progress of these improvements may be described as follows : the net of hemp was supplanted by the cotton net, the use of the cotton net brought luggers and cutters into use instead of the old clumsy "hookers"; and the use of new nets and ships caused the capture to increase five-fold in fifteen years. The cotton net therefore gave the impulse to the thorough revival of the fishery; *and the cotton net could not have been used under the Grand Fishery Regulation,* 1827, *which prescribed all nets to be made of hemp yarn.*

An eminent shipowner, Mr. A. E. Maas, of Scheveningen, was the first to import cotton herring-nets from Lowestoft, about 1857 ; and at the outset used those nets in bumboats only. The superior catching power of the nets at once became apparent. Being much lighter than hemp, larger fleets could be used, and more water covered ; and at the same time their depth could be made greater without the weight causing the upper meshes to contract, and be of no avail. But, as a set-off to their lightness, cotton nets were found subject to more wear and tear than the solid net of the ancestors. Mr. Maas spent some years in tanning and boiling experiments to make them as durable as hemp ; and cotton prices being at the time up, in consequence of the American war, it was not till 1865 that the use of cotton nets fairly began to spread among herring ship-owners.

Several causes besides the dearth of cotton meantime counteracted the effect of the new law. Both shipowners and dealers had to get accustomed to liberty before learning how to turn it to account. A body of men brought up from childhood to strict observation of a set of rules precluding all innovation whatever, could scarcely be expected, immediately upon the withdrawal of those rules, to turn their attention to novelties, and invest money in experiments, or look abroad for examples, all of which operations they had been taught to regard as the breaking of sacred laws. Fetter a man down through life, and when set free he will be some time in recovering the use of his limbs. Besides these psychological causes for a continued stagnation, positive checks at first kept the herring-fishery down. Years elapsed before an enlightened administration, advised by a College of competent men, could, under the salt excise law of 1857, regulate the conditions of freedom of salt excise for fishermen in such a manner as not to thwart the development of the several branches of sea-fishery. The herring seasons of 1857–1861 were in general unfavourable, and the returns below the average, and sometimes bad. Much capital had of late been lost in the business; and the state of suspense in which it had been kept between 1850 and 1857, when bounties were gradually withdrawn and uncertainty prevailed as to future fishing liberty, had especially done much to reduce it, and scare fresh capital away. Extensive markets, such as those of Northern Germany, Hamburg, Bremen, and Stettin, which in former centuries were supplied by Dutch brand-herring exclusively, were now entirely lost; and customs tariffs in some countries thwarted an extension of exports, while Scotch herring was prevalent everywhere, and very far ahead in the race. The commercial treaty with Belgium expired on January 1st, 1858; and the severe prejudice caused to Dutch fisheries by the elevation of tariffs attendant upon the event was by no means counterbalanced by the abolition of differential duties against importation of Dutch fish in Russia, which took place in the next year. But the greatest enemies of Dutch herring in the markets abroad, it must be owned, were Dutch dealers. Prices of good Dutch brand-herring were then still as a rule above those of Scotch; and no sooner was importation of herring permitted than some Dutch dealers hastened to import Scotch herring of anything but the best quality, and export it repacked, not under the new Dutch crown-brand, but in old barrels marked with the *abolished* brand, consisting of the figure of a lion. The fraud was generally detected too late by foreign buyers, because the change in the brand had not been efficiently brought to the knowledge of dealers abroad; and when detected and reported on it could not be punished, because it had been omitted to enact penalties against the use of abolished brands. Thus the liberty to forego assay was at first misapplied for purposes of delusion, and the perpetrators of the fraud of course were themselves the victims of their short-sighted artifice. The alteration of assay rules in 1858 contributed to spoil the market. Under the Regulation of 1827 herring was assayed and sorted with tolerable accuracy immediately upon being landed, and a preliminary mark was generally put on the barrels to certify the result. The large barrels, loosely packed as they were on board, where close and careful packing of herring was an impossibility, were next sold to wholesale dealers, and by them delivered into the hands of *packers*, who transferred the fish to barrels of the regulation size, shape and construction, and the article was, by this re-packing, prepared to receive the official brand for exportation. These *packers*, who were alone entitled to transfer herring from the "sea barrel" (*ton zeestuks*) into the brand-barrel, were public officials, and under oath, like the assayers themselves, whence there was a fair certainty that the contents of the "sea-barrels" should be transferred to the exportation barrel without any tampering; and the barrels issuing from the packers' hands could be, and were generally, branded by the assayer with the exportation brand, without renewed examination of their contents. Under the Regulation of 1858, which was the first piece of work prepared by the new College (and owned by them in their Report for 1859 to have been deficient in several points) there were no sworn "packers," and the assayers' own verification was required for the exportation brand as well as for the first marking of the sea-barrel; the latter operation being still a requisite to shield first-hand buyers against fraud. Now, however diligent the assayers (and as to their diligence and honesty there are no serious complaints to my knowledge) it was beyond their power to effectually and *twice* control the immense quantities of fish subjected to them under the spur and hurry of the early "hunting" days of the season, when every dealer was anxious to have thousands of barrels branded and exported at once. The first assay upon landing was done as usual, and the first sale of the herring to the inland wholesale dealer was effected upon its credit ; but for thoroughly performing the second there was no time left, and the inspection previous to giving the crown-brand was generally very superficial, allowing much refuse of the Scotch fisheries to obtain the Dutch brand, and spoil its renown abroad. A revision of the branding rules in 1860, and another in 1861,* intended to introduce an easier mode of control, and prevent foreign herring from obtaining the Dutch brand, failed to accomplish the purpose. Both the old and new brands continued to be put on bad foreign herring ; and the fraud was even turned into open connivance with foreign dealers, who had " Scotch herring in Dutch fustage," consigned to them at prices above those of Scotch and under those of genuine Dutch fish, and in their turn made their clients pay the latter. Although of course highly prejudicial to the sale of the genuine article, these dealings could not be stopped ; and they went on, on a scale more or less extensive as herring prices ruled higher or lower, until the average prices of Dutch brand gradually came down to a level with, and even below, those of Scotch crown-brand, chiefly owing to the frauds described. Then, of course, there was no longer a profit in selling Scotch herring for Dutch ; and the only way of making fraudulent gain lay in obtaining the Dutch " full," or " maatjes," crown-brand for herring of inferior quality, which practice never could be stopped entirely until the official brand was finally abolished altogether. Assayers always did their utmost ;

* Decrees of March 4th, 1860 (*Staatsblad*, No. 11) and February 24th, 1861 (*Staatsblad*, No. 13).

but their control was not now more efficient than it was in former centuries, when we have seen foreign dealers frequently complain of bad herring being sold under Dutch prime brands.

Such were the principal reasons which in the first ten years after the legislative reform counteracted actual improvement, the progress of which shall now be described.

Cotton nets had been first used in bum-boats, as said above, about 1857, and were in a keeled vessel in 1861. In 1865 about one-third of the fleet had some cotton nets on board, but not a vessel could use many of them; for on account of their lightness they did not sufficiently steady the clumsy "hookers" while lying before the fleet. The virtue which increased the catching power of the nets was a defect as regards navigation; and whenever a fleet chiefly composed of cotton nets was tried, the vessel was apt, as soon as part of the nets was got on board, in rough weather to drift across the rest. The evil might have been stopped by enlarging the fleets; but there is, of course, a limit to the surface of net that can be managed in one ship of a given size. Experience soon showed that light vessels were required to get the full avail out of cotton fleets; and this seems to have been the reason why they were at first principally used in bumboats, two of which, belonging to Mr. Maas, tried the Shetland seas in 1862, being the first Dutch flat-bottomed vessels ever seen in those waters. But if bum-boats were light, they on the other hand afforded too little stowage for an abundant catch. The point to be gained was to have a vessel at once light enough to manage a cotton fleet in all weathers, and capacious enough to carry as much herring as could be caught in such a fleet.

Mr. Maas, now as formerly ahead in fishery innovation,

solved this problem in 1866, by sending out a lugger built upon a model from Boulogne. The vessel had as yet more hemp than cotton in her fleet; she had upon the whole not a favourable catch, and she began to fish three weeks late, and thence did not share in "hunting" prices. In spite of these disadvantages, she covered her building and equipping expenses, including two complete fleets in six voyages, and in the first year yielded a net return of thirty-seven per cent. The splendid success of this first lugger in the Dutch fleet, named by her owner the *Scheveningen*, after his residence, was the signal of a rapid revolution in the country's herring-fishery. Four luggers were launched in 1866; and the number increased very rapidly in the next years. All new ships built were either luggers or cutters; and the wharves on the Maas had a busy time of it. The old "hookers" were sometimes sold off before being worn out; and the transformation was so rapid that, in 1872-3 and 1875-6, there was actually a decrease in the strength of the herring fleet,* owing solely to old vessels being sold off faster than new ones could be built. The following figures show the progress of this most important reform:

Years.	Hookers and sloops.	Luggers and cutters.	Years.	Hookers and sloops.	Luggers and cutters.
1867	85	4	1875	25	90
1868	80	11	1876	17	92
1869	79	28	1877	19	94
1870	69	51	1878	18	109
1871	58	64	1879	14	114
1872	44	64†	1880	12	121
1873	34	68	1881	11	127
1874	31	83			

* See Appendix K.
† The stand-still in lugger-building in 1872 is apparent, not real. Six luggers were in that year transferred to a German herring company formed at Emden, whose directors prevailed upon a Dutch

Improvements in other fishing material went hand in hand with this renovation of the fleet. Sea-fishery exhibitions, as will be remembered, were very frequent about the time now spoken of; and in each of them the Netherlands exhibits outshone those of preceding years. Objects considered and reported upon as novelties at Amsterdam in 1861, and at Bergen (Norway) in 1865, proved antiquated in 1867 at the Hague. British cotton net-yarns created a sensation at the first-named exhibition; Dutch cotton yarns, and nets made out of them, the produce of several inland factories which did a brisk business in them, were medalled at the latter. And it is to be noticed that this strenuous expansion of the whole of the fishery business was obtained without a single florin of subsidy. Up to 1861 Government had contributed towards equipping a "hospital ship," the nature of which has been explained in a former chapter. The subsidy had been gradually lessened, and declined by the common herring shipowners in 1861, since when no "hospital-ship' was sent out.

The organization of the herring shipowning business in

---

shipowner to sell them the whole of his ships and materials, and take the direction of their business. Any one inclined to pursue patriotism into superstition may read a warning against selling the nationality of a ship or a business in this Emden company's fate. Their ships, managers, and management were Dutch; they fished in the same seas and seasons as Dutch; and yet they never could make catches or returns like Dutch vessels of exactly the same description. While Dutch shipowners, being entirely unprotected, were making handsome dividends, the Emdeners, who have a "protective" customs tariff to shield, and an immense national market to support them, have for ten years hardly shown their shareholders the colour of their money, and were in 1881 still deeply indebted to their Government for subsidial loans not paid back.

the same period likewise underwent a material change. New vessels of course demanded considerable capital, and as their catch averaged from forty to one hundred per cent. above that of the "hookers," capital was invested in them freely enough. Shipowning companies, limited, sprang up, and superseded the partnerships of the old type, many of which liquidated as their hookers were broken up or sold off. The institution of "sale-hunting" shared the general reform. The Herring-hunting Association, which, as said before, was in a previous period formed every year to carry home early herring from the fleet, had continued annually since the law of 1857 had abolished the "hunting" privilege and restriction, and any shipowner was free to carry herring home at such a time and in such quantities as he chose. One firm only kept outside from the beginning; most shipowners found it expedient to be partners in the association for some of their vessels, in order to secure the enormous prices of the opening season, or "hunting time," for some part of their catch; but the association's general expenses were so high as gradually to drive out many vessels; and owners, while they kept some of theirs on the association's books, left out an increasing percentage. The association's mode of operating was also materially altered. It had, till now, kept up the old traditions. Partners bound themselves not to have their ships home before a date annually fixed by common consent, unless with an exceptional cargo; and the fish brought home before that date in the association's "hunters" was sold at certain minimum prices, and kept on hand if prices in the early season were unfavourable. The latter practice was now abandoned, and the whole stock sold in auction for the partners' account as soon as landed. Thus the institution of "hunting" became what it should have been from the beginning: an annual contract of carriage for common account between shipowners, and lost the monopolising character it had adopted in the height of the regulation period.

As for innovations in fishing properly said, the main feature of the period now spoken of, is the mixing up of the two branches formerly known as grand and small fishery. Fresh herring or "*steurharing*" began to be brought home in luggers, whose crews thereby managed to turn to account portions of their catch which there was no time to cure, and sometimes, when the catch in the ordinary herring waters was not favourable, went into seas where no keeled vessels were permitted to go by the law of 1818, and made the capture of fresh-herring their business for the time. On the other hand, the pickling of herring in coast bumboats increased exceedingly fast in the years succeeding 1870; so that both the curing and the fresh herring monopoly of old were now not only abolished by law, but had actually fallen into entire disuse among fishermen, and there was no longer a grand fishery in keeled, and a small fishery in flat vessels. The latter fished for herring as early, and in the same waters, as luggers and cutters, which in their turn sometimes invaded the continental shore waters, and did bumboats' work. A glance at the figures in Appendix K will show that not a vestige was ever felt of the dread consequences which we have, in former parts of this work, seen both parties predict as sure to attend such mutual competition. There was indeed a decline in pickle-herring prices, partly occasioned, as has been shown, by dealers tampering with the brand; but the average prices of fresh-herring and "bucking" at the same time showed a tendency to rise, owing to the widening of the market for the latter; and in both branches of the business, the liberty to choose a fishing place, a fishing gear, and a curing process according to the state of the season and the market, amply made up for increased competition.

The brand, and the more and more apparent impossibility of preventing abuse of it, still continued to thwart progress. I shall conclude this account of Dutch herring-fishery by briefly relating how this last monument of Government interference with it came to be abolished like the rest.

From lugger fishery, as stated just now, there ensued a promiscuousness of the herring-fishery's produce. Besides deep-sea herring as of old, luggers in 1867, and subsequently, brought home fish caught off the continental coasts, which in quality was decidedly inferior. Now, the branding regulations of 1860 and 1861 had ordained distinct brands, certifying herring to have been caught either in the high seas (V. Z. V., or high-sea catch brand), under the coast (K. V., or coast-catch brand) or in the Zuider Zee. The latter brand was never or very seldom given, as Zuider Zee herring of late years has ultimately proved unfit for curage; but lugger skippers were in the habit, although they often fished under the coast, of declaring all their cured-herring as high-sea catch. They generally obtained the V. Z. V. brand for inferior fish, as an efficient control never could be carried into execution. Bumboat owners, on the other hand, not only cured herring on a large scale, but actually sometimes cured it *ashore*, contrary to all ancient notions and prescriptions; and fish thus cured, though certainly much inferior to fish cured on the day of the capture, obtained the same brand as the latter. It became, in short, an impossibility under the new fishery *regimen* to certify where herring had been caught; and a new regulation approved by Royal Decree of May 11th, 1868 (Staatsblad

No. 66), accordingly ordained the V. Z. V. or K. V. brands to certify, not where fish should have been *caught*, but where it should have been *cured*, *i.e.* whether at sea or ashore. At the same time, as the promiscuous use of the several fishing methods led to promiscuous results, the main stress of the brand certificate was laid, not as formerly on the place where herring should have been either caught or prepared, but on its *actual quality;* and a new sub-division was introduced into the three great descriptions of Dutch brand herring (full, "maatjes," and "ylen"), each of which was to be furthermore stamped either 1A, 2A, or 3A, according to its quality upon test. This arrangement of course greatly increased the assayers' task and responsibility; and as accurate verification of the contents of each barrel became more utterly impossible in proportion as the yields of the annual catches increased, it soon became customary to brand herring as Full 1A, Maatjes 1A, or ylen 1A, as the case might be, upon little besides the owner's authority. The circumstance of course by no means increased the brands' repute abroad. Moreover, the change in the brands proved an evil in itself, inasmuch as in some foreign markets confusion once more ensued between the old brands and the new.

To abolish the Government brand was the only way out of these several difficulties, as the Sea-Fishery Board clearly saw; but they did not venture to advise the measure unless Great Britain should cease to brand at the same time. Foreign correspondents averred herring not bearing an official mark to be unsaleable so long as Scotch branded herring should be in the market; and overtures made by the Dutch to the British Government about a simultaneous abolition of brands were received in a very friendly and congenial spirit, but ultimately led to nothing, owing to circumstances which it is unnecessary here to mention. Dutch brands gradually lost most of their reputation ; and the loss was the worse, as *no unbranded herring was exported as long as the brand existed*, upon the representations of the dealers' correspondents abroad.* Thus, as a fact, the brand, after having been for three centuries and a half held on all hands to be the *palladium* of Holland's greatness in the herring market, was now found out to be the main stumbling-block in the path of its progress.

The quality brands, or 1A, 2A, and 3A marks, instituted in 1868, were given up in 1875† on account of the difficulties just now exposed, and the simple brand in use till 1868, stating, besides the year of the catch and the place of curage, the herring's quality as full, "maatjes," or "ylen," was reinstated. No change for the better ensued ; and the Fishery Board, after taking the opinion of many considerable herring shipowners and dealers, in their report for 1875 earnestly advised to abolish the brand, *without waiting for England's co-operation*. It was high time, in the Board's opinion, for Government to stop warranting the quality of an article of which it knew little or nothing, to the detriment of trade in an important article of exportation. The advice was followed, and a Bill for the abolition of the official brand laid before Parliament in June 1877. An intervening political crisis delayed the measure for about a year ; and when adopted by Parliament it was too late to put it into operation for the herring-

---

* Nearly none of the herring cured in bumboats was indeed branded upon landing, but nearly the whole of the fish was carried to Vlaardingen to be mixed up with the lugger-herring landed there, and exported under crown-brand.

† Royal Decree, March 27th, 1875 (*Stbl.* No. 31).

season of 1878 ;* and June 1st, 1879, was determined upon for its execution. From this date downward assayers appointed by the College have still continued to examine any pickle-herring presented to them, but the operation now bears a strictly private commercial character. The assayer's task is now no other than that of a common commercial expert; and he gives no official certificate whatever. Penalties have this time been enacted against the use of the abolished brands, and as a consequence no complaints of this abuse have arisen. Four seasons have elapsed since the measure was taken ; and its effects have been decidedly very beneficial. As long as there were Government brands, dealers but too often sought profit in obtaining those brands for fish undeserving of them. Since the brand was abolished they have been obliged, like dealers in any other article, to get their own trade-marks respected and sought abroad by strictly attending to the quality of the goods. The measure was, in fact, nothing but a final link in the chain of consequent fishery reform, and a completion of the system adopted in 1857, viz. to make parties concerned look for profit to nothing but their own vigilance, industry, and honesty, and stop their ancestral habit of leaning upon Government measures taken in their behalf. The law of 1857 had put a stop to the herring fishery's utter rottenness ; it was reserved for the law of 1878 to bring about a state of entire soundness in its stead.

Of such a thorough soundness the herring business has indeed since 1879 given the most substantial proofs. By the aid of very favourable seasons, both fishing returns and exports have, as shown by Appendix K, increased in the

* Law of May 7th, 1878 (*Stbl.* No. 37).

late years at a rate hitherto unknown.* Care has been taken that the law of 1878 should be known on every foreign market in time before its coming into vigour ; and foreign dealers in the season of 1879 were fully aware that there was no longer a Dutch official crown brand. Far from showing a diffidence towards herring not bearing that mark, they may be said to have ceased to mistrust Dutch fish since the removal of a Government certificate, the fallacy of which had been proved to satiety. Several markets, where in the course of the present century Dutch cured herring had ceased to appear, are now taking the article with increasing eagerness. Prices, which under the brand system had fallen below those of Scotch herring, are once more steadily rising above them, as regards the better descriptions of the article. The south of Germany is, as formerly, the greatest market for Dutch pickle-herring, in spite of the German tariff. Exports to Belgium have much increased since a new treaty of commerce was concluded with that power ; the United States have of late years become a market of importance ; and the North German markets, upon which we have in former parts of this work seen Dutch herring predominant, are being, so to say, re-conquered by the sheer force of the article's worth. Stettin herring statistics are conclusive evidence to the fact. No Dutch herring had been seen on that market for years ; whereas the quantities brought in, and nearly

* The Fishery Report for 1882 has not been published while this is being written, and will not appear before a couple of months are over. It should therefore be remembered that the above statements can be backed by official statistics only as to the years including 1881. It can, however, be stated now that the year 1882 has also been a very favourable one as regards catch, exports, and prices. Dutch herring fishers and dealers are now quite confident to sell the whole of their produce at good prices, however fast the supply may increase.

THE HISTORY OF DUTCH SEA FISHERIES. 275

all sold off at the end of each year have in the latter years been as follows:

Years.	Barrels.	Years.	Barrels.
1875	302	1879	3,663
1876	530	1880	13,584
1877	848	1881	5,915
1878	1,446	1882	10,593

I have now, as throughout the present work, treated matters relative to Dutch herring fishery with particular care, for the obvious reason that this branch is the one most closely connected with legislation on fisheries, and therefore directly responding to the subject given for the present essay. A few words still remain to be said of the other branches since 1857; some of which, although unconnected with legislation, are still of considerable importance.

The fate of hook-fishery (for cod, flat-fish, &c.) may be resumed in the simple statement: that it is now carried on in the North Sea exclusively, and is gradually being absorbed in, or superseded by, the herring business, and is chiefly kept going by the capture of fresh fish, not of cod for salting. Bumboat owners of Scheveningen, Katwijk and Noordwijk, are gradually abandoning the hooks, or *beugvaart*, and occupy the time between herring seasons chiefly by trawling for fresh fish. In the two villages of Egmond and Zandvoort, where herring fishery has become unusual, the trawl is likewise the implement most used. Herring ships continue hook-fishery between herring seasons, i.e. in winter and spring ; but the returns often amount to a clear loss, and the reason why many ships are not kept at home between herring seasons is chiefly to keep their crews together, and have men ready in June. At the same time, luggers sometimes use the trawl instead of the hooks and lines in winter and spring ; whereas a trawl-net and a keeled vessel were formerly held as objects entirely incompatible. What remains of the once important "*beugvaart*" is exercised by vessels of all descriptions and hailing from many parts of the country ; and it is therefore difficult to give anything like complete statistics of the business. The figures contained in Appendix L, and relative to exports of salt cod, will show that cod-fishery, the only branch in which no other gear than hooks can be used, has not shared the increase of other branches. The maintenance of prohibitive tariffs on foreign salt-cod in France has contributed much to keep the salt cod business down. Two more important causes have of late years likewise checked its progress. Firstly, a series of circumstances have contributed to keep the fish called *geep*, the usual bait for cod-hooks, at inconveniently high prices. Secondly, profits are much greater in fresh fishery than in the salt-cod industry. The two are indeed much mixed up ; for most of the flat-fish and haddock brought home from hooking trips to the North Sea is sold fresh.

Of fresh fishery it is difficult to give accurate statistics, owing to the same circumstance just stated for hook-fishery. Vessels of every description and from every fishing port and coast locality are now employed in this lucrative business ; and it is carried on with implements of several descriptions, and in part jointly with fishery for cod to be salted. Its actual importance can, like that of the latter, best be shown by export figures; which have been collected in Appendix M. The reasons why exports of fresh fish should have increased at the very fast rate shown by this table, may be evident to any one upon the very slightest reflection. It is, simply, the increase of railway traffic, and the care now taken by continental railway directors to provide cheap and fast conveyance for fish. Fresh fish caught by Dutch vessels may, owing to the said circumstance, any day be eaten all over Belgium; and the importance of the German market on this score is being keenly realised by Dutch dealers. Packing in ice is of course increasing at the same rate, as exports of fresh fish; and companies exclusively destined to work this new mine have sprung up of late years, and are in a flourishing condition. Nieuwediep, particularly well situated in the centre of the North Sea and Zuider Zee fresh fisheries, and for years past directly connected with all Europe by rail, is fast increasing in importance as a fresh fish market. Ymuiden, the new North Sea port of Amsterdam, seems by its geographical position to be destined to a similar importance; and fresh fishery may be susceptible of any degree of increase in the towns of Vlaardingen and Maassluis, when the plan for giving them a direct communication by rail with Rotterdam, and the rest of the world, shall have been fully carried out, as it will be soon. Rapid conveyance is of course the mainspring of the fresh-fish business; and it cannot be denied that in this respect, as applied to the fishery interest, Holland has much to learn from foreign countries. Still we are now very far from the days of yore when "*de neeringhe van den versche*" was a despised business, fit for small men without capital, and yielding a pittance. A shadow, however, seems to impend over this flourishing trade; to wit, complaints of impaired catch. It is said by some, that the North Sea is showing signs of exhaustion, possibly by over-trawling.

The latest Fishery Board Reports mention the circumstance more than once; and not a fortnight ere this is written, bumboat trawlers from Scheveningen reported that "the sea seemed fished out (*doodgevischt*)." We have in former chapters seen similar complaints raised at more than one period; and if they were unfounded *then*, the case may be different now the number of trawlers of all nations in the North Sea has very much increased. Trawling prohibitions, shrimping restrictions, &c., may possibly within a few years become once more the fishery topic of the day.

Measures of a similar nature, i.e. to prevent the extinction of fish-life, have since years been the preoccupation of Government as regards the Zuider Zee. It has been remarked in an earlier part of this work, that whatever may be the probabilities of the North Sea being exhausted, the inlet called Zuider Zee, being small and very shallow, is certainly more liable to exhaustion than the wide main; and we have seen, in former centuries, men of the provinces surrounding this gulf engaged in long-winded disputes, and even in actual contests, to secure the conservation of a stock of fish. As a fact, in the last fifteen years the yield of pan-herring and flat-fish from the Zuider Zee has been declining ;* and complaints of exhaus-

---

* Some figures relative to Zuider Zee fishery since 1857 have been collected into Appendix N. They are anything but complete; for pan-herring caught in the said water has during this period been brought to several other markets besides Monnickendam, and the fresh-fish returns (plaice, flounder, sole, turbot, eel, &c.) form no part of the table.

tion of the water have not unfrequently occurred ever since 1857, becoming towards 1880 constant and loud. A local inquiry instituted by delegates from the Sea Fishery College in 1878 showed that the peculiar species of small herrings caught in the Zuider Zee and sold as "pan-herring" were indeed liable to be destroyed by the use of narrow nets, and that anchovy-fishery with very narrow pocket-nets, dragged through the water at a great speed, either between two vessels or between two beams rigged out from one boat, might be presumed to extirpate herring, as fry of herring was caught in those nets in great quantities, and thrown away or sold as manure. Some Zuider Zee fishermen, it appears, were actually in the habit of "fishing for manure" in this manner, when no full-grown fish could be caught. The pocket-nets alluded to, and especially the net used between two boats and called *wonderkuil* from the astonishing returns of small fish yielded by it, could not however be prohibited altogether; for without them it was not possible to catch anchovy, which article, as shown by Appendix N, continues to be of much importance in the Zuider Zee. Anchovy is not a fish resident in the said water, but visits it in the early summer, generally between May 15th and July 15th, when there is no pan-herring fishery of importance; and the plain way to conciliate the interests of both trades was, therefore, to allow the use of the incriminated pocket-nets between the said dates, and to prohibit it at all other times. A statute to that effect has accordingly been established by law of June 21st, 1881 (Staatsblad No. 76), which, further to prevent the destruction of herring, flounder, and smelt, prohibits at any time to buy or sell, transport, possess, or use fish of those descriptions inferior to certain dimensions. In a word, statutes analogous to those described in Part III. chapter IV., have been called into life again, and are in vigour at this moment.

The same law of June 21st, 1881, in which these statutes are contained, regulates a few more subjects relative to fishery, of which brief mention ought to be made in the present work.

The tenth clause of the law empowers Government to prohibit the killing of seals in certain parts of the Northern seas, and during certain seasons. The enactment existed before, and has only been repeated in the law of 1881 in order to collect all legislative dispositions relative to fisheries into one single statute ; the unrepealed clauses of the law of 1857 being likewise repeated in 1881 for the same reason. The Government's faculty to restrict seal-killing by Dutchmen was first established by law of Dec. 31st, 1876 (Staatsblad No. 289) and executed by Royal Decree of February 15th, 1877 (Staatsblad No. 19), by which Dutchmen were prohibited from killing seals in certain high latitudes before April 3rd of each year. The measure was enacted upon the invitation of the British Government ; it was at the time, and is now, of no importance whatever for the Netherlands, as the last enterprise of seal and walrus-killing in the Northern seas had come to an infelicitous termination in 1875, the year before the law, and the business has not been since resumed. Walrus-killing in latter years only deserves mention because it has been, so to say, the last glimpse of the once flourishing trade of whaling. I have stated in a former chapter that the latter business was kept up late in the present century by two vessels from Harlingen under the stimulus of premiums, without which it would have been given up much earlier. The last whales were caught by these vessels in 1851 and 1852, each of which seasons produced *one* fish ; and they have since made it their sole business to knock the seal on the head and kill the walrus in the Arctic seas, this also having been given up in 1875, on account of insufficient returns. A few seals are still annually killed in the Zuider Zee and Zealand estuaries. But of the bold spirit which caused Dutchmen of old to look for gain, and find plenty, in the Northern seas, a spark has survived the utter ruin of Dutch whaling. A seaman of spirit and experience, Mr. Bottemanne,* in 1869 prevailed upon some capitalists to invest in a whaling enterprise, the aim of which was to kill the animals, not by harpoons thrown from boats, but by the modern contrivance of the rocket-shell-harpoon shot from a gun on board a steamer. A company was formed, and fitted out a whaling vessel of this description, under Mr. Bottemanne as commander. He made his first voyage in 1870, and secured only one fish, owing to inexperience in the use of the artillery. In the next year better aim was taken and 26 whales were shot, but half of them lost, mainly owing to deficiencies in the lines and gear. The returns of 1872 were still worse; and the Whaling Company of Rotterdam, which had chartered the steamer, was forced to liquidate. Another attempt to create a similar company was made in 1875, but failed for want of partners; and whaling, once the second in importance of the Dutch sea-fisheries,

---

* Any one who writes a *complete* history of Dutch sea-fisheries in the last quarter of a century will have to make very frequent mention of this remarkable personage. With a sailor's love for salt-water Mr. Bottemanne combines a scientist's interest for, and extensive knowledge of, the creatures that live in it. He has been a merchant-captain and a whaler; he is now Inspector of the Fisheries in the Schelde and Zealand Estuaries, and his thorough and practical ichthyological acquirements have made him the constant adviser, in matters of salmon fishery, oyster-culture, and similar subjects, of both the Government and the Sea-Fishery Board.

is now quite extinct. Cod-fishery off Iceland, the former extent of which has been spoken of in the course of the present work, has shared the same fate. The last voyages North with the cod-lines were made a few years after 1857, and all attempts to revive the business have since been in vain.

Before closing this account of Dutch sea-fisheries I have to mention a subject in which some of the men employed in them are viewed in a light not altogether favourable, to wit, the conduct of Dutch fishing crews towards their patrons and towards their foreign colleagues. The subject were perhaps best avoided ; but, as it has occasioned legislative measures, the present work would be incomplete without a brief statement of its bearings.

It is a painful fact that ever since Dutch sea-fishery has begun to increase fast, the great demand for able hands has caused fishing sailors not only to raise their pretensions as to wages, which is but natural, but also in many cases to adopt a most unjustifiable behaviour towards their employers. As trained fishermen became scarce, Dutchmen and foreigners, ill-acquainted with the business, have had to be intrusted with vessels and nets, and, what is worse, with the cure of herring ; and many native able fishermen, finding the demand for their trained labour to acquire the proportions of sharp competition between employers, have resorted to the baleful habit of desertion, i.e., breaking contracts of service whenever they were tempted from them by higher bidders, or had earned enough to indulge in idleness for a time. Wages in Dutch sea-fisheries uniformly take the shape of a share in the raw returns, generally averaging about one-third ; and the contracts upon which this share is determined are now, as we have found them in former centuries,* intricate and apt to give rise to many disputes. Part of the crew's shares in the returns is under the habitual contracts not paid in money, but prepaid in fish; and this of course promotes the men's tendency to help themselves to all they can get. It would be highly interesting fully to investigate the effects of socialism, as embodied in this system, upon the fishing population, both from a moral and an economical point of view. As regards the effects of the sailors' behaviour upon the business, they have for a series of years been highly deleterious, and have seriously retarded the several fisheries' progress. Instances of vessels kept at home in the height of a favourable season by the crews' desertion have been frequent of late years; and the lawlessness prevailing in the connections between fishing shipowners and men might have ended in the ruin of both employed and employers, had not the legislative power intervened, upon the urgent representations of all ship-owners and of the Board appointed to second their interests. There is a law on discipline in merchant shipping, dated 1857, on the Netherlands statute-book; but this law has been pronounced by the supreme judicial authority not to apply to fishing-vessels. The new Penal Code enacts penalties against desertion by fishermen; but this Code, although now a law of the realm, has not yet been put to execution, owing to several combined circumstances; and a special law upon the subject was therefore enacted on June 20th, 1881 (Staatsblad No. 98). Imprisonment for from one to thirty days now attends desertion, consisting in non-fulfilment of contracts of service in Dutch sea-fishing

* Part iii. chapter iii.

vessels. The law is as yet of too fresh a date for a fair judgment of its effects to be formed. In the meantime, *lack of able crews* is still a drawback upon Dutch sea-fisheries ; a circumstance which in itself proves their expansive vitality.

Desertion till 1881 was not the only offence frequently laid at the doors of Dutch fishing-crews. We have seen in earlier parts of this work that a peculiar standard of notions on private property seems from early times downward to have existed among sea-fishermen at large ; that they appear never to have strictly respected each other's possessions, and have from time immemorial been given to acts of petty piracy, which, when carried on between crews of different nationality, frequently took the aspect of private warfare. This state of things, inherent in the nature of both the men and the trade, has of course become worse in proportion as fishery in the North Sea developed in the several countries surrounding it. The available fishing-grounds have of late become very much crowded by vessels of many descriptions and nationalities, using herring-nets, trawls, and hook-and-line gear, of increasing dimensions, every one of which implements is liable, either by accident or wilful mismanagement, to injure or destroy others. A man may sometimes be in the necessity of cutting his neighbours' fleet, and is often tempted to do it, and to appropriate them afterwards, by having so formidable an instrument of destruction as a trawl in the water at the time. To pilfer nets from the fleet of a vessel lying helpless miles away is often a hard temptation for a conscience no stronger than a fisherman's appears but too frequently to be ; and, though most of the evidence on this head now before me is relative to outrages committed by British fishers upon Dutch, I do not mean to say that the latter are as a rule much more scrupulous. At any rate, mutual remonstrances relative to acts of either wilful outrage or deliberate piracy have of late years occasioned much correspondence between the Foreign Offices of the North Sea fishing states, and between those of Great Britain and the Netherlands especially ; and, although in some cases offenders have been detected and punished, the impossibility either to take them *in flagranti* or identify them afterwards has generally been the reason of their escaping. This is not a place for dwelling on so painful a subject ; neither does the scope of the present work include an exposition of the Convention concluded at the Hague on May 6th, 1882, for the future prevention of similar outrages, and the establishment of an international police in the North Sea A Bill for the ratification of the said treaty has been laid before the Netherlands Parliament, not many weeks before this is being written, and has not as yet been taken into consideration ; and the subject therefore cannot as yet be said to belong to the history of Dutch sea-fisheries, or of legislation respecting them. The only statute for the prevention of ill-doings by Dutch fishermen as yet on the Netherlands statue-book, besides of course the common penal laws, is contained in articles 2-5, 14, and 20 of the above-mentioned law of June 21st, 1881, which is at present the sea-fishery code of the realm. The obligation for every Dutch fishing-vessel to carry on her bows and sails letters and a number, stating her home port, name, and owner, and never to hide or obliterate those letters and numbers, is contained in the said law, together with the necessary penal and administrative dispositions to ensure the precaution being carried into effect.

APPENDIX A.

STATISTICAL ACCOUNT OF THE GRAND OR CURED-HERRING FISHERY BETWEEN 1750 AND 1794.

Years.	Maassluis.	Vlaardingen	Enkhuizen.	Amsterdam.	De Rijp.	Zwartetraal.	Delfshaven.	Rotterdam.	Schiedam.	Den Briel.	Delft.	Graft.	Egmond aan Zee.	Total.	Market-hunters (ventjagers.)
\multicolumn{14}{c}{Number of busses sailed from each of the following places:—}		
1750	22	111	56	..	16	..	12	13	5	..	..	..	..	235	27
1751	20	113	57	..	17	..	14	13	5	..	..	..	..	239	26
1752	22	118	55	..	17	..	16	12	8	1	..	..	..	249	28
1753	23	111	57	..	16	..	17	12	9	1	..	..	..	246	30
1754	22	101	58	..	16	..	17	10	10	..	..	..	..	234	31
1755	20	102	58	..	16	..	18	10	10	..	..	..	..	234	26
1756	20	99	58	..	16	..	17	8	10	..	..	..	..	228	24
1757	16	90	59	..	16	..	17	8	10	..	..	..	..	216	24
1758	15	80	56	..	14	..	17	5	6	..	..	..	..	193	17
1759	12	68	44	..	14	..	12	6	7	..	..	..	..	163	15
1760	10	63	43	..	14	..	11	6	7	..	..	..	..	154	13
1761	7	59	40	..	14	..	5	5	4	..	..	..	..	134	15
1762	7	59	39	..	14	..	5	6	5	..	..	..	..	135	15
1763	7	64	40	..	14	..	7	7	5	..	..	..	..	144	15
1764	14	71	40	..	14	..	9	6	6	..	..	..	..	160	17
1765	15	69	40	..	14	..	9	6	7	..	..	..	..	160	17
1766	14	60	40	..	14	..	8	2	11	..	..	..	..	149	17
1767	14	58	40	..	16	..	7	2	11	..	..	..	..	148	17
1768	12	61	41	..	15	..	7	2	10	..	..	..	..	148	17
1769	12	64	41	..	14	..	7	2	9	..	..	..	..	149	20
1770	14	62	41	..	14	..	7	3	8	..	..	..	..	149	20
1771	14	64	41	..	14	..	7	5	7	..	1	1	..	153	20
1772	15	68	42	..	13	..	7	7	7	..	..	1	..	160	23
1773	18	76	44	..	13	..	7	7	5	..	..	1	..	171	20
1774	18	74	44	..	14	..	7	6	2	..	..	1	..	166	20
1775	17	66	41	..	16	..	6	6	2	..	..	2	1	158	20
1776	21	84	41	..	16	..	6	6	2	..	..	2	1	179	22
1777	23	76	41	..	15	..	6	4	2	..	..	2	1	170	22
1778	20	71	41	..	15	..	6	4	1	..	..	2	..	160	18
1779	17	75	41	..	16	..	6	4	1	..	..	2	1	163	21
1780	16	67	40	..	15	..	6	4	1	..	..	2	..	151	20
1781) 1782)	\multicolumn{14}{l}{No business done on account of the war.}														
1783	..	60	43	..	17	..	..	..	..	..	..	..	..	120	..
1784	25	74	43	..	18	..	3	2	1	..	..	..	..	166	15
1785	23	74	45	4	18	..	3	2	1	.,	..	..	..	170	15
1786	24	77	44	5	17	..	4	2	1	..	..	..	..	174	15
1787	24	81	44	6	17	..	4	2	1	..	..	..	..	179	15
1788	25	84	45	6	17	..	2	1	1	..	..	..	..	181	15
1789	27	82	44	6	17	..	3	1	..	..	..	..	..	180	15
1790	29	85	44	4	17	..	3	1	..	..	..	..	..	183	15
1791	28	93	44	4	17	..	2	1	..	..	..	..	..	189	15
1792	30	103	44	1	18	..	2	1	..	..	..	..	..	199	15
1793	31	104	44	1	11	2	1	..	..	..	..	..	..	194	15
1794	35	96	44	1	17	1	2	..	..	..	..	..	..	196	11

APPENDIX B.

Statistics of Dutch Whaling, 1670–1794.

Years.	Vessels sailed to Greenland.	Whales caught off Greenland.	Vessels sailed to Davis Straits.	Whales caught in Davis Straits.
1670	148	792		
1671	155	$630\frac{1}{2}$		
1672				
1673	The Greenland trade in these years was forbidden because of the troublous times.			
1674				
1675	148	$881\frac{1}{2}$		
1676	145	$808\frac{2}{3}$		
1677	149	686		
1678	110	$1118\frac{3}{4}$		
1679	126	831		
1680	148	1373		
1681	172	889		
1682	186	1470		
1683	242	1343		
1684	246	1185		
1685	212	$1383\frac{1}{4}$		
1686	189	639		
1687	194	617		
1688	214	345		
1689	163	243		
1690	117	$818\frac{1}{2}$		
1691	2	(Sailed from Hamburg and Bremen, whaling being prohibited throughout the Republic.)		
1692	32	62		
1693	89	175		
1694	62	$156\frac{1}{4}$		
1695	96	201		
1696	100	380		
1697	111	$1274\frac{1}{2}$		
1698	140	$1488\frac{1}{2}$		
1699	151	$775\frac{1}{2}$		
1700	173	907		
1701	207	$2071\frac{3}{4}$		
1702	225	$697\frac{3}{4}$		
1703	208	$646\frac{1}{2}$		
1704	130	$651\frac{1}{2}$		
1705	157	$1664\frac{1}{2}$		
1706	149	$452\frac{1}{2}$		
1707	131	128		
1708	121	$525\frac{1}{4}$		
1709	127	$190\frac{1}{2}$		
1710	137	62		

APPENDIX B.—STATISTICS OF DUTCH WHALING—*continued.*

Years.	Vessels sailed to Greenland.	Whales caught off Greenland.	Vessels sailed to Davis Straits.	Whales caught in Davis Straits.
1711	117	$630\frac{1}{2}$		
1712	108	$370\frac{1}{2}$		
1713	94	256		
1714	108	1234		
1715	134	$696\frac{1}{2}$		
1716	153	519		
1717	180	391		
1718	194	$281\frac{3}{4}$		
1719	182	308		
1719–1728	1504	3439	748	1251
1729–1738	858	2198	975	1929
1737	88	149	106	355
1738	74	113	112	360
1739	58	$51\frac{3}{4}$	133	$676\frac{1}{2}$
1740	..	..	..	..
1741	..	..	..	...
1742	48	50	125	$508\frac{1}{2}$
1743	49	$74\frac{1}{2}$	137	$850\frac{1}{2}$
1744	39	$182\frac{1}{2}$	148	1311
1745	31	$206\frac{1}{2}$	153	$362\frac{1}{2}$
1746	40	341	130	820
1747	37	$135\frac{1}{4}$	128	820
1748	..	..	93	217
1749	116	$470\frac{7}{8}$	41	206
1750	112	$533\frac{1}{2}$	46	$62\frac{1}{2}$
1751	117	$264\frac{11}{12}$	45	$65\frac{1}{2}$
1752	117	$438\frac{3}{4}$	42	$107\frac{1}{2}$
1753	118	$539\frac{1}{2}$	48	100
1754	135	$654\frac{11}{12}$	36	18
1755	152	$685\frac{1}{2}$	29	31
1756	160	$529\frac{1}{2}$	26	39
1757	159	$413\frac{1}{2}$	20	10
1758	151	..	7	..
1759	133	425	22	39
1760	139	$376\frac{1}{2}$	15	78
1761	138	$287\frac{1}{2}$	23	70
1762	139	124	26	$65\frac{3}{4}$
1763	127	565	35	132
1764	126	193	38	31
1765	130	394	35	82
1766	135	$156\frac{2}{3}$	31	32
1767	132	$102\frac{1}{2}$	33	83
1768	124	392	36	$207\frac{1}{2}$
1769	111	684	43	$154\frac{1}{2}$
1770	105	$434\frac{1}{2}$	45	$85\frac{1}{2}$
1771	110	$105\frac{2}{3}$	40	38
1772	93	$546\frac{1}{12}$	38	$239\frac{1}{2}$
1773	91	$193\frac{1}{12}$	43	$247\frac{1}{2}$
1774	72	281	48	179
1775	88	86	41	19
1776	84	$364\frac{1}{2}$	39	$153\frac{1}{2}$
1777	75	$250\frac{1}{4}$	42	$177\frac{1}{2}$
1778	64	252	47	$54\frac{1}{2}$

THE HISTORY OF DUTCH SEA FISHERIES.

APPENDIX B.—STATISTICS OF DUTCH WHALING—*continued*.

Years.	Vessels sailed to Greenland.	Whales caught off Greenland.	Vessels sailed to Davis Straits.	Whales caught in Davis Straits.
1779	59	$132\frac{1}{4}$	45	36
1780	46	$383\frac{1}{2}$	36	91
1781 1782	\multicolumn{4}{c}{No business done on account of the war.}			
1783	46	$325\frac{1}{2}$	9	2
1784	57	$163\frac{1}{2}$	4	8
1785	65	328	1	5
1786	?	..	?	..
1787	60	$198\frac{1}{2}$	7	41
1788	58	167	11	21
1789	53	$481\frac{3}{4}$	8	23
1790	52	$103\frac{1}{2}$	14	10
1791	49	$61\frac{3}{8}$	13	$17\frac{1}{2}$
1792	47	200	14	2
1793	31	72	1	
1794	55	$92\frac{1}{2}$	3	$13\frac{1}{2}$

APPENDIX C.

COD FISHERY OFF ICELAND, 1751–1790.

Years.	Number of vessels.	Average number of lasts caught by each vessel.	Years.	Number of vessels.	Average number of lasts caught by each vessel.
1751	73	12	1772	121	7
1752	64	7	1773	107	5
1753	56	20	1774	83	8
1754	95	11	1775	78	5
1755	76	15	1776	36	9
1756	95	2, 3, or 4	1777	22	16
1757	111	a few lasts only.	1778	24	{even better than in 1770.
1758	94				
1759	124		1779	61	16
1760	..	15	1780	63	20
1761	123	20	1781 1782	\multicolumn{2}{c}{Stopped by war.}
1762	142				
1763	148		1783	..	very bad.
1764	113		1784	49	unfavourable.
1765	140		1785	52	,,
1766	155	10	1786	58	
1767	157		1787	2	
1768	160	5	1788	1	
1769	137	8	1789	None.	
1770	126	14	1790	,,	
1771	145	6			

APPENDIX D.

Text of the Law on Herring Fishery, dated March 12th, 1818 (*Staatsblad*, No. 15); literally translated.

WE, WILLIAM, by the grace of God, King of the Netherlands, Prince of Orange-Nassau, Grand Duke of Luxemburg, &c., &c.
To all who shall see these, or hear them read, Our greeting.
Whereas We have considered, that the Grand or Herring Fishery of this Kingdom has always been an object of the Government's solicitude and protection;
That measures have at several times been taken to prevent prejudice by all such doings and evil practices as might endanger and diminish the renown of Herring caught and cured by the Fisheries of this Kingdom;
That the happy result of these measures yields constant proof of their suitableness, whence there is reason to forcibly maintain them;
Considering, moreover, that the said Fishery is not exercised in the same manner in all provinces of this Kingdom, and that care ought to be taken lest a protection of both fisheries should lead to their doing each other a prejudice; the object being, on the contrary, that both shall contribute to the welfare of this branch of general industry;
We have, after taking the advice of the Council of State, and upon common deliberation with the States-General, decreed, and hereby do decree as follows:

GENERAL RULES.

Art. 1.—Herring-fishery under the Netherlands colours shall be exercised only for the account of inhabitants of this Kingdom, and in vessels owned by them.

2.—No one shall, under a penalty of 2000 florins, let any foreigner have a share in a herring-fishing enterprise, or lend his name to a foreigner for such enterprise.

THE HISTORY OF DUTCH SEA FISHERIES. 291

3.—All inhabitants of this Kingdom are forbidden, under the same penalty, to participate, even indirectly, in any herring-fishery under foreign colours.

4.—Any person who shall undertake either directly or indirectly to entice inhabitants of this Kingdom to exercise herring-fishery in a foreign country, shall forfeit a penalty of 2000 florins, or be imprisoned for one year.

5.—Any fisherman who shall have either exercised herring-fishery abroad, or engaged there to exercise such fishery, shall be imprisoned for six months.

6.—No foreign herring, whether fresh, cured, salted or smoked, shall be imported into this Kingdom, on pain of forfeiture of the herring, and a fine of 500 florins for every barrel of salted pickle-herring, or 5 florins per hundred of herrings fresh or smoked.

GENERAL SUPERINTENDENCE AND POLICE OF THE HERRING FISHERY.

7.—The external police, or general superintendence of the herring-fishery, shall be governed by uniform rules all over the Kingdom, established by law and by Royal Decrees based upon the law.

8.—The internal police, or detailed regulations for these fisheries, shall be established for each sea-bound Province, by the Provincial States; but the said regulations shall not be contrary to the general rules.

9.—The internal police of the herring fisheries includes : the details of equipment, the rules relative to applying for, and obtaining, permission to fish for herring, the mode of preparing, sorting and salting herring, and the necessary precautions relative to vessels going for cod-fish and having some herring nets on board.

10.—In every sea-province where it shall be found useful, the Provincial States shall, subject to Our approval, appoint a College to have the direction of all things concerning the herring fishery.

11.—In provinces where herring-fishery has not sufficient importance to require a separate College, it shall be lawful for the Provincial States to confide the care of that fishery to such Boards as shall have the direction of other fisheries in such provinces.

12.—Any persons exercising herring-fishery without being authorized thereto in the manner stipulated by the Provincial States, shall be liable, viz. the equipper of the vessel to a fine ranging from 300 florins to 3000 florins, and her steersman to imprisonment for not less than fourteen days and not more than two months.

OF THE SEVERAL HERRING-FISHERIES.

13.—The Grand, or Pickle-herring Fishery is exercised in the summer or autumn, in keeled vessels, off Hitland [Shetlands] and Edinburgh, and under the coasts of England.

14.—The object of this fishery is, to catch herring of the best quality, and to cure, salt and barrel such herring at sea, both for exportation and home consumption.

15.—The Small, or Fresh-herring Fishery is exercised in the high sea, generally in the so-called Deep Water, about east of Yarmouth, in flat-bottomed and keelless vessels which commonly do not enter any port, but go ashore on the sea-beach.

16.—It shall be provisionally interdicted as heretofore, to cure herring from the latter-named fishery, either at sea or ashore, under the following penalties, viz. one month's imprisonment for the steersman, and a fine of 5 florins per hundred of herrings to be forfeited by the shipowner and all other delinquents, besides forfeiture of the herring. It shall, however, be lawful for the King upon advice of the Provincial States to ordain how, in how far, and at what time herring from the Small Fishery shall be allowed to be cured and made into pickle-herring, without prejudice either to the interests of the Grand Fishery or to the renown of Netherlands herring.

17.—The Pan-herring fishery is exercised, with or without vessels, in the entire extent of the Kingdom in the rivers, river-mouths, inner seas, and within one hour's distance from the outer sea-shores.

18.—All fishermen, equippers of vessels, dealers, and persons whatsoever are prohibited, on pain of one month's imprisonment and a fine of 5 florins per hundred of herrings, besides forfeiture of the herring, to cure or salt as pickle-herring any herring from the fishery last named.

19.—All dispositions further required respecting the said fishery shall be enacted by the States of the several Provinces, who shall be entitled to comminate penalties against breach of their

THE HISTORY OF DUTCH SEA FISHERIES. 293

rules, viz. from fourteen days' to two months' imprisonment, and fines up to 300 florins, whether separately or in cumulation.

FISHERMEN'S DUTIES DURING THEIR VOYAGES OUT AND HOME.

20.—All steersmen of herring-ships shall be obliged to carry the herring caught by them into this Kingdom, on pain of one month's imprisonment and a fine of 50 florins.

21.—All herring fishermen, having left their port or place of equipment, shall be bound, time and weather serving, to sail straight to their fishing water, and likewise to sail straight home thence

22.—They shall not, unless in case of urgent necessity, enter any foreign port, or port belonging to another province than where the vessel was equipped.

23.—All fishermen are prohibited, on pain of one month's imprisonment and a fine of 100 florins, from selling, bartering, exchanging, or giving away at sea, any herring caught by them.

24.—They are prohibited, under the same penalties, from buying herring either abroad or at sea, for the purpose of bringing such herring into this Kingdom.

25.—Any shipowner convicted of having, after the close of the fishery, given his vessel another destination besides the usual and lawful one, i.e. destined her to buy herring at sea or abroad, or sell his own in a foreign country, shall be fined 50 florins per barrel of foreign herring brought home, and 300 florins if he shall have sold his own abroad.

LIMITS OF THE HERRING-FISHING SEASON.

26.—No inhabitant of this Kingdom shall be allowed to shoot nets for herring fishery in the open sea earlier than June 24th, at night, or later than December 31st. Any steersman contravening this enactment shall be imprisoned for one month, and fined 50 florins. The vessel's owner shall be fined 1000 florins, if privy to the transgressions.

27.—The aforesaid prohibition is not applicable to vessels mentioned in Article 9, sailing for cod-fish and having some herring nets on board. Dispositions relative to such vessels shall be enacted by the Provincial States.

28.—Muster-rolls shall be made out, and signed by the steersman and crew of each herring-fishing vessel; the forms for such muster-rolls shall be determined by the Provincial States.

29.—The Provincial States shall be entitled to determine the date on which herring fishermen shall be allowed to enter port, cases of urgent necessity and extraordinary capture excepted.

30.—The Provincial States are likewise entitled to determine the opening of the Small or Fresh-herring Fishery; and to comminate fines not exceeding 100 florins against transgressors of this and the last article.

OF SALE-HUNTING (*Jagery*).

31.—It shall be permitted annually to send some vessels out to the herring fleet, there to take on board herring *of the first capture*, in order to bring them speedily into this Kingdom.

32.—The said vessels, known as herring-hunters (*haring-jagers*), shall not carry the herring taken on board by them anywhere but to the port whence they have sailed.

33.—The opening and closing dates of herring-hunting shall be determined by the Provincial States.

34.—Articles 20, 21, 22, 23, 24, and 25 of the present law shall apply to the owners and skippers of herring-hunters.

RULES TO BE OBSERVED WHILE IN FISHING WATER.

35.—All herring fishermen from this Kingdom are prohibited from fishing for herring, at any time, between the sand-bars and rocks of Norway, Ireland, and Scotland.

36.—Any injury or damage done by one herring-fisher to another at sea shall be subject to a fine ranging between 10 florins and 100 florins, and imprisonment from 10 days to one month; without prejudice to an action for damages and interests.

37.—All vessels and fishing implements shall be marked with convenient marks, to be determined by the Provincial States.

OF THE ASSAYING OF PICKLE-HERRING, AND BRANDING OF BARRELS USED FOR SALTING AND PACKING SUCH HERRING.

38.—No pickle-herring shall be sold, or carried from the place where landed, unless the fish be previously assayed by sworn assayers (*keurmeesters*), and the barrel branded with the name of the place where such herring was brought ashore.

39.—Pickle-herring transported from one province into another shall be allowed to be exported abroad in the same barrel, and only marked with the local brand; but if repacked into another barrel, such herring shall not be exported abroad unless branded with the name or escutcheon of the province where it was landed.

40.—No province-brands shall be apposed to barrels unless previously marked with the peculiar signs to be determined by provincial regulations.

41.—Any brander who shall have apposed the provincial or local brand to barrels known by him to contain foreign herring, or herring from another province, shall be liable to imprisonment for one year.

42.—All barrels, great or small, used in salting herring, shall be previously tested by sworn assayers.

43.—The assayers, both of herring and barrels, and the branders, both of local and provincial marks, shall be appointed and sworn by the municipal magistrates.

44.—The Provincial States shall draw up the assayers' and branders' instructions, and determine the peculiar marks to be apposed to barrels in order to certify the year when the herring was caught, its quality and sort.

45.—Any person selling or expediting herring in this Kingdom, whether to a home or foreign destination, shall be liable to a fine of 20 florins for each barrel, great or small, not provided with the prescribed brands.

ADDITIONAL CLAUSES.

46.—The premiums proffered for herring-fishery shall be regulated by the King in a fair proportion, in consideration of the expenses of the several kinds of equipment.

47.—All provincial and municipal statutes not in contradiction to the terms of the present law shall remain in force till ulteriorly provided for by the Provincial States.

The which We order and command to be inserted into the Statute-Book (*Staatsblad*), and that all ministerial departments and authorities, colleges and officers whatsoever shall see to the strict execution of the same.

Given at the Hague, on March 12th of the year 1818, the Fifth of Our Reign.

(*Signed*) WILLIAM,

By the King's Order,

(*Signed*) A. R. FALCK.

APPENDIX E.

STATISTICAL ACCOUNT OF THE "GRAND" OR CURED-HERRING FISHERY, 1814-1853.

Years.	Number of Busses.	Total number of lasts of herrings.	Average number of lasts brought in by each buss.
1814	98	1862	19
1815	137	3558	26
1816	159	3498	22
1817	160	3360	21
1818	168	1680	10
1819	169	1521	9
1820	153	1380	9
1821	168	2856	17
1822	160	1600	10
1823	128	1792	14
1824	123	2214	18
1825	111	2664	24
1826	130	3120	24
1827	130	3250	25
1828	133	3059	23
1829	131	1965	15
1830	173	4329	25
1831	132	2178	16
1832	120	2520	21
1833	107	2568	24
1834	116	2900	25
1835	113	2260	20
1836	117	2925	25
1837	117	3550	31
1838	121	3267	27
1839	120	2280	19
1840	122	2318	19
1841	123	2706	22
1842	129	2964	23
1843	127	1150	9
1844	126	2800	23
1845	127	1263	10
1846	116	1283	11
1847	115	2149	19
1848	107	2900	28
1849	110	2260	20
1850	102	2515	$24\frac{1}{2}$
1851	97	2454	25
1852	93	1499	16
1853	92	2284	25

APPENDIX F.

STATISTICAL ACCOUNT OF THE FISHERY OF SALT HERRING FOR SMOKING (*Steurharing*), CARRIED ON IN VESSELS FROM THE COAST VILLAGES OF SCHEVENINGEN, KATWIJK, AND NOORDWIJK, 1823-1853.

Years.	Number of boats.	Herrings brought home.	Average number of herrings per boat.
1823	35	4,202,000	121,200
1824	41	3,102,000	75,658
1825	43	2,378,000	55,502
1826	40	3,192,000	79,800
1827	45	4,615,000	102,555
1828	47	4,476,000	95,650
1829	43	6,150,000	143,023
1830	51	3,641,000	71,419
1831	39	1,282,000	32,872
1832	36	930,000	25,833
1833	39	4,199,400	107,677
1834	45	2,699,000	59,311
1835	49	3,430,000	69,592
1836	52	6,952,200	133,700
1837	71	10,503,000	147,930
1838	83	7,138,000	86,000
1839	93	8,630,000	92,800
1840	101	9,539,000	94,445
1841	100	8,215,000	82,150
1842	106	8,942,600	84,364
1843	100	5,695,000	56,950
1844	89	7,632,000	85,752
1845	89	8,932,000	100,358
1846	94	8,716,000	92,723
1847	96	12,398,000	129,146
1848	96	9,520,600	99,166
1849	98	10,906,000	112,204
1850	102	9,767,000	95,755
1851	111	14,000,000	126,207
1852	117	15,918,000	136,569
1853	118	23,433,000	198,585

APPENDIX G.

GENERAL ACCOUNT OF THE DUTCH HERRING FISHERIES BETWEEN 1834 AND 1853.

Years.	Cure-herring caught.	Salt herring (*steur-haring*) caught.	Fresh or "pan herring" caught.
1834	32,480,000	2,699,000	31,920,000
1835	25,312,000	3,430,000	29,890,000
1836	32,760,000	6,952,200	16,550,000
1837	39,760,000	10,503,000	5,730,000
1838	39,590,400	7,138,000	2,270,000
1839	25,536,000	8,630,000	3,410,000
1840	25,961,600	9,539,000	4,590,000
1841	30,307,200	8,215,000	9,560,000
1842	33,196,800	8,942,600	12,140,000
1843	12,880,000	5,695,000	11,090,000
1844	31,360,000	7,632,000	8,360,000
1845	14,145,600	8,932,000	14,240,000
1846	14,369,600	8,716,000	17,680,000
1847	24,068,800	12,398,000	12,940,000
1848	32,480,000	9,520,000	23,820,000
1849	25,312,000	10,906,000	14,120,000
1850	28,168,000	9,767,000	22,520,000
1851	27,484,800	14,000,000	18,260,000
1852	16,788,800	15,918,000	16,500,000
1853	25,580,800	23,433,000	11,920,000

APPENDIX II.

Account of the Iceland Cod Fishery between 1844 and 1853.

Years.	Number of ships, each making one voyage.	Total returns. Lasts of salt cod of divers kinds.
1844	2	50
1845	2	51
1846	2	58
1847	3	$84\frac{1}{2}$
1848	5	176
1849	6	176
1850	3	93
1851	3	108
1852	5	155
1853	6	141

APPENDIX I.

ACCOUNT OF THE NORTH SEA HOOK FISHERY IN WINTER, FOR COD, HADDOCK, PLAICE, &C. (*beugvisscherij*), BETWEEN 1844 AND 1853.

Years.	Number of Ships.	Number of Voyages.	Total catch.	
			Barrels of salt cod and haddock, plaice, &c.	Numbers of cod, haddock, plaice, &c., brought home alive.
1844	41	147	7,122	31,141
1845	36	119	4,307	17,132
1846	38	139	7,607	21,946
1847	39	136	6,334	19,062
1848	30	105	4,316	9,919
1849	35	98	4,423	11,897
1850	32	110	4,993	9,958
1851	26	97	7,464	15,010
1852	38	144	11,939	16,924
1853	35	112	8,078	14,185

APPENDIX J.

ACCOUNT OF THE TRAWLING RETURNS OBTAINED BY TRAWLERS OF KATWIJK, 1821-1850.

Years.	Number of trawl boats.	Total returns.	Average return per boat.
1821	38	fl. 112,302	fl. 2955.26
1822	37	79,128	2138.85
1823	34	65,047	1913.15
1824	31	70,573	2276.58
1825	30	75,169	2505.62
1826	31	78,413	2529.45
1827	31	68,678	2215.40
1828	32	55,872	1746.00
1829	33	57,560	1743.63
1830	33	69,577	2108.00
1831	27	49,055	1816.75
1832	27	48,905	1811.22
1833	28	51,690	1846.00
1834	29	59,091	2037.62
1835	29	61,316	2114.30
1836	29	55,753	1922.50
1837	27	60,539	2242.20
1838	32	64,400	2012.51^5
1839	36	84,376	2343.80
1840	42	79,762	1899.09^5
1841	46	61,793	1343.33^5
1842	50	69,377	1387.54^5
1843	50	86,638	1732.76
1844	49	89,653	1829.45^5
1845	43	73,769	1715.56
1846	48	58,162	1211.71
1847	47	79,593	1693.49
1848	50	80,437	1608.74^5
1849	50	76,223	1524.46
1850	48	78,902	1643.78

APPENDIX

NORTH SEA HERRING FISHERIES
THE REPEAL OF

Years.	Vessels employed.		HERRING BROUGHT HOME.			
			Cured herring (barrels) by		Fresh herring salted preparatory to smoking (*steurharing*) (thousands), by	
	Keeled boats.	Bumboats.	Keeled vessels.	Bumboats.	Keeled vessels.	Bumboats.
1	2	3	4	5	6	7
1856	82	147	35,924	106		36,295
1857	91	157	21,924	210		29,803
1858	95	175	16,940	548		24,969
1859	79	178	23,226	1,398		27,768
1860	92	174	26,222	295		22,545
1861	91	181	29,260	165		20,568
1862	90	181	51,108	136		32,011
1863	86	170	35,056	127		38,612
1864	80	180	26,946	140		33,535
1865	81	186	29,388	419		57,372
1866	82	195	22,856	3,096‡		48,498
1867	89	198	27,664	2,811		46,928
1868	91	202	38,515	4,714		74,043
1869	104	192	29,900	3,827	1,539	27,323
1870	120	189	70,868	4,130	5,265	59,025
1871	122	200	77,897	21,544	5,366	86,699
1872	108	208	60,442	22,248	1,655	39,350
1873	102	205	77,412	39,962	2,710	53,295
1874	114	218	66,118	46,519	1,349	27,582
1875	115	222	59,483	42,478	826	19,439
1876	109	229	50,102	58,221	1,021	37,478
1877	113	244	71,585	69,414	2,013	38,932
1878	127	265	70,355	41,176	2,628	30,465
1879	128	268	78,103	87,750	1,764	44,260
1880	133	284	134,275	83,724	9,989	56,741
1881	139	269	110,110	88,788	3,323	50,279

* Column 9. Smoked herring from the Zuider Zee is comprised in these figures.
† Column 10. A considerable part of these figures, in the earlier years especially, represents This fraud ceased in later years, when Dutch-brand herring was neither dearer, nor expected
‡ Column 5. Most, and in latter years the whole, of this pickle herring from the coast was not luggers, and branded and exported along with such herring.
§ Column 8. The export figures for 1879 and following years are taken from Custom-house over Custom-house declarations in it. The figures down to 1879 are collected from the College's for exportation, and their figures are constantly at variance with Custom-house statistics.

K.

IN THE NETHERLANDS, FROM THE LAW OF 1818.

EXPORTS.		IMPORTS.	HIGHEST AND LOWEST PRICES. Of "full"-cured herring brought			
Of cured herring (barrels).	Of smoked herring or "bucking." (thousands)*	Of cured herring for consumption (barrels).	(a) in keeled vessels, after the close of hunting time (barrels containing 800 herrings).		(b) in bumboats from Scheveningen (barrels containing 620 herrings).	
8	9	10†	11 H. fl.	12 L. fl.	13 H. fl.	14 L. fl.
	33,099					
	28,001					
17,140	30,919	4,098	69	36	78	20
15,355	27,863	3,787	38	33	34	21
14,490	25,803	about 8,000	48.25	47.50	26	21
15,040	27,244	5,276	83	43.50	88	23
22,236	25,184	6,069	32	21	24	16
22,250	41,310	less than 4,000	42	20	38	22
14,726	42,698	8,364	50	26	27.50	17.50
17,224	49,404	9,715	45	25	45	16
13,023	66,072	14,822	51	27.25	27	20
15,098	53,729	12,280	63	20	22.10	17.25
22,152	71,275	5,400	60	19	28	12
15,921	55,086	21,060	66	25	28	12
39,435	59,032	16,734	40	24	f.24	
48,437	84,176	2,709	44	25	28	13
46,839	67,916	1,984	76	28	24	15
58,388	47,645	3,415	29.25	21	27	17
68,306	44,928	2,080	39.75	27.50	28	18
68,142	27,486	1,770	45	24.25	36.50	17.50
68,430	23,166	2,830	61	34.75	34.25	26.50
88,843	42,201	1,205	98	22	26.50	16
76,004	33,345	475	31.25	18	26	14.50
90,841§	45,216	2,033	56	23	33.25	19
138,986	52,470	480	22.75	14.50	32.50	10.50
134,620	41,427	220	35	25	27	17.50

Scotch herring imported and re-exported after being transferred to Dutch-branded barrels. to be better than Scotch.
branded upon coming ashore, but carried to Vlaardingen and mixed up with herring caught in

statistics, and are probably inexact, as the article is duty free, and there is no sufficient control reports, who were enabled, before the said year, to state the exact number of barrels branded

APPENDIX L.

Exports of Salt Cod.

Years.	Quantities exported to		Total of exports.
	Belgium.	Germany.	
	Barrels.	Barrels.	Barrels
1857	456	1,949	2,883
1858	498	2,118	3,274
1859	280	2,445	2,886
1860	402	1,474	3,564
1861	333	2,384	3,774
1862	200	2,494	3,590
1863	244	2,956	3,592
1864	1,530*	19,980*	21,780*
1865	2,390	2,030	6,630
1866	4,160	2,000	7,550
1867	1,250	1,810	3,510
1868	3,480	1,640	5,840
1869	4,260	2,750	7,790
1870	3,900	2,530	6,600
1871	2,210	1,540	4,030
1872	about 2,440	1,460	3,900
1873	546†	200†	764†
1874	about 272	404	676
1875	257	323	580
1876	528	415	943
1877	539	434	973
1878	337	263	600
1879	648	245	893
1880	274	202	533
1881	302	223	575

* These figures, although taken from Custom-house statistics, are obviously erroneous.
† In consequence of a change in the arrangement of Custom-house statistics, exports of salt cod are given in *thousands of kilogrammes* from 1872 downwards.

APPENDIX M.

EXPORTS OF FRESH SEA FISH.
(*In thousands of kilogrammes.*)

Years.	Fresh fish exported to		Total of exports.
	Belgium	Germany.	
1857	983	440	1498
1858	999	802	1863
1859	750	689	1611
1860	716	830	1653
1861	520	526	1163
1862	820	593	1499
1863	1362	406	1915
1864	1394	758	2256
1865	1599	474	2095
1866	1445	152	1914
1867	1617	157	2110
1868	1207	276	1499
1869	1961	327	2302
1870	2745	390	3140
1871	2614	416	3114
1872	2617	420	3120
1873	4327	633	5459
1874	4456	583	5584
1875	5491	470	6911
1876	5452	375	6779
1877	3637	375	4236
1878	4671	603	5354
1879	5952	416	6638
1880	6445	443	6959
1881	3943	463	4800

APPENDIX N

ZUIDER ZEE FISHERIES, 1854-1881.

Years.	Pan-herring brought to sale at Monnickendam (in thousands).*	Anchovies caught (in "ankers," or 50lb. barrels).	Highest prices of anchovy caught and sold in the same year (per anker).
			f.
1854	13,160	10,000	12
1855	10,674	2,000	16.50
1856	15,390	2,000	21
1857	11,980	10,000	17
1858	13,880	60,000	9.50
1859	14,920	30,000	11
1860	13,071	6,000	7.50
1861	16,460	5,000	9
1862	16,232	7,000	9.25
1863	25,755	1,000	20
1864	20,278	2,000	20
1865	16,179	1,000	52
1866	20,326	65,000	20
1867	19,472	10,000	18
1868	17,105	1,000	29
1869	18,657	75,000	15
1870	11,435	4,000	17
1871	15,336	7,000	23.50
1872	6,694*	9,000	25.75
1873	9,158	30,000	31
1874	6,106	40,000	27.50
1875	8,364	55,000	25.50
1876	5,605	46,000	22.75
1877	6,496	6,000	22
1878	1,823	1,400	29
1879	4,635	3,000	43
1880	12,566	1,000	78
1881	7,770	15,000	66

* The total quantities of pan-herring caught in the Zuider Zee are about double the quantities mentioned in this column as regards the earlier years. Since 1872 most Zuider Zee herring has been carried direct to the inland markets; and the decline of the sales at Monnickendam is no sign of corresponding decline in the business.

www.ingramcontent.com/pod-product-compliance
Lightning Source LLC
Chambersburg PA
CBHW022105230426
43672CB00008B/1290